MULTIMODAL COMPOSING

MULTIMODAL COMPOSING

Strategies for Twenty-First-Century Writing Consultations

EDITED BY
LINDSAY A. SABATINO
BRIAN FALLON

UTAH STATE UNIVERSITY PRESS
Logan

© 2019 by University Press of Colorado

Published by Utah State University Press
An imprint of University Press of Colorado
245 Century Circle, Suite 202
Louisville, Colorado 80027

The University Press of Colorado is a proud member of
the Association of University Presses.

The University Press of Colorado is a cooperative publishing enterprise supported, in part, by Adams State University, Colorado State University, Fort Lewis College, Metropolitan State University of Denver, University of Colorado, University of Northern Colorado, Utah State University, and Western State Colorado University.

∞ This paper meets the requirements of the ANSI/NISO Z39.48–1992 (Permanence of Paper)

ISBN: 978-1-60732-845-2 (paperback)
ISBN: 978-1-60732-846-9 (ebook)
DOI: https://doi.org/10.7330/9781607328469

Library of Congress Cataloging-in-Publication Data

Names: Sabatino, Lindsay A. (Lindsay Ann), author. | Fallon, Brian (Brian J.), author.
Title: Multimodal composing : strategies for twenty-first-century writing consultations / Lindsay A. Sabatino, Brian Fallon.
Description: Logan : Utah State University Press, [2019] | Includes bibliographical references and index.
Identifiers: LCCN 2018050267 | ISBN 9781607328452 (pbk.) | ISBN 9781607328469 (ebook)
Subjects: LCSH: English language—Rhetoric—Study and teaching (Higher) | Mass media—Authorship—Study and teaching (Higher) | Visual communication. | Oral communication.
Classification: LCC PE1404 .S23 2019 | DDC 808/.0420711—dc23
LC record available at https://lccn.loc.gov/2018050267

For Ben Rafoth—
teacher, mentor, and friend.

CONTENTS

PREFACE

Brian Fallon
Fashion Institute of Technology, SUNY

Lindsay A. Sabatino
Wagner College

We began writing this book on an airplane. We were on our way home from the 2015 International Writing Centers Association conference in Pittsburgh, where Lindsay led a roundtable discussion on tutoring multimodalities. Brian had been at that roundtable because, like many of the other participants, he was looking for resources to share with his consultants to prepare them for the variety of multimodal projects students bring to the Writing Studio at FIT. It just so happened we were seated next to each other on our flight home, and by the time we got to Charlotte, North Carolina, we had decided we would put together an edited collection that would cover a number of frequently seen multimodal projects in the writing center.

We both studied at Indiana University of Pennsylvania under the guidance of our shared mentor and dissertation director, Ben Rafoth. For years, we have grabbed Ben's *A Tutor's Guide* off our shelves to provide consultants insight on any number of tutoring situations. We thought it would be great to have a book similar to Ben's that covers multimodal projects, offering consultants strategies and background information. The structure of the chapters for this book is inspired by Ben's careful and thoughtful attention to the learning needs and interests of consultants. We owe Ben a great deal of thanks not only for his example but also for his advice as we worked our way through this process.

As the options for effective communication become more visually and technologically demanding, writing center consultants are more likely to come across texts that are dynamic and multimodal.

DOI: 10.7330/9781607328469.c000

In our writing centers, we often work with students who bring texts that involve visual media, design principles, social media, and digital composing. As we began to consider the best ways to assist writers with these types of composing practices, we noticed our consultants have few resources to turn to when it comes to strategies for working with these texts. While there are a lot of excellent consultant guides and great publications on new media, design, and digital writing, few are dedicated to strategies for tutoring digital texts, new media, and visual elements.

In her "New Media Matters: Tutoring in the Late Age of Print," Jackie Grutsch McKinney (2014) notes this lack of guidance and offers some reasons as to why writing center scholars have cautiously considered whether or not to teach consultants how to work with twenty-first-century texts. Assessing the types and focus of tutor-training guides currently available to writing center practitioners, she builds an argument for how some of the central tenets of "good" tutoring have been built on shifting ground. For example, Grutsch McKinney notes how traditional approaches to tutoring like reading aloud, looking beyond the text, and HOCs over LOCs must evolve to better accommodate twenty-first-century texts. Grutsch McKinney concludes her thoughtful and instructive chapter rather persuasively with the following admonition: "Writing has evolved with new composing technologies and media, and we must evolve, too, because we are in the writing business. A radical shift in the way that writers communicate . . . necessitates a radical re-imagining and re-understanding of our practices, purposes, and goals" (255). Like Grutsch McKinney, we wondered about what to do for our consultants when most tutor-training guides tend to address aspects of tutoring focused exclusively on written texts or on the process of tutoring traditional written texts. While what we have learned from these texts provides much of the backbone of our work with consultants and students, we recognized that a genre-based approach to building tutoring strategies is useful when opening the writing center's doors to multimodal composing.

With that said, this book has three major aims: (1) build on and evolve tutoring practices and strategies for multimodal texts, (2) introduce consultants to important features and practices in a variety of multimodal texts, and (3) start a conversation about the relationship among rhetorical choices, design thinking, and technological awareness in the writing center. One of the most comprehensive overviews of the tutoring process can be found in Lauren Fitzgerald and Melissa Ianetta's *The Oxford Guide for Writing Tutors: Practice and Research*. What's

[handwritten marginal note: argues for development of our practices]

great about their chapter on tutoring practices is that it covers both the practical elements of a tutoring session and the intellectual, emotional, and collaborative demands of tutoring. Fitzgerald and Ianetta (2016) instruct consultants on a range of disciplinary and genre-based approaches to tutoring, and their discussion of those topics provides an essential foundation for the work this collection addresses. The contribution this book makes is a focused conversation on how rhetorical, design, and multimodal principles inform consultation strategies, especially when working with genres less familiar or traditional. We know consultants are already asked to do a lot; they teach, mentor, research, collaborate, learn, anticipate problems, and negotiate complex social relationships. The goal of this book is to provide consultants resources and strategies so they can continue to do all these important writing center tasks while also attending to the ways writing is changing.

Consequently, we wanted *Multimodal Composing: Strategies for Twenty-First-Century Writing Consultations* and its companion website www.multi modalwritingcenter.org to provide writing center consultants with instructive and practical approaches to tutoring writers whose texts are visual, technological, creative, and performative. As an edited collection, *Multimodal Composing* covers multimodal and visual topics many writing centers are more frequently encountering.

Lindsay's introduction to this book is a foundational overview of design principles consultants will read about in each of the chapters. It's written as a crash course for consultants with no or little design experience. Each subsequent chapter in this collection adheres to a specific organization, offering the following sections:

illustrative example—a concrete example or story of a particular kind of text or issue in working with visually rich and technologically-advanced communication

background information—the context and foundation for the issue or text, highlighting the essentials

consultation strategies for tutoring—suggestions and strategies for consultants to employ when working with writers on the particular text or issues presented in the illustrative example

activity—an activity that enhances consultants' understanding and knowledge of the topic and provides them with the experience needed to help writers make decisions about multimodal projects

conclusion—wrap-up that brings together the strategies and activity, putting them in context with the background information

resources—helpful resources on the text or issue that allow consultants and directors to follow up on the topic *key search terms*—a list of helpful search-engine terms on the topic under discussion, especially as new information and technologies become available

references—a complete list of references at the end of each chapter

We encourage readers to visit the collection's companion website: www.multimodalwritingcenter.org. On this site, readers have access to color images, videos, podcasts, and other dynamic resources that are difficult to reproduce in print. The website also provides updated links to resources and tools, especially given the ever-changing nature of technology.

In this collection, we refer to those who are working with students as *consultants* rather than *tutors*, partly due to the kinds of texts under discussion. In many cases, consultants play the roles of expert users, listeners, viewers, and readers of the different multimodal projects discussed by our contributors. At times, we use *consultant* interchangeably with titles like *tutor* and *coach*. What's important is that we believe writing centers can offer students working on design-focused, multimodal projects a unique rhetorical perspective in a one-to-one or small-group environment. Likewise, this collection asks us to cast the traditional writers visiting our centers as artists, designers, creators, filmmakers, podcasters, and makers of all sorts. Understanding and appreciating the multiple roles consultants and students play while working on communication across modalities creates collaborative experiences predicated on design thinking, innovation, and aesthetic meaning making.

Finally, we would like to thank the consultants who worked at the FIT Writing Studio and the University of North Carolina Greensboro Digital ACT Studio in the spring semester of 2017. Our peer consultants tested all the activities included in this collection, providing ample feedback on what worked and what needed work in the chapters. They challenged us to see things from a student and consultant perspective and helped us produce a stronger collection. We thank Sarah Blazer, Sasha Graybosch, Melissa Ianetta, and Nicole Stockburger for their feedback and support throughout the process of compiling this collection and editing chapters. We are also grateful to Rachael Levay, Laura Furney, Kylie Haggen, Daniel Pratt, and Beth Svinarich at Utah State University Press for their support throughout the publication process. Additionally, we are indebted to Jacob Babb, Nicole Caswell, and Kami Day, who provided insight and feedback that profoundly shaped this collection and strengthened the text on every level.

On a personal note, we'd like to thank Aries Jurwei Liang and Linda and Robert Sabatino for their love and support.

REFERENCES

Fitzgerald, Lauren, and Melissa Ianetta. 2016. *The Oxford Guide for Writing Tutors: Practice and Research.* New York: Oxford University Press.

McKinney, Jackie Grutsch. 2014. "New Media Matters: Tutoring in the Late Age of Print." In *The Routledge Reader on Writing Centers and New Media,* edited by Sohui Lee and Russell Carpenter, 242–56. New York: Routledge.

Rafoth, Ben A., ed. 2005. *A Tutors Guide: Helping Writers One to One.* 2nd ed. Portsmouth, NH: Boynton/Cook.

MULTIMODAL COMPOSING

1

INTRODUCTION
Design Theory and Multimodal Consulting

Lindsay A. Sabatino
Wagner College

As Brian and I sat down to discuss this book, we explored the different theoretical underpinnings that inform our concepts about multiliteracies, multimodality, and digital composing. We recognized that writing centers are increasingly becoming sites for feedback on multimodal projects, especially as educators are expanding their concepts of literacy to encompass "the burgeoning variety of text forms associated with information and multimedia technologies" (Cazden et al. 1996, 61). More specifically, instructors are including assignments that ask students to negotiate multiple modes (words, images, colors, gestures, movement) in order to communicate effectively to their audiences. An interdisciplinary group of scholars called the New London Group encourages more comprehensive understandings of literacy, especially in light of all the means of communication available to us in today's culturally and linguistically diverse world. Simply put, they explain that "new communication media are reshaping the way we use language" (64). Given that consultants are in the writing business, as Jackie Grutsch McKinney (2014) reminds us, and that the business of writing is evolving, we must prepare to work with students being asked to explore new ways of communicating and thinking about language use. Moreover, we believe multimodal composing provides consultants with an opportunity to expand the ways writers think about language and connecting to audiences. The multiliteracy center John Trimbur (2000) imagined as a place where consultants will begin seeing assignments that move beyond the printed text is upon us. This collection is designed to prepare consultants to offer feedback on those projects by providing them with an overview of visual and audio design principles, the rhetorical nature of multimodal composing, and a variety of multimodal genres.

DOI: 10.7330/9781607328469.c001

Given this starting point, we specifically found ourselves drawn to concepts put forth by the New London Group, Claire Wyatt-Smith and Kay Kimber, the Gestalt principles of design, and Theo van Leeuwen's sound theory. Through this book, we aim to pull from the New London Group's emphasis on six design elements in the meaning-making process: "Linguistic Meaning, Visual Meaning, Audio Meaning, Gestural Meaning, Spatial Meaning, and the Multimodal patterns of meaning that relate the first five modes of meaning to each other" (Cazden et al. 1996, 65). By critically examining these six meaning-making elements, consultants can assist writers as they learn how to effectively compose projects that explore the use of multiple modes:

- *linguistic meaning*—"emphasi[s on] the productive and innovative potential of language as a meaning-making system" (79) that has linguistic features including delivery, vocabulary, positioning, word choice, information structures, and the overall organizational properties of the text
- *visual meaning*—colors, images, font, page layout, perspective, and screen formats
- *audio meaning*—noise, music, and sound effects
- *gestural meaning*—body language, behavior, and sensuality
- *spatial meaning*—the arrangement of elements on a physical plane, environmental spaces and architectural spaces
- *multimodal*—the dynamic relationship among all these modes

Meaning is shaped by the interaction among the different modes (linguistic, visual, audio, gestural, spatial, and multimodal) and how they are combined to create a message. How these modes are used or implemented to shape meaning depends on the modal affordances (Wyatt-Smith and Kimber 2009). These affordances refer to the potentials and limitations for a particular mode. According to Carey Jewitt (2013), affordance "is a complex concept connected to both the material *and* cultural, social and historical use of a mode. Modal affordance is shaped by how a mode has been used, what it has been repeatedly used to mean and do and the social conventions that inform its use in context" (254). Understanding modal affordances provides consultants with opportunities to discuss the social conventions surrounding modes and how the possibilities of the mode impact the ways writers communicate. For example, as Wyatt-Smith and Kimber (2009) explain, "The affordance of still images are governed by the logic of space and simultaneity, while the affordance of speech is governed by temporal logic" (76). It is difficult to avoid the logic of time sequence when dealing with speech because "one sound is uttered after another, one word after another, one syntactic and textual element after another" (Jewitt 2013, 254). Images, on the other hand, have an impact based on the time, setting, and context in which they are taken and viewed. Images can also be influenced by the material in which they are presented, such as through a screen or on a poster. Therefore, the use of particular modes shapes the meaning of the message in ways other modes might not.

In order to create unity within a text, cohesion must occur. Cohesion "refers to the ways in which the selected visual, verbal and even aural elements are displayed and combined to achieve unity. Headings, sub-headings, lexical choices and cohesive ties directly affect cognitive structuring and meaning-making" (Wyatt-Smith and Kimber 2009, 78). Writers can create greater cohesion by taking into account the individual modal affordances, as well as the meaning created through the combination of those modes. Effective communication involves the meaning-making process that occurs across multiple modes. We use these concepts of multimodality and the meaning-making process from the New London Group and Wyatt-Smith and Kimber to provide consultants an opportunity to reconceptualize how they interact with writers and texts.

As you make your way through this book, looking at specific areas of design, remember the basis of meaning making that occurs through multiple modes. All these areas of design are closely associated with the essential rhetorical choices of design.

RHETORICAL CHOICES AND NARRATIVE

Rhetorical situations are applicable to all projects a student designs. As Pamela Takayoshi and Cynthia Selfe (2007) argue, "Conventional rhetorical principles such as audience awareness, exigence, organization, correctness, arrangement, and rhetorical appeals are necessary considerations for authors of successful audio and visual compositions" (5). The three main rhetorical elements essential to communicating effectively involve taking into consideration the writer's purpose, audience, and context:

- *purpose*—the goal of the writer's communication. Consultants can ask writers what they expect the audience to do with the information they receive. Does the purpose match up with the intended audience? Is the writing aiming to inform or persuade the audience in a certain way? Is there a call to action?
- *audience*—whom the writer is aiming their communication towards. Consultants and writers can discuss the audience's age range,

education, culture, race, class, gender, and familiarity with the topic. Who will be receiving the message? What background knowledge do they have on the topic? What is their previous experience with the type of communication the writer is designing?

- *context*—where the communication is taking place: "the physical and temporal circumstances in which readers will use your communication" (Kostelnick and Roberts 2011, 5). Consultants can inquire about the surrounding setting of where the writer intends to display their communication. Is the writer interacting with the audience, or is the project standing alone? Will the writer see their audience, or is the audience in cyberspace responding remotely? Is the audience expected to glance at or skim the information, or should they be pondering the concepts?

Effective communication requires the writer to determine the various elements associated with the rhetorical situation. First, writers need to understand their purpose for writing; they need to know what story they are trying to tell and to be able to succinctly summarize that story for their audience. Similar to working with writers on text-based papers, consultants help writers effectively articulate their purpose for multimodal projects. Once they know their storyline or purpose, they are able to tailor the story for their particular audience, taking into account language choices, familiarity with subject matter, and comfort level with the mode of communication. In considering new media and rhetorical situations, Andrea Lunsford and Lisa Ede (2014), who are experts in audience and collaboration, note that "as writers and audience merge and shift places in online environments, participating in both brief and extended collaborations, it is more obvious than ever that writers seldom, if ever, write alone" (196). Writing center consultants know this better than most, and they have the unique opportunity to respond as engaged audience members/ collaborators to help writers process these areas. Consultants can "help designers think and learn about rhetorical choices (audience, context, purpose), aesthetic elements and visual design, the designing process, goals and plans for revisions, and design products" (Sabatino 2014, 41). For example, Brian Fallon's chapter in this collection on artist statements calls attention to the ways artists communicate their work to audiences both visually and verbally using these familiar rhetorical principles.

VISUAL DESIGN PRINCIPLES

In order to assist writers in areas of design, consultants need a basic understanding of visual-design principles to provide meaningful feedback on projects—specifically applying the Gestalt principles of psychology to discuss visual-design basics. *Gestalt* means "form" or "wholeness" (Kostelnick and Roberts 1998, 52), and the principles come from a German movement in psychology that refers to the ways we organize information and perceive objects in relation to the whole visual field. Therefore, the "gestalt principles cover a wide range of perceptual experiences" (Kostelnick and Roberts 2011, 52). Susan Hilligoss and Tharon Howard (2002) state that "in visual communication, the principles of Gestalt psychology are flexible, powerful tools for interpreting many kinds of visual information and for creating successful documents, pages, and screens" (9). For a more detailed compilation of Gestalt principles applied to art design, see Rudolf Arnheim's book *Art and Visual Perception: A Psychology of the Creative Eye* (1960). In other places in this collection, authors draw upon similar practices called the "CRAP" (contrast, repetition, alignment, and proximity) principles presented by Robin Williams (2008)—these principles are outlined in detail in Shawn Apostel's chapter on visual aids for presentations. Similar to the Gestalt principles, the CRAP principles help focus the audience's attention to visual details. While there are many different Gestalt principles, this introduction focuses on three that provide practical guidance when working with multimodal writers: figure-ground, grouping, and color.

Figure-Ground

Figure-ground is the distinction between the figure and ground. Figure-ground contrast is "our ability to separate one image from another, to distinguish what stands in the front and what stands in the back" (Kostelnick and Roberts 2011, 52). As shown in figure 1.1, there is clear figure-ground contrast, as the white triangles (figure) stand out on the dark black circle (the ground).

Whenever we view images, we actively engage in making the figure-ground distinction. The level of distinction might vary depending on the contrast created between the images and the overall purpose of the image. Figure-ground contrast is important when designing because it creates a visual distinction between objects and creates the context for the how the image will be viewed. The level of figure-ground contrast depends on the writer's purpose for the visual and how the writer intends the audience to interact with that visual.

Ambiguous figure-ground contrast occurs when we cannot easily determine what is in the front and what is in the back (Hilligoss and Howard 2002). For example, in figure 1.2, image A has a clearer distinction between the triangles and circle than does image B. Ambiguous

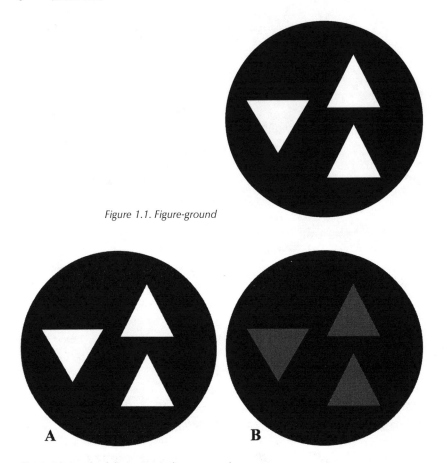

Figure 1.1. Figure-ground

Figure 1.2. Levels of distinction in figure-ground contrast

figure-ground contrast can be effective when designing optical illusions, but if that is not the writer's goal, the lack of distinction between the objects only acts as a hindrance for the audience. With strong figure-ground contrast, the writer is clearly indicating to the audience how to perceive the visual, whereas ambiguous figure-ground contrast puts more responsibility on the audience to determine the elements and goals of the visual. By sharing their perceptions of the writer's figure-ground contrast, consultants can help writers determine their intended meaning.

Grouping

Another important Gestalt principle for consultants to be aware of involves the ways our eyes organize information and group them together. This visual arrangement is the act of our minds grouping information and determining how objects differ from one another. As explained by Kostelnick and Roberts (2011), "Visual arrangement also involves spatial orientation within a field, as in left and right, up and down" (15). In this process, we create a hierarchy, or queuing, of information. We prioritize objects based on how we group them, as well as how they look in relation to one another.

Visual grouping involves sorting through parts and differentiating the objects the eyes are seeing. This important step in design helps the reader understand the organization of the project. Effective grouping practices are significant for visual projects, such as slide presentations, posters, brochures, infographics, and web design. Kostelnick and Roberts (2011) state that "grouping is a powerful tool for structuring the parts of a document—pieces of text, pictures, icons, lines, bullets, and so on. By threading these parts together into manageable units, grouping enables readers to sort through the parts of a document more efficiently" (59). Specifically, in order for our minds to make sense of the information we are receiving, we begin to group objects together in two ways: (1) proximity or (2) similarity. Proximity refers to grouping objects together based on how close the objects are in relation to each other (see fig. 1.3). Objects grouped together based on similarity are organized by their similarity in shape, orientation, color, or texture. Figure 1.4 demonstrates grouping by similarity.

As seen in the example of proximity, based on the distance of the objects from one another, the brain comfortably organizes the circles in three sets of objects: a vertical line and two triangles. By grouping the circles through proximity, the eyes can quickly organize the information on the page in order to make sense of it. Proximity is a grouping method that creates unity based on where the objects are in relation to one another. In the similarity example, the objects are grouped together based on their shapes: triangles and squares. Due to the similarity of the shapes, the eye is more likely to group figure 1.4 into vertical columns instead of horizontal rows. The repetition of these shapes creates an association and grouping for the eye to follow. Similarity can be a powerful grouping method because it is used to create unity among objects.

Effectively grouped items can be used to create meaning for the viewer. Poorly grouped items create confusion and make it difficult to differentiate the message the writer is trying to send. Consultants and writers can discuss the path their eyes follow and which visuals their eyes are drawn to first. The ways a reader groups information are influenced by their cultural background and context. Therefore, as explained by

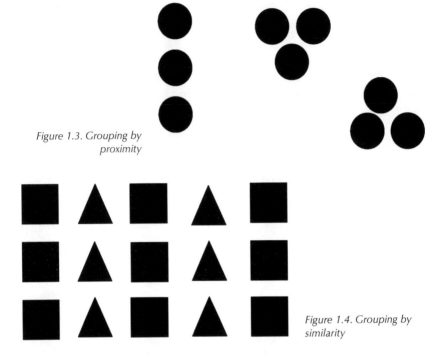

Figure 1.3. Grouping by proximity

Figure 1.4. Grouping by similarity

Ray Kristof and Amy Satran (1995), in Western languages readers identify the following conventions:

- text will read from top left to bottom right
- larger items are more significant than smaller items
- items higher on the page have more priority than those lower down
- signals of continuation ("more to come") appear at bottom center or bottom right (quoted in Hilligoss and Howard 2002, 22).

When grouping information, the writer must be aware of their audience's cultural background. Consultants can help writers reach their audience by explaining their knowledge of the visual practices of a culture.

Color

Color is another powerful way of grouping information; it can also be used to evoke emotion and create an emphasis or distinction. Color can be used to effectively distinguish and group items of similar topics together. As powerful and effective as color can be, it can equally cause distraction or overwhelm readers. Since the goal of this chapter is to introduce you to basics of color, this section is focused on color character-istics, contrast, and figure-ground and will provide a simplified overview about color choices. Color versions of the images in this collection and additional resources are available at www.multimodalwritingcenter.org.

Color consists of three characteristics: hue, saturation, and value.

- *Hue* is the color, such as yellow, red, blue, and so forth.
- *Saturation* is the purity or the strength of the color. The higher the saturation the more vivid or bright the hue appears.
- *Value* is the lightness or darkness of the color based on the amount of black or white in the color.

Value is used to distinguish a figure from the ground. More specifi-cally, "Value is a graphics term meaning the relative lightness or dark-ness of a color. The lightest is white; the darkest is black. Use very dark text on light backgrounds. Alternatively, use light text on very dark backgrounds" (Hilligoss and Howard 2002, 98). In order to distinguish the figure from the ground effectively, there must be a contrast in the colors used in order for the figure to stand out. Without proper contrast in color, the audience must strain their eyes and might not be able to receive the intended meaning.

Avoid using colors that strain the eyes.

Instead, consultants should encourage writers to use colors that are complementary and contrastive. As a result, there is a distinction between the colors of the figure and the ground, and the message is more easily deciphered

Use contrasting colors.

In addition to discussing contrasting colors, it is important for con-sultants to remind writers to use colors consistently throughout the text. If the writer establishes green to indicate subheadings on a poster, it will be disorienting for the audience if that green switches to orange halfway down the poster. Obviously, the concept of cohesion is key, and one way to achieve cohesion in a project is to make sure the colors are consistent throughout the design.

All colors used in a project should have a purpose. Each color chosen should take into consideration the purpose, audience, and context. The color should also reflect the tone and content of the project. For example, some writers might cringe at the thought of using bright pink as a back-ground color in a project, but if the topic is breast-cancer awareness, the use of pink fits the content and rhetorical situation. Consultants can ask writers why they've chosen the colors used in their project and encourage writers to explore what the colors convey to their audience.

Additionally, colors are contextually compatible with meaning—sensitive to contexts and cultures. For example, according to a 2016 post by SmarterTraveler on the Huffington Post blog *Life*, in Western cultures, the color blue represents melancholy and "is also a symbol of masculinity and represents the birth of a boy—the opposite of China, where blue is considered a feminine color." Consideration of intended audience is particularly important when choosing color because some choices can be seen as insulting. For example, according to SmartTraveler, in Western cultures, green is typically meant to represent money, greed, freshness, or spring. Whereas "most Eastern and Asian cultures relate green with new and eternal life, new beginnings, fertility, youth, health, and prosperity . . . in Chinese culture, wearing a green colored hat for men is a taboo because it suggests the man's wife is cheating on him." During a session, consultants can help writers research the meaning behind colors in order to appropriately address their audience. For more information about color and using the color palette, see color .adobe.com or paletton.com.

FONT

Font, or typeface, is the design of all alphabetic and numerical characters and punctuation of documents and projects. In order to provide you with suggestions for discussing font with writers, this section focuses on the Gestalt principles, legibility research done by Miles A. Tinker, and the scholarship produced by Susan Hilligoss and Tharon Howard, and Rob Carter, Ben Day, and Philip Meggs. These tips are to help writers effectively use font based on their rhetorical situation and accepted practices in Western genres.

The legibility of a font is determined by the ability to read it rapidly and easily. As explained by Tinker (1963), legibility refers to "perceiving letters and words, and with the reading of continuous textual material. The shape of letters must be discriminated, the characteristic word forms perceived, and continuous text read accurately, rapidly, easily, and with understanding" (7–8). Other factors that affect the font's legibility "include the medium of the document (page or screen), readers' genre knowledge, and their goals for reading" (Hilligoss and Howard 2002, 124). Legibility is an important aspect of choosing the appropriate font.

Serif versus Sans Serif

Serif fonts have small strokes, or "tails," at the end of the letters, such as Times New Roman or Cambria, whereas sans serif fonts do not, such as Arial or Helvetica.

Serif   **Sans Serif**

Serif font strokes also have varying weights, or thicknesses; "A typeface that is too light or too heavy has diminished legibility," as the letters merge visually, making it hard to discern (Carter, Day, and Meggs 1993, 91). When choosing between a serif and sans serif font, the writer must consider the context in which the document or project will be viewed. Serif fonts tend to be used more often for printed text and longer bodies of work, whereas sans serif fonts tend to be more legible on screens and on the web. The research into the legibility of serif versus sans serif font has been inconclusive.

When designing a document or project, the writer should use no more than two or three different fonts. Hilligoss and Howard (2002) describe how to create a structural contrast between serif and sans serif fonts within one document: "Use sans serif fonts like Arial or Helvetica for headings and display type. Use Old Style serif font like Times New Roman, Palatino, Garamond, or Goudy Old Style for body type. These contrast in structure. The built-in styles for body text and headings of many word processing programs incorporate this basic concept. The more traditional the audience and rigid the genre, the more likely that this combination will serve well" (129). In general, sans serif fonts are viewed as cleaner, friendlier, and more modern, while serif fonts appear more classic and formal. Information about choosing the best fonts for accessibility will be discussed later in this chapter.

Font and Tone

The font a designer chooses must match the rhetorical situation in which the information is presented. Therefore, consultants should encourage writers not to choose a font solely based on personal preference but by examining how purpose, audience, and context inform font choices. For example, if the heading below was printed in a medical journal, would the audience take it seriously?

Depression and War

No, this font does not match the purpose or seriousness of the topic. Instead, this font would more likely be found on a birthday invitation or a bakery storefront. If a writer does not choose a font that matches the tone or purpose of the project, the audience will question the credibility of the designer or wonder whether the designer is mocking the topic.

Depression and War

A more appropriate font might include Georgia (shown above) because of its traditional yet modern look, and the weight behind the strokes makes it more serious in appearance. The tone of the font sets the precedent for how the content should be read. As Shawn Apostel's chapter in this collection mentions, the weight of the font can impact how the audience perceives the information. It is important to make sure the font is sending the right message. James Truman outlines how font impacts personal branding in his chapter on professional identity.

Creating Emphasis

Italics, bold, all capitals, and color changes are some ways designers emphasize text within a document. These changes in text can be a helpful tool to signal to the audience the importance of information. When using signals, the designer should be consistent with the signal they choose and only use one.

Bolding text can be used to create a hierarchy of information. Bolding "should not be employed for large amounts of text" (Tinker 1963, 65) but instead should only be used for a word or phrase. *Italics* and text in ALL CAPITALS can impede reading or cause the reader to slow down (Carter, Day, and Meggs 1993, 89, 91; Tinker 1963, 65). Therefore, italics "should be restricted to those rare occasions when added emphasis is needed" (Tinker 1963, 65). Additionally, italics should be avoided when information is being presented on a screen. As described by Hilligoss and Howard (2002), "Italics are harder to read. On screen, the combination of thin, slanted lines and the ***pixellation*** (jagged, dot-like appearance) of letters is particularly hard to decipher" (128). Similarly, "If a text is set entirely in capital letters, it suffers a loss of legibility and the reader is placed at a significant disadvantage" (Carter, Day, and Meggs 1993, 89). Text in all capitals also takes up more space on the page or screen.

Color is another tool designers use in order to emphasize a point. Similar to the other signals, color should only be used to create emphasis for a word or phrase. As previously discussed with figure-ground contrast, being able to discern the text from the background is crucial for legibility (Hilligoss and Howard 2002, 124). Typically, body text is most readable when it is on the black or white scale. As explained by Rob Carter, Ben Day, and Philip Meggs (1993), "Large amounts of text are most legible as black on white, rather than the reverse" (92). Also, following their suggestion of using black or white text, the introduction of color to signal the importance of text makes it stand out even more.

Making decisions about font requires practice and experimentation. This process can be time consuming, but it is necessary in order to make good choices. Additionally, it is helpful to test out the font in the context in which it will be presented. If designing materials for a printed brochure, the writer cannot solely judge the font based on what appears on the screen. The printing process might result in a font looking smaller or bigger than the writer intended. As both Russell Carpenter and Courtnie Morin's and Sohui Lee and Jarret Krone's chapters advise, consultants should encourage designers to print a prototype of their project in order to see whether the elements change when moving from the screen to a tactile, physical version. While there are numerous font options available, consultants can help designers make quality choices that have the right impact on the audience.

AUDIO-DESIGN PRINCIPLES

Similar to visual design, there are principles and concepts for consultants to consider when helping students create multimodal texts that include audio elements. Drawing from Theo van Leeuwen (1999), Gunther Kress and Theo van Leeuwen (2001), and the National Communication Association (NCA), this section provides consultants with an introduction to sound theory and basic concepts and language for discussing audio components of multimodal projects with writers.

When utilizing sound in composing projects, writers should consider the planes or layers of sound:

- *figure or foreground*—the most important sound. This is the sound the listener must be immediately aware of and identify with.
- *ground or middle ground*—contextual sounds the listener is aware of but pays little attention to. These sounds are ones that "we take for granted and only notice when it is not there any longer" (van Leeuwen 1999, 23).
- *field or background*—sounds added to the foreground in order to simulate real-world conditions and natural reality. These sounds can also come in the form of music and are meant to create a particular mood or emotion. While these sounds are a part of the listener's physical world, they are not ones the listener pays close attention to.

By identifying these layers and understanding their function, consultants can help writers create a soundscape and perspective for the audience. The figure, ground, and field can change depending on the listener's perspective; for example, "Even sounds which are clearly intended to stand out, such as bells, alarms, and sirens, may become Ground, for instance in a big city. It all depends on the position of the listener" (van Leeuwen 1999, 17). When creating soundscapes, the writer must determine the perspective from which the listener is engaging and interacting with the audio components. Brenta Blevins's chapter on podcasting also reminds us of the importance of paying attention not only to sound but also to the impact of silence. As explained by van Leeuwen (1999), "Sound is dynamic: it can move us *towards* or *away from* a certain position, it can *change* our relation to what we hear" (18). In order to accomplish this, writers should be able to distinguish the layers in order to recognize their impact on the audience.

Voice and Delivery

Narration can be used in audio and video projects as a way for the writer to create a connection with and engage an audience, develop a storyline, and prompt critical thinking. Similar to written text, when crafting the narration, writers must be selective with language, choosing words appropriate to the topic, audience, purpose, and context. Text written for an academic paper is not always suitable for audiences who will only be following along with the spoken word. The writing in this scenario should be designed for a listening audience, which means the language tends to be more conversational, specific, and direct. When responding to audio-based projects, consultants can help writers develop a script or storyboard, provide feedback as writers practice delivery, and remind writers to check the quality of their microphone. Brandy Ball Blake and Karen Head's chapter provides resources, templates, and guidelines for creating different types of storyboards.

In addition to the language chosen, delivery and voice quality also impact the message. Delivery includes employing vocal varieties in pitch, rate, and intensity. The aspects of vocal delivery and voice quality are outlined by Kress and van Leeuwen in *Multimodal Discourse: The Modes and Media of Contemporary Communication*:

- *tension*—tightness or constriction of muscles in one's throat producing a strained or sharper sound
- *roughness*—hoarseness, raspiness

- *breathiness*—heavy breathing, soft tone; typically associated with intimacy (Kress and van Leeuwen 2001, 83)
- *loudness range*—level of noise produced and the range of territory it can cover, which "is strongly related to power and domination" (Kress and van Leeuwen 2001, 83)
- *pitch range*—highness or lowness
- *vibrato*—tremble in sounds, typically associated with emotion

The combination of these material qualities of voice and delivery influence the way a message is received. By being mindful of these concepts and manipulating these aspects of voice quality, consultants can help writers make an emotional impact on the audience. These concepts help writers understand the importance of using vocal variety to heighten and maintain interest and of using intensity appropriate for the message and audible to the audience (National Communication Association). Brenta Blevins's chapter on podcasting helps consultants think about how writers communicate in a nonvisual medium.

UNIVERSAL AND ACCESSIBILITY DESIGN

The goal of universal design when creating multimodal projects is to make them accessible to all audiences. As explained by the Centre for Excellence in Universal Design, "The designer is not expected to find one design solution that accommodates the needs of 100% of the population, as Universal Design is not one size fits all. Rather, designers are urged to explore design solutions that are more inclusive; those designs that push the boundaries as far out as possible without compromising the integrity or quality of the product." While addressing all aspects of universal design in multimodal projects is beyond the scope of this book, I'd like to highlight a few concepts: color, font, images, captioning, and transcripts. For more information about accessibility for particular genres, please see Russell Carpenter and Courtnie Morin's chapter on poster design, Shawn Apostel's chapter on slide presentations, Clint Gardner, Joe McCormick, and Jarrod Barben's chapter on web design, Brenta Blevins's chapter on podcasting, and Patrick Anderson and Florence Davies's chapter on video project.

Color

Not everyone sees color the same; as a result, when designing, careful consideration must be taken when choosing colors. High-contrast colors, such as black and white, work best for audience members who have a color-vision deficiency or color blindness. Designers should avoid combining colors (text and background or images) in the red and green or blue and yellow color families because they are not easily distinguishable. As explained by Mario Parisé (2005), "For most people, red and green contrast very well. But red and green are common color deficiencies. For example, if you use purple, brown or orange, all of which have red in them, I'll get lost. What seems clear to most people may seem blurry or indistinguishable to others." There are resources available to help writers address color concerns, such as uploading any image to color blindness simulation websites (http://www.color-blindness.com/coblis -color-blindness-simulator/) to see how they will appear or color universal design (CUD) software in Photoshop (http://www.adobe.com /accessibility/products/photoshop.html).

Font

In addition to helping writers create well-contrasted text, consultants can also encourage writers to use fonts that are accessible for all audiences. Some qualities of accessible fonts include sans serif, open letters, medium weight, and evenly spaced letters and words. Consultants can remind writers to choose fonts that have easily discernible letters, such as the distinction between a lowercase *l*, uppercase *L*, and the number *1*. As mentioned above, consultants can help writers think about the legibility of their font options. In their research on accessible fonts for people with dyslexia, Luz Rello and Ricardo Baeza-Yates (2013) determined that the best fonts for writers to use are "*Helvetica, Courier, Arial, Verdana* and *CMU*, taking into consideration both, [*sic*] reading performance and subjective preferences. Also, *sans serif, monospaced,* and *roman* font types increased significantly the reading performance, while *italic* fonts decreased reading performance" ("Conclusion"). Together, consultants and writers can discuss how font can impact their audience and ways to make choices that promote inclusivity.

Images

Poor use of images in web-based or digital projects can make them inaccessible for some users. Text-to-speech readers cannot accurately represent an image if it is missing alternate text or proper descriptions. When placing an image in a website or digital project, it is important to:

- specify alternate text, which appears when the mouse or pointer hovers over the item;

- provide a long, detailed description of a table or image, which should allow the audience to have a clear understanding of the essential aspects, such as data points;
- avoid putting essential text, large paragraphs, or navigational information in images (Centre for Excellence in Universal Design).

For a more detailed discussion about using alternative text in web design, refer to Clint Gardner, Joe McCormick, and Jarrod Barben's web-design chapter.

Captioning and Transcripts

Captioning and transcripts are important tools when creating podcasts, videos, or public service announcements that will reach a wider audience. They allow the viewer to follow along with a text representation of the audio. Captioning and transcripts are useful for a number of reasons; specifically, they allow the audience to move at their own pace and are helpful for audiences who might have difficulty hearing or processing auditory information. Captioning and transcripts are also helpful for people who are not proficient in the language in which the audio is being delivered, who are in noisy environments, or who have low bandwidth (Henry 2014).

Creating a script or text version before recording makes it easier to add captioning in the editing stages. Consultants should encourage students to develop a script for a podcast or video in the early planning stages of the project. Then, the consultant and student can revisit the script and make adjustments in order to ensure it lines up with what was recorded and what remained after editing. This script can then be used for creating captions and transcripts. Both Brenta Blevins's chapter and Patrick Anderson and Florence Davies's chapter provide details on creating scripts and transcripts for podcasts and videos, respectively.

The audio, visual, and accessibility design principles presented in this chapter are in no way exhaustive. The goal of providing this information is to help consultants develop a language to use when working with writers on multimodal projects. Additionally, these concepts help readers understand basic elements of design in order to effectively navigate through this book.

NAVIGATING MULTIMODAL COMPOSING

The chapters in this collection were written for writing consultants developing skills and abilities to meet the needs of students using the writing center for multimodal and design-focused purposes. *Multimodal Composing* introduces consultants to key elements in design, technology, sound, and visual media and how they relate to the rhetorical and expressive nature of written, visual, and spoken communication. The text is organized as a kind of journey through multimodalities, starting from more traditional text-based experiences that exist at the intersection of language, information, and images and moving toward more dynamic online and video-based compositions. This collection begins with Brandy Ball Blake and Karen Head's chapter on storyboarding, which lays a foundation for many of the following chapters that involve planning and organizing multimodal projects.

A number of chapters focus consultants' attention on the relationship between texts and images, as well as on the how to present linguistic and visual information persuasively. Brian Fallon's chapter on artist statements introduces why and how artists should discuss their visual work. Both Russell Carpenter and Courtnie Morin's chapter and Sohui Lee and Jarret Krone's chapter focus attention on design thinking, layout, and presenting information in rhetorically savvy and aesthetically pleasing research posters and brochures, respectively. Presentation slides are often under discussion during sessions at our writing centers, and Shawn Apostel offers consultants helpful strategies for choosing presentation platforms and making design decisions. Alyse Knorr's chapter on infographics demonstrates the power of visualizing complex data.

As the collection continues, the topics move toward navigating online tools and environments and using video and sound. Lauri Dietz and Kate Flom Derrick's chapter on ePortfolios provides insight into the purposes of ePortfolios, especially as tools for demonstrating students' accomplishments in logical and comprehensive ways. Clint Gardner, Joe McCormick, and Jarrod Barben move the discussion of ePortfolios to web design using a CMS and how consultants can serve as test users for web designers, providing key information on how users interface with web pages. Brenta Blevins brings the collection into the realm of sonic literacy and provides an overview of the world of podcasts. Patrick Anderson and Florence Davies introduce consultants to working with film and video projects, laying out some basic concepts that will help them discuss planning and editing video projects. Additionally, Alice Johnston Myatt looks at public service announcements, which can exist as video, audio, or written text, stressing the importance of connecting audience and purpose in multimodal texts. In the penultimate chapter, James Truman asks consultants to consider their professional identities online in order to help students think through personal branding and social media.

Finally, Brian and I chose to conclude this collection with Molly Schoen and Sarah Blazer's chapter on copyright and citation when it comes to multimodal and visual sources. In our experience, discussing attribution in the era of online sharing is always tricky, especially when we don't feel completely confident ourselves about what must be cited, how it should be cited, and whether we even have permission to use an image, sound clip, video, and so forth. Since the entire collection tends to focus on what we might consider nontraditional texts, we thought consultants would find it helpful to know the basics when it comes to fair use, attribution, and due diligence in finding out where multimodal sources originate.

Along this journey, readers will get a glimpse into the practices and values of different writing and multiliteracy centers that have been engaging in multimodal work. Each contributor offers peer, graduate-student, and professional consultants practical information and strategies based on first-hand experience. We encourage readers to adapt the activities for your own purposes and centers: individual use, classroom use, staff education, and so forth. Ultimately, the book is designed to be a go-to resource that guides consultants who are new to multimodal projects in their conversations with students.

REFERENCES

Arnheim, Rudolf. 1960. *Art and Visual Perception: A Psychology of the Creative Eye.* Los Angeles: University of California Press.
Carter, Rob, Ben Day, and Philip Meggs. 1993. *Typography Design: Form and Communication.* New York: Van Nostrand Reinhold.
Cazden, Courtney, Bill Cope, Norman Fairclough, and Jim Gee. 1996. "A Pedagogy of Multiliteracies: Designing Social Futures." *Harvard Educational Review 66* (1): 60–92.
Centre of Excellence in Universal Design. N.d. "Avoid Using Images to Display Text." Accessed June 14, 2017. http://universaldesign.ie/UniversalDesign/Technology-ICT/Web-accessibility-techniques/Designer-s-introduction-and-index/Images-Section-4-of-6-/DES-4–3-Avoid-using-images-to-display-text.html.
Henry, Shawn Lawton. 2014. "Transcripts on the Web: Getting People to Your Podcasts and Videos." uiAccess. http://www.uiaccess.com/transcripts/transcripts_on_the_web.html.
Hilligoss, Susan, and Tharon Howard. 2002. *Visual Communication: A Writer's Guide.* New York: Longman.
Jewitt, Carey. 2013. "Multimodal Methods for Researching Digital Technologies." In *The SAGE Handbook of Digital Technology Research*, edited by Sara Price, Carey Jewitt, and Barry Brown, 250–65. Los Angeles, CA: SAGE.
Kostelnick, Charles, and David D. Roberts. 1998. *Designing Visual Language: Strategies for Professional Communicators.* Boston, MA: Allyn & Bacon.
Kostelnick, Charles, and David D. Roberts. 2011. *Designing Visual Language: Strategies for Professional Communicators.* Boston, MA: Allyn & Bacon.

Kress, Gunther, and Theo van Leeuwen. 2001. *Multimodal Discourse: The Modes and Media of Contemporary Communication*. New York: Oxford University Press.

Kristof, Ray, and Amy Satran. 1995. *Interactivity by Design: Creating and Communicating with New Media*. Mountain View, CA: Adobe.

Lunsford, Andrea A., and Lisa Ede. 2014. "Among the Audience: On Audience in an Age of New Literacies." In *The Routledge Reader on Writing Centers and New Media*, edited by Sohui Lee and Russell Carpenter, 194–209. New York: Routledge.

McKinney, Jackie Grutsch. 2014. "New Media Matters: Tutoring in the Late Age of Print." In *The Routledge Reader on Writing Centers and New Media*, edited by Sohui Lee and Russell Carpenter, 242–56. New York: Routledge.

National Communication Association. N.d. "Learning Outcomes and Assessment." *Natcom.org*. Accessed June 9, 2016. https://www.natcom.org/assessmentresources/.

Parisé, Mario. 2005. "Color Theory for the Color-blind." Digital Web Magazine. http://www.digital-web.com/articles/color_theory_for_the_colorblind/.

Rello, Luz, and Baeza-Yates, Ricardo. 2013. "Good Fonts for Dyslexia." Paper presented at ACM SIGACCESS International Conference on Computers and Accessibility, Bellevue, WA, October 21–23, 2013. http://dyslexiahelp.umich.edu/sites/default/files/good_fonts_for_dyslexia_study.pdf.

Sabatino, Lindsay A. 2014. "Back to the Center: University of North Carolina Greensboro's Digital ACT Studio." *Southern Discourse in the Center: A Journal of Multiliteracy and Innovation* 19 (1): 41–45

Takayoshi, Pamela, and Cynthia L. Selfe. 2007. "Thinking about Multimodality." In *Multimodal Composition: Resources for Teachers*, edited by Cynthia L. Selfe, 1–12. Cresskill, NJ: Hampton.

Tinker, Miles A. 1963. *Legibility of Print*. Ames: Iowa State University Press.

Trimbur, John. 2000. "Multiliteracies, Social Futures, and Writing Centers." *Writing Center Journal* 30 (1): 88–91.

Van Leeuwen, Theo. 1999. *Speech, Music, Sound*. New York: St. Martin's.

Williams, Robin. 2008. *The Non-Designers Design Book: Design and Typography Principles for the Visual Novice*. Berkeley, CA: Peachpit.

Wyatt-Smith, Claire, and Kay Kimber. 2009. "Working Multimodally: Challenges for Assessment." *English Teacher: Practice and Critique* 8 (3): 70–90.

2

STORYBOARD(ING)
Multimodal Tool and Artifact

Brandy Ball Blake and Karen J. Head

The Georgia Institute of Technology

CHAPTER OVERVIEW

As a communication tool, storyboarding has its roots in the film-production industry. In the same way film designers and producers use storyboarding to capture details that represent the larger project goals, students can use storyboarding to integrate visual modes into projects that increasingly require them to negotiate a myriad of communication-related challenges. The need to communicate complex ideas is nothing new, but the need to do so in ways that address the needs of wide-ranging audiences is changing. For instance, the growing emphasis in the science, technology, engineering, and mathematics (STEM) fields on what is often more generally labeled *communicating science to the public* has many students in those fields visiting writing centers to ask for multimodal/multiliteracy tutoring. Storyboarding provides an excellent tool for consultants to use to help students reenvision the ideas they need to communicate, but storyboarding is also a viable, and often-overlooked, communication artifact.

ILLUSTRATIVE EXAMPLE: THE MANY PURPOSES OF STORYBOARDING

When Stephanie walked into the center, she already seemed frustrated. After some initial small talk, she explained she had a storyboarding assignment, and she didn't understand the point. "We're not making a video or anything," she complained. "We're just going to write some instructions. I don't understand what storyboarding has to do with that." That Stephanie was perplexed by her assignment seemed related to the course: an upper-level biomedical engineering seminar. She was struggling to understand how and why a visualization of using an MRI

DOI: 10.7330/9781607328469.c002

machine would help her write better instructions for new students entering labs.

The consultant asked Stephanie to show her the draft of her storyboard and immediately saw part of the problem; Stephanie was falling into a common trap for people new to storyboarding—a tendency to conflate storyboarding with different brainstorming techniques, particularly outlining, listing, mapping/clustering, and graphing, which focus on creating categories or subtopics, organizing ideas, and laying out visuals. While they have a lot in common with storyboarding, these techniques differ significantly, and Stephanie's draft, a combination of outlining and clustering, looked more like a draft of word-heavy slides rather than a storyboard. However, Stephanie's main problem was that she didn't understand how storyboarding was useful for her assignment.

The consultant tried a different approach. She took out a piece of paper and started drawing. "Think of a storyboard like a comic. It hits the highlights of a story—the key points or moments—and designs them very deliberately using visuals and linguistic representations of sound. Comics can show a wide variety of perspectives and angles, but they always focus in on key points because you can't have a box for each individual moment. Instead, your brain fills in the gaps between those highlights." The consultant drew a quick three-frame comic of two stick figures in a tutoring session, putting in speech bubbles for a few of the comments she and Stephanie had discussed.

Stephanie's face lit up at the mention of comics. "I guess I never thought about it like that." She and the consultant moved on, talking about the key points of Stephanie's draft, but Stephanie soon started to look puzzled again. "So I get how it's like a comic. I did a simple storyboard in my first-year English class, but that was to help us make a video. We planned out the most important scenes in the video so that we knew how to emphasize our point . . . our story." She paused, the frustration coming back into her face. "But what does that have to do with writing instructions for an MRI machine?"

Stephanie had been so caught up in the traditional definition of storyboards she could not understand how the assignment related to her or why she would ever use the form. She needed to expand her understanding of the form and of how it could be used in order to see how it could help *her*.

The consultant walked Stephanie through an example she might apply to her own storyboard development. The sample storyboard, "How to Give an Elevator Pitch" (figure 2.1), helped the author decide which ideas were the most important and how they wanted to explain

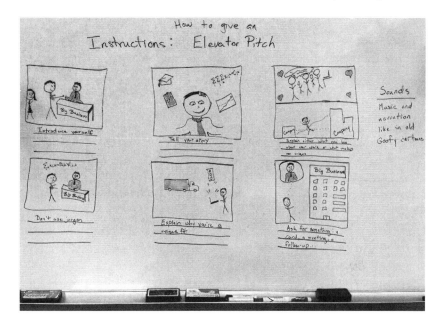

Figure 2.1. A rough draft of a storyboard completed on a whiteboard

them. Looking at this example alleviated the anxiety associated with the actual assignment and illustrated the overall process of storyboarding. Stephanie was able to see how the images, angles, words, and sound descriptions worked together to explain the process of giving a pitch.

Once Stephanie felt comfortable, the consultant returned to the MRI draft, drawing a general storyboard template on the whiteboard and asking Stephanie to sketch her ideas out roughly as they talked through the instructions. They discussed what visuals should go in the frames in order to match her key points, what kind of "shot" to use, what language to incorporate to clarify the story, and what audio would go best alongside the instructions. As she sketched and talked about the ideas, Stephanie became more enthusiastic about storyboards, realizing as she worked her way through the process how it helped her clarify her instructions and focus on her main points.

BACKGROUND INFORMATION: FROM TRADITIONAL USES TO MULTIMODAL COMMUNICATION AND LEARNING TOOL

Used traditionally, storyboarding helps artists, authors, filmmakers, and other creators plan out stories while addressing multiple modes within the work, including the six design elements of meaning making discussed in this book's introduction: linguistic meaning, visual meaning, audio meaning, gestural meaning, spatial meaning, and multimodal meaning. In particular, the form helps creators break down moments from a story and examine the best way to present those moments for maximum impact. Perspective, camera angle, shot, positioning of characters and objects, sound (music, narrator comments, background noise, etc.), dialogue, transitions, and numerous other elements are considered and, depending on the exact purpose of the storyboard, included or addressed. Visit the www.multimodalwritingcenter.org for links to examples of film storyboards, and, in particular, find the link to a sample storyboard from the movie *Apocalypse Now*. Notice how storyboard artists Alex Tavoularis and Tom Wright (2013) walk the audience through the scene, emphasizing the music, the important characters and their attitudes, the movement and formations of the helicopters, the camera angles, and so forth in order to underscore the tone of power and intimidation.

Despite its consistent use in film design and preparation, storyboarding has many uses outside the film industry, and storyboarding assignments have become common in K–12 and higher education. Such assignments can be used at any level to help students develop film or video projects, websites, works of fiction, and formal or informal presentations. Specifically, storyboarding helps creators

- develop the story of a work;
- develop or come to recognize main points; and
- organize, visualize, and declutter work.

More complex than outlines or clustering, the development of a storyboard forces students to make very specific choices in how information or stories are presented. What moments are the most important? What ideas must be emphasized? How does the visual and auditory presentation of these ideas affect how they will be interpreted by others?

However, because storyboarding methodologies focus so strongly on the choices made by the creator of a work, they can also be useful in analytical as well as creative assignments. Students can use storyboards to examine existing works in order to

- discover main points and author emphasis;
- analyze and reflect on the themes, characters, and so forth;
- visualize the work; and
- consider a work from multiple angles/modes.

Because storyboards help students organize, analyze, and create while simultaneously helping them concentrate on multiple modes of communication, diverse fields—from English and film to science and engineering—can benefit from the structure. As we've learned at our center, STEM students in particular can benefit from using storyboarding because it is similar to drafting and design techniques foundational to the work they do in their fields; they simply haven't thought of those practices in relationship to communication elements in their projects.

Additionally, storyboarding can help all students better communicate scientific and technical data—a critical skill for STEM, humanities, and social science projects. Quantitative physiology professors at MIT found that students "often find themselves at a loss of what to do with the data tables and figures they have produced" and "are likely to simply dump raw data tables into laboratory reports with the claim that the data support a given theory" (Poe, Lerner, and Craig 2010, 115). Frustrated that the students seemed unable to show the meaning of their data, they began teaching students to storyboard.

In incorporating the storyboarding approach, quantitative physiology faculty identified three underlying concepts to storyboarding they wanted students to learn:

1. Data drive scientific research. Organize and locate trends in data before beginning to write the supporting text.
2. Each figure in a report tells its own story. Design figures that make the point that you want to make.
3. In sum, the figures in a report tell a narrative of the research. Consider if the data make a logical sequence from one figure to the next figure. (Poe, Lerner, and Craig 2010,118)

Because students in STEM focus so strongly on showing their process, they often forget to contextualize their information and emphasize the point of their research. Storyboarding can help such students better understand their major points, how their data visualizations fit into the points, and how to show the meaning behind the numbers.

As mentioned earlier, comics are a familiar kind of storyboarding to many people and are therefore a compelling way to help students find better ways to communicate ideas by incorporating visuals. Over the past seventy years, educators have slowly expanded the role of comics in the classroom, in some cases analyzing them as multimodal works but in many cases using them as a foundation for transmitting information.

As seen in *Understanding Rhetoric: A Graphic Guide to Writing* (Losh et al. 2014) and the comic dissertation *Unflattening* (Sousanis 2015), comics

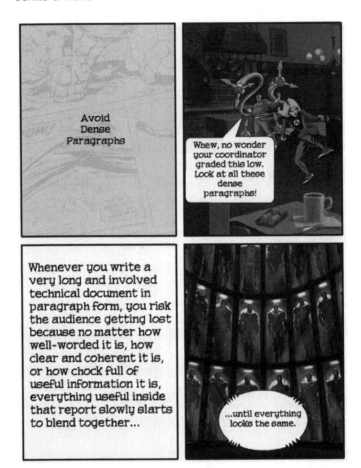

Figure 2.2. An excerpt from an unpublished comic on technical writing by Brandy Ball Blake, designed using Marvel.com's Create Your Own Comic website

break down information in engaging and approachable ways, and a strong foundation in comic conventions can help students explain and visualize ideas across fields. Take the following example from Brandy Ball Blake's unpublished technical-writing manual in figure 2.2. The sample incorporates traditional text into comic-book formatting (panels, gutters, images, word boxes, etc.) in order to make a point about readability—that in technical communication, the visual formatting of a work contributes to or detracts from the readability and, therefore, the consumption of information. Storyboards, like comics, allow students to play with the interconnections among linguistic, visual, audio, gestural, and spatial meaning—not only learning how they interact but also discovering how those interactions create multimodal meaning in and of themselves.

From a center perspective, storyboarding is also one of the easiest practices to implement. Where multimodal/multiliteracy projects are concerned, there is often the misconception that expensive tools are necessary. While a SMARTboard or other similar technologies are useful, they are not imperative. All anyone needs to employ storyboarding is a blank space to "capture" ideas (whiteboard, chalkboard, design-based software, or paper all suffice). Almost any center could make a small investment in crayons or colored pencils and a few rolls of large-format paper that would allow consultants to easily integrate storyboarding into their daily tutoring practices. Rolling whiteboards, which require a larger front-end investment, provide a more sustainable option in the long term. However, the employment of reusable materials also means providing a way for students to save their work—perhaps the easiest solution is a photograph taken with a smartphone. Ultimately, the most important consideration is providing students with an artifact to reinforce that a storyboard isn't only a means to an end; it has value as a stand-alone artifact, much in the way architectural drawings continue to be important long after a structure is built.

CONSULTATION STRATEGIES FOR STORYBOARDING
Practical Strategies
Be Familiar with Storyboarding Materials

Many tools and materials are needed for a productive storyboarding tutoring session (templates, colored pencils, erasers, storyboarding programs, etc.). Storyboarding templates are easily accessible online, and they can be modified to fit numerous assignments. Following is a basic eight-panel storyboarding template.

A simple template like the one shown in figure 2.3 helps students understand the foundational elements of storyboarding, visually encouraging students to fill in both graphic and textual components. Even if students or consultants don't want to fill in the template, it can still serve as a structural reminder that guides more creative design approaches (perhaps on an interactive SMARTboard that could allow for the insertion of high-resolution photographs, as one example).

Practice Drawing Simple Visual Icons

Students might be nervous about drawing, so developing a simple visual vocabulary allows consultants to help students more quickly and provide

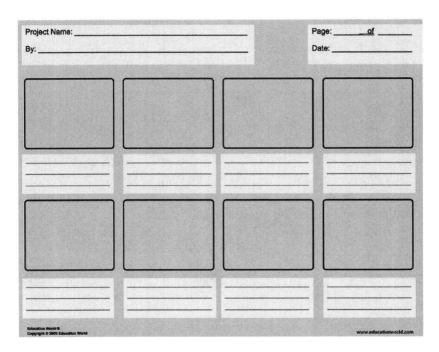

Figure 2.3. A storyboard template from the website Education World: Connecting Educators to What Works

them with tools they could use for storyboarding, brainstorming and note taking (see books such as *The Sketchnote Handbook* [Rohde 2013], *The Doodle Revolution* [Brown 2015], and *100+1 Drawing Ideas* [Toselli 2016] for additional information on this topic and for help with simple pictograms). Consultants can demonstrate these techniques to students and ask them to practice a few simple drawings in the session.

Ask Students to Sketch/Write as They Talk through Their Ideas

Encourage students to make preliminary sketches while brainstorming during the session. Assure them the sketches should be rough and that no one is judging their drawing capabilities. Spending a session on this activity will help students break through their initial resistance to incorporating visuals into a work, and it will also help them link the concepts of visualizing and brainstorming, hopefully encouraging them to make this type of multiliteracy a habit.

When working with visually impaired students, tutors should expect to create the textual equivalent of a storyboard—using all the same elements (panels, key moments, design, sound, etc.) but without the pictures. Screen readers rely on alternate text to depict images, so visually impaired students are likely to be familiar with this method of description. During brainstorming sessions, encourage them to practice verbally "sketching" the different panels using text and help them become more familiar with applying textual description to a storyboard template.

Show Students Storyboard Templates

Teach students how to find templates for storyboarding and discuss the ways different templates emphasize different information or modes. A Google Image search using the words *storyboard templates* or an internet search using the phrase *how to create a storyboard* will provide you with numerous options—some from educational websites, corporate websites, and even WikiHow. Templates are available for free on many of these sites.

Rhetorical Strategies

Determine Context and Purpose of the Assignment

There are many reasons to create a storyboard (a storyboard by itself, a storyboard in preparation for a video or presentation, a storyboard for analysis, etc.). These differences could change the focus of the storyboard. For example, when storyboarding is used for analysis, the focus should be on using the format to emphasize examining an analytical argument rather than explaining an idea or telling a story. In preparation for a video, students should consider the limitations they face in creating the final video while designing the storyboard. Storyboards might also help students think outside the box about other types of media. In one session, a consultant working with a student who was using storyboarding as the first step in designing a research poster simply switched the orientation of the template from horizontal to vertical. This simple action helped the student imagine a presentation strategy she had never considered. Her data was much easier to represent in a vertical format, and storyboarding was the "window" through which she could see that format taking shape.

Become Familiar with Some Filmmaking Concepts

Knowing a little about types of shots, camera angle, and point of view can help consultants better understand the variation within the storyboarding form and better explain the available options to the students. Consultants can learn more about filmmaking concepts in Patrick Anderson and Florence Davies's chapter on video projects in this collection.

Address the Six Design Elements of Meaning Making

The design elements of meaning making are discussed in the introduction of this collection. Here's how consultants can address these elements in regard to storyboarding: linguistic meaning (the text of the storyboard); visual meaning, gestural meaning, spatial meaning (color, placement, perspective, grouping, angle, and nonverbal meaning within the images); audio meaning (sound, narration, or music that could be incorporated); and multimodal meaning (how each of these elements work together to provide greater meaning).

Keep Storyboards from Getting Too Cluttered or Incoherent

If students are trying to incorporate every idea they have or are worrying over the inclusion of every design element, help them focus on the most important points/choices. Storyboards generally hit the highlights, so too much information can make them more intimidating or cause them to be incoherent.

ACTIVITY

Every year, the Alan Alda Center for Communicating Science at Stony Brook University promotes the Flame Challenge, a competition designed to help people learn how to explain complex scientific concepts in clear and simple ways. The competition's topics (*What is energy? What is sleep? What is sound?*) are determined by eleven-year-olds, the target audience for the entries. Therefore, in order to communicate clearly with this audience, the competitors must concentrate on core ideas, discuss them in straightforward terms, and create explanatory (but entertaining) visuals. Entries are short: videos are under five minutes, and written entries are less than three hundred words. The brevity of these materials will help you easily find core ideas to focus on as you develop storyboards.

This activity will allow you to practice creating storyboards from abstract concepts. As you practice, consider how the experience would help support a student during a storyboarding session. The process will help you prepare to

- talk to students about the purpose of storyboards,
- sketch concepts quickly,
- create storyboards on topics in multiple fields,
- explain connections between presenting and storytelling (whether in humanities or STEM fields), and
- visualize information in different ways.

Throughout the activity, you will need access to storyboard templates, but feel free to try out different technologies—from paper and pencils to whiteboards to SMARTboards to storyboarding software, ideally finding what works best for you at your center.

1. On the Aldi-Kavli Learning Center for Science Communication website (http://www.aldakavlilearningcenter.org/practice/flame -challenge), find a Flame Challenge question that interests you. Each challenge has two winning entries—a video and a written answer.

2. First, watch the video, and as you watch, pay particular attention to the main points and the visuals used to explain the scientific concept. Feel free to pause the talk as you go and consider how the concept is being explained—how the visuals work together, how the editing and flow of the video would keep the audience engaged, and so forth. Then, complete the following:

    a. Consider what the storyboard for the video would look like. How would it be broken down? How many core ideas are being discussed? How much time does the video give to each of these core ideas? Using a storyboarding template, break up the video into main concepts and figure out how many frames you would allot to each one. At this stage, feel free to use text only.

    b. Once you've completed the breakdown, look at the number of frames you've allotted to the video. How many main points did you choose to include in your storyboard? How many frames did you allot for each? Are there any that are redundant, unnecessary, or that don't focus on a major point? How does the storyboarding format make you narrow down and focus in on main points?

    c. Choose two topics from your frames. Look back at the video, and pause it on the most important image. Quickly sketch a simplified version of the image in your frame.

    d. Watch the video again, but this time, take notes on how sound is used during the frames you focus on. How is sound contributing to the explanation or retaining the attention of the audience?

    e. How does storyboarding change your perception of the video?

3. Next, read over the winning written entry on the topic. Consider how you would turn that entry into a video, and plan out that video using a storyboard. (While you can use ideas from the winning video entry, try to branch out and create something different.) Consider the following as you create a simple storyboard draft:

    a. What are main points in the written entry? What parts are critical to a clear explanation of the scientific concept? How does the storyboarding format make you narrow down, focus in on, and choose between main points?

b. What should be said and what should be shown in order for the audience to understand the concept? What visuals should you include to help explain the points and keep the eleven-year-olds' attention, and how do you incorporate those visuals into your explanation?

c. When sketching visuals for the storyboard, how much detail are you using? What images should be more detailed, and what images can be simplified? How much time do you spend on each image in order to get general gist across? How would you adjust that in a tutoring session?

d. How did you incorporate sound into the storyboard?

e. How does storyboarding the written entry change your perception of the concept? Of the written entry? Of the video entry?

4. Flesh out the storyboard on a whiteboard or using storyboarding software (such as StoryboardThat, StoryBoard Pro, Storyboard Fountain, or Storyboard Composer) in order to create a more finalized draft. Once the storyboard is complete, consider the following questions:

a. How do you balance the number of boxes included in the storyboard? How do you keep from having too many (mapping out every tiny point) or not having enough (only including main points)?

b. How do you cover the different elements of the explanation in the storyboarding template? What information should go in the boxes, and what information should be described in the spaces surrounding the boxes?

c. How do the six design elements of meaning making (linguistic meaning, visual meaning, audio meaning, gestural meaning, spatial meaning, and multimodal meaning) come together in this storyboard?

d. How can this activity prepare you for working with students on storyboards?

Additional Storyboarding Activity Ideas:

- Create a storyboard for a purely linguistic essay previously written. How does storyboarding it change your perspective of the work? Of the organization, the linguistic meaning, visual meaning, audio meaning, gestural meaning, spatial meaning, multimodal meaning, and so on.
- Look at storyboards for movies that have already been released. Analyze the choices made by the storyboarder, its similarities to and differences from the final cut, and so on.
- Storyboard a tutoring session (real, pretend, or typical). Emphasize important choices in the session.

CONCLUSION

So how does a consultant take it to the next step? While many professors assign storyboards, they mostly do so in connection with film, websites, or presentations. However, just because a professor did not assign it does not mean it's not appropriate in a tutoring session. Storyboarding is a creative way to visualize information and to focus on multiple modes, and once students understand how it does that, storyboarding can be used for a number of different purposes. Consultants should attempt to incorporate storyboards into tutoring sessions, particularly in cases in which the student needs a better understanding of how to manage the narrative of a large work/project and to better visualize data/examples. Furthermore, storyboarding can illuminate how

- main points emerge from secondary ideas,
- organization and sequence matter,
- visual-design elements require revision,
- procedural artifacts illuminate the wider process(es) inherent in a project, and
- different modes create interesting tension in an assignment.

While tutoring might be the primary focus for introducing story-boarding, consultants who encourage (and students who use) story-boarding in the same way and for the same purpose as brainstorming, mapping, and clustering are missing the contextualized sense of the storyboard as an artifact in and of itself. Therefore, consultants should always take time to explain to students that storyboarding is both a useful tool and another way to visualize and present information—helping students understand storyboards as one of many potential presentation choices, along with traditional slides, posters, and so forth.

Because storyboarding provides an increased focus on creating better "stories"—narratives that incorporate visuals, sound, and text in more integrated ways—consultants should be educated to consider story-boarding as part of their tutoring practices. However, consultants should also understand storyboards as multimodal artifacts that might provide the exact format to communicate an idea most effectively, no matter what a student's discipline may be.

RESOURCES

Further Reading

Archer, Arlene. 2011. "Dealing with Multimodal Assignments in Writing Centers." *Writing Lab Newsletter* 35 (9–10): 10–13.

Brown, Sunni. 2015. *The Doodle Revolution*. New York: Portfolio.
Harring, Suzanne L. 1994. "An Author's Storyboard Technique as a Prewriting Strategy." *Reading Teacher* 48 (3): 283–86.
Hickey, Dona, and Joe Essid. 2002. "It's a Wrap: Digital Video and Tutor Training." *Writing Lab Newsletter* 26 (6): 13–16.
McCloud, Scott. 1993. *Understanding Comics: The Invisible Art*. New York: HarperPerennial.
Rohde, Mike. 2013. *The Sketchnote Handbook*. Berkeley, CA: Peachpit.
"The Flame Challenge. Explaining Science to an 11-Year-Old." N.d. Alan Alda Center for Communicating Science. https://www.aldacenter.org/outreach/flame-challenge. http://www.aldakavlilearningcenter.org/practice/flame-challenge.
Toselli, Mauro. 2016. *100+1 Drawing Ideas*. Create Space.

Storyboard Templates

Cinemek Storyboard Composer: http://cinemek.com/storyboard/.
Education World: Connecting Educators to What Works. "8-panel Storyboard Template." http://www.educationworld.com/tools_templates/template_strybrd_8panels.doc.
Storyboard Fountain: http://storyboardfountain.com/.
StoryboardThat: http://www.storyboardthat.com/.
Toon Boom StoryBoard Pro: https://www.toonboom.com/products/storyboardpro.

KEY SEARCH TERMS

storyboard; storyboard template; storyboard examples; comic; Flame Challenge; visual representation of research; visual rhetoric; mapping; meaning making; multimodal; multiliteracies; brainstorming; outline; visual artifacts; narrative; data visualization; communicating science; ADA; alternate text; Toon Boom StoryBoard Pro; Cinemek Storyboard Composer; Storyboard Fountain; StoryboardThat

REFERENCES

Blake, Brandy Ball. "Avoid Dense Paragraphs." In *The Adventures of Senior Design Team Awesome: A Technical Manual for Georgia Tech's Industrial and Systems Engineering Majors*. Unpublished manuscript.
Brown, Sunni. 2015. *The Doodle Revolution*. New York: Portfolio.
Education World: Connecting Educators to What Works. N.d. "8-panel Storyboard Template." Accessed June 12, 2017. http://www.educationworld.com/tools_templates/template_strybrd_8panels.doc.
"The Flame Challenge: Explaining Science to an 11-Year-Old." N.d. Alan Alda Center for Communicating Science https://www.aldacenter.org/outreach/flame-challenge.
Losh, Elizabeth, Jonathan Alexander, Kevin Cannon, and Zander Cannon. 2014. *Understanding Rhetoric: A Graphic Guide to Writing*. Boston, MA: Bedford/St. Martin's.
Poe, Mya, Neal Lerner, and Jennifer Craig. 2010. *Learning to Communicate in Science and Engineering: Case Studies from MIT*. Cambridge, MA: MIT.
Rohde, Mike. 2013. *The Sketchnote Handbook*. Berkeley, CA: Peachpit.
Sousanis, Nick. 2015. *Unflattening*. Cambridge, MA: Harvard University Press.

Tavoularis, Alex, and Tom Wright. 2013. "Napalm in the Morning." *DGA Quarterly*, Spring 2013. https://www.dga.org/Craft/DGAQ/All-Articles/1302-Spring-2013/Drawing -Board-Apocalypse-Now.aspx.

Toselli, Mauro. 2016. *100+1 Drawing Ideas*. Create Space.

3

ARTIST AND DESIGN STATEMENTS
When Text and Image Make Meaning Together

Brian Fallon
Fashion Institute of Technology, SUNY

CHAPTER OVERVIEW

Artist and design statements offer creative individuals opportunities to communicate the purpose, philosophy, and inspiration of their visual work through the written or spoken word. This chapter offers an overview of artist statements and provides consultants with strategies to help artists and designers make connections between the images and texts they create. In discussing their personal collection of artwork, Gael Mendelsohn and Michael Mendelsohn note that "every collection of art tells a story about the person who assembled it, just as surely as a work of art tells a story about the person who created it" (2000, 11). Consultants can help artists connect to language that best illuminates their work, process, and philosophy.

ILLUSTRATIVE EXAMPLE: A DESIGNER WRITES AND REVAMPS

Every year at the Fashion Institute of Technology (FIT), fashion design students prepare collection statements for a scholarship competition run by the Council of Fashion Designers of America (CFDA). FIT is only one school of many that competes in the CFDA scholarship program, and students work hurriedly to pull together swatches, sketches, color stories, mood boards, and, of course, an essay. Over the years, the CFDA has changed its expectations for the written portion of the portfolio from a design philosophy statement to its latest incarnation, a collection statement that includes an explanation of the idea, narrative, and process. Now the CFDA also asks students to prepare a resumé and bio in addition to a video self-introduction. Despite these new expectations for communicating a designer's identity, experience,

DOI: 10.7330/9781607328469.c003

and approach, a constant requirement over the years has been that the design concept is clearly articulated in the statement and executed in the collection. In reviewing past comments from judges, it's clear the CFDA wants students to be able to communicate their design motivations and concepts. The concept must resonate throughout the collection, and what we've learned from doing this work year after year is that artist statements should be developed as a part of the design process. If and when the looks in a collection evolve, so should the statement.

Years ago, I worked with a designer named Bella. Bella was using kente cloth in her collection because she felt a personal connection with the traditions and heritage kente cloth represented. As we sat down to work on Bella's statement and I started asking questions about why her fabric choices were significant to her, she admitted she didn't know very much about kente cloth. Bella began to research, learning the meanings of the colors in the cloth and the differences between *Asante* and *Ewe* kente. She also realized that the swatch of kente she had been using in her collection was inauthentic, having been mass produced in textile mills that had no ties to Africa or African culture.

Working on her statement led Bella to replace swatches in her collection and to think globally about her work as a designer. She could see how decisions about materials could run counter to the message she wanted her collection to send, and, in some sense, Bella began to see herself as a kind of designer-intellectual. The reason I think Bella's story is so important to tell is that it demonstrates how artist statements can achieve multiple goals in one short text.

The power of the statement was not just in Bella's ability to bring personal meaning to her concept and material selection; it provided the reflection and analysis needed for Bella to engage her work on a deeper intellectual, cultural, and political level.

BACKGROUND INFORMATION: WHAT CONSULTANTS NEED TO KNOW ABOUT ARTIST AND DESIGN STATEMENTS

Just as in the case of Bella, artists and designers often need to communicate the purpose, philosophy, and inspiration of their visual work through the written or spoken word. According to visual communications professor Lisa Graham (2010), there are a number of reasons artists or designers might need to write about their work, and an artist statement can be a useful tool for accomplishing any number of the following goals:

- self-analysis and reflection;
- promoting one's work;
- translating, explaining, or enhancing a concept;
- describing inspiration, process, or concept;
- representing a point of view, motivation, or philosophy.

Many chapters in this book address the interplay between text and image, specifically addressing the ways writers use visual media to persuade, inform, and entertain. This chapter focuses on how makers and creators of visual media write about their own work, describe their design process and aesthetic, and elaborate on the concepts that motivate and inspire their creativity.

One specific way writers communicate their aesthetic and process is through artist and design statements. These statements can vary from one field to the next and can differ depending on the purpose of writing the statement. For instance, artists working in the applied arts might be more concerned with clients or customers when describing their work, while fine artists might be more concerned with aesthetics. Regardless of the purpose, artist and design statements can help artists engage in reflection while offering viewers insight into their work. And, as Graham (2010) notes, "A well-written, informative statement strengthens a creative individual's position as serious in their profession" (20).

As mentioned earlier, there are a variety of artist and design statements that serve a number of purposes. Some artist statements are intended to accompany a gallery show or collection while others provide general insight into a creative type's design aesthetic and process. These statements are often used for promotional reasons, but they also provide insight into an artist's body of work, sometimes offering a reflection on inspiration and philosophy.

It's important to note that some visual artists might not feel confident about their writing. Furthermore, they are used to expressing themselves through visual media and might even argue that their work shouldn't need written explanation. That is obviously fine in some cases, but artist statements don't simply exist to explain what a work of art means. In fact, an artist statement is more likely to clue viewers into an artist's way of seeing and thinking rather than dictate how to view the work, meaning that the statement can sometimes be more about the relationship between artist and viewer than between viewer and art.

To make a point about interpretation, language, and visual work, I turn to Vincent van Gogh. At some point, whether as art lovers, art history students, or just casual observers of culture, most people have encountered

Figure 3.1. Vincent van Gogh, Wheatfield with Crows, *1890, oil on canvas, 20.125 × 39.75 in. (50.5 × 103 cm), Amsterdam, Rijksmuseum.*

his work and might even know something about his life. Figure 3.1 is van Gogh's *Wheatfield with Crows*, which happens to be an important work for a very specific reason. Take a minute to observe this painting and reflect on the feelings, memories, and associations it brings to mind.

This particular work provides a great example of how a little bit of text can bring about profoundly new interpretations of images, and vice versa. As John Berger (1973) points out in his *Ways of Seeing*, this image takes on totally new meaning when it is juxtaposed with the sentence "This is the last picture that van Gogh painted before he killed himself" (21). If viewers didn't already know this fact, the sentence might compel them to contemplate how this information shifts what the work communicates, and they might even see the work from a different perspective. As Berger notes, "It is hard to define exactly how the words have changed the image but undoubtedly they have. The image now illustrates the sentence" (21).

When we bring language to visual works, we do more than just explain what we see. We bring new meanings to the work while simultaneously assigning new responsibilities for the artwork. In this case, this pastoral scene illustrates a somber beauty that might not have been as apparent before we knew it was van Gogh's last work before taking his own life. This kind of insight is part of the reason a good artist/design statement matters. The language artists choose to shed light on their work, process, and design aesthetic allows appreciators of a work to reach a deeper level of interpretation and understanding. It also creates possibilities for images to represent an array of rhetorical and expressive situations that benefit from a thought-provoking visual illustration.

Furthermore, artwork, like writing, can be and often is rhetorical in nature. In fact, there are many similarities between the way writing theorists think of rhetorical situations and the way creative types think about visual literacy and the messages visuals communicate. In her *A Primer of Visual Literacy*, Donis Dondis (1973) explains, "Meaning lies as much in the eye of the beholder as in the talents of the creator. The end result of all visual experience, in nature but primarily in design, lies in the interaction of duplex polarities: first, the forces of content (message, medium, and arrangement); and second, the effect on each other of the articulator (designer, artist, craftsman) and the receiver (audience)" (104). What Dondis addresses here is similar to a writing scholar's consideration of the relationships among readers, writers, and texts. For Dondis, it's clear the works artists produce will be interpreted by audiences in ways never intended by the creator. She concludes, "The message is cast by the creator and modified by the observer" (104).

Given the obvious connections between how artists and writers express meaning and how audiences interpret their work, there's always a place to start when discussing the rhetorical situation of a statement. The introduction of this book discusses the significance of purpose, audience, and context for visual work. Artist statements that help readers understand the story of a particular design or artwork make for more compelling experiences when viewing artwork. However, the statement cannot stand in for the artwork—it can be both crucial and ancillary at the same time. As Diana George (2002) has pointed out about twenty-first-century students, "Questions of communication and composition will include the visual, not as attendant to the verbal but as complex communication intricately related to the world around them" (32). George is reminding us that the visual holds its own meaning and rhetorical power and that when images and texts make meaning together, they don't necessarily accomplish that by one form simply supplementing the other. In this sense, it is important for consultants to help artists figure out how their written and visual work communicate their world-view or philosophy in tandem.

Purpose of an Artist Statement

Artist statements are commonly used for self-reflection, promoting work, and describing a concept, process, motivation, or philosophy. Given the wide array of purposes, artists might be asked to write many different kinds of statements. In some ways, consultants can be helpful by just assisting the artist with pinpointing their purpose for writing the statement.

As mentioned earlier, statements might tell different stories or take on different purposes based on the art and design field. For example, let's consider how a statement written for the applied arts might differ from one written in the fine arts. A statement written by a fashion designer might include a customer profile, especially if a collection's concept is directly influenced by its muse. Similarly, an interior designer or architect might have a serious obligation to consider human factors in their design statement because the nature of their work involves built environments suitable for living. On the other hand, fine artists might be more interested in discussing the political, social, historical, or cultural observations embedded in their work, producing a statement focused on ideology rather than function.

In our work at FIT, we've come across the following kinds of statements: autobiography, (self) promotion, call to action/participation, individual work of art, gallery show, collection, and portfolio. Some of these are self-evident, like a collection statement, but others, like the call to action or participation statement, are a bit more nuanced. An example of this type might be a work of art that asks viewers to interact with the exhibit. In this case, the statement provides viewers with instructions on how to experience the work.

There are likely a number of reasons to write the statement, so hearing from the writer what they're trying to communicate can help them clearly state a purpose while also helping the audience learn more about the work. The audience might want to know about the philosophy, concept, or inspiration. Additionally, discussing process, materials, and aesthetics can satisfy the interests of an audience as well. Consequently, there are lots of types of statements artists might choose to draft depending on their field and the needs of the work they've created. While one artist might call their statement a *design philosophy*, another might refer to it as an *artist statement*; no matter what, knowing the purpose, audience, and context can help artists make decisions about discussing myriad issues such as concept, process, philosophy, methods, materials, and inspiration.

CONSULTATION STRATEGIES FOR ARTIST AND DESIGN STATEMENTS
Determine Statement Type, Purpose, and Audience Needs

Depending on the situation, a creative person might have to write a statement that focuses on specific aspects of their process, their collection of work, or an individual work. Table 3.1 can help consultants guide an artist through the process of considering the rhetorical situation of

Table 3.1. Artist statement context, purpose, and audience analysis

What's the context for this artist/design statement?	
Autobiography (Self-) promotion Call to action/participation Individual work of art Gallery show Collection Portfolio	NOTES:
The purpose of this statement is to:	
Analyze Describe Educate Enhance Explain Inform Promote Reflect	NOTES:
Given the context and purpose, what does the audience need to know about your work?	

Philosophy/ideology
Concept
Process
Materials
Customer profile/muse
Aesthetic
Elements of art: line, color, shape, form,
   texture
Principles of art: balance, emphasis, move-
   ment, proportion, rhythm, unity, variety
	NOTES:

an artist statement, keeping in mind that creative types might be writing statements that include a number of different purposes and approaches. Asking questions about the goals of the statement and how the artist would like to use the statement is a good place to begin. Once the general context of the statement is determined, a consultant can ask students about their purpose for writing. Is it to inform or educate the viewer? Will the statement explain, describe, or promote the work? Does it try to enhance or translate the concept?

Helping artists pick and choose their way through these different elements is important for helping them develop a focused and appropriate statement, but it can be daunting. Table 3.1 offers a worksheet that breaks down the consulting process into a series of questions and potential options for a statement.

As with any other type of writing, audience is key in figuring out what must happen with any given statement. For instance, an artist being asked to write a statement for a competition must likely consider what the judges expect to read and see in that work. But if the same artist writing about the same collection of work is asked to prepare a statement for a gallery show, they will likely consider what a general audience might want or need to know to understand the collection's story.

In either case, the audience determines what the statement really needs to be effective. In the case of the competition, the writer might need to clearly align concept with the goals of the competition. However, for a gallery show, viewers might be more interested in how the artist's experiences resulted in the collection, making the statement more autobiographical in nature. One other key factor to keep in mind, however, is that the nature of the collection, and how an audience receives it, will also influence the statement. The visual and verbal texts reach an audience together, not separately.

Create Dialogue about the Visual Work

Many artists can be reluctant to prepare a statement. As noted earlier, some artists might contend that their work speaks for itself and therefore needs no linguistic interpretation. While any individual is certainly entitled to this line of thinking, it's good to point out that this isn't simply an either/or situation. It can be a both/and scenario. A consultant can offer an artist their perspective on the work and ask how that squares with the artist's intentions. Opening up a dialogue about interpretation might encourage the artist to complement the visual work with a statement.

All too often, a statement can be treated like an afterthought when in reality it can be a meaningful and reflective addition to a body of work. It can be poetic, explanatory, autobiographical, and/or philosophical in nature, which means there's a lot a good statement can do to enhance an individual work or collection.

Decide on Style and Voice

As mentioned above, statements can take on any number of forms to help readers/viewers gain special insight into an artist's work. There's no one right way to accomplish this writing task, so it's important to talk to artists about achieving the best voice for a particular statement. In some cases, artists might want to personalize their connection to the work and locate themselves within it in order to engender a particular feeling for the viewer. In other cases, statements will involve research and take on a more academic tone.

Translate the Visual to the Verbal

Some artists can benefit from a conversation on what they visually create. The back and forth of conversation allows these writers to grow their vocabulary, creating opportunities for them to practice new ways of communicating their visual work in speaking and writing. While descriptive language is obviously key to helping artists elucidate their work, it's also important consultants learn about the language artists use to describe their work and their process. Learning about the Gestalt principles discussed in the introduction of this collection can be helpful, and the "Resources" section of this chapter provides links to elements and principles of art vocabulary and a comprehensive glossary available on Steven Zucker and Beth Harris's (2015) website smarthistory.org. Consultants can help artists bring together their knowledge of good design and artistic practice with language that most captivates readers.

Work with the Visuals

Similar to the last tip, we have learned over the years at FIT that working with the visuals makes a world of difference when helping artists write about their work. In fact, it's nearly impossible to adequately assist with an artist statement without any of the work present. Ask writers to show where in their work a particular concept plays out or how their process informed the product. This can help the consultant get a better understanding of what the artist is trying to communicate, but it also ensures the artist is adequately conveying what's significant to the readers.

Develop a Concise yet Meaningful Statement

Finally, many artist statements are fairly brief. Therefore, a lot of rich meaning gets packed into a fairly short text. Helping artists be concise is an important part of the consultant's job. Consultants should be honest about any difficulties they have following the ideas or concepts presented in the statement. It's likely the writer has gotten off track, and consultants can help steer them back in the right direction. This aspect of the statement might be one of the most difficult because it involves careful decision-making on which aspects of this work are most important for viewers to know. That's rather difficult given the highly interpretive nature of artistic work. A good statement succinctly guides viewers toward a deeper level of meaning without necessarily telling them what to think or how to interpret a particular work or collection.

ACTIVITY

To best help creative types find language that conveys their process, design aesthetic, collections, series, and individual works in new and meaningful ways, consultants should help them think carefully about what is known and what is unknown about their work. In order to practice with this, let's turn to the work of landscape architect Maya Lin. Maya Lin is most known as the designer of the Vietnam Veterans Memorial in Washington DC, but we are going to focus on her *Storm King Wavefield*. *Wavefield* is a massive installation at the Storm King Art Center, which is the world's leading sculpture park, located in the Hudson Valley of New York.

For this activity, we will start with the image in figure 3.2 and begin to layer it with written, spoken, and visual information. The goal is to note how our understanding of *Wavefield* transforms both visually and philosophically as the image and texts coalesce. This activity can be done individually or with a group, and links to videos and images can also be found on www.multimodalwritingcenters.org.

1. The first step in this activity is to examine the image in front of you without doing any research. There's no right or wrong answer—it's about your take on this image. Look at the image and begin to describe what you see.

   - As a viewer, what stands out to you most in this picture?
   - How would you describe this exhibition to a friend?
   - In your opinion, what's the message encoded in this work?

2. Next, read the Storm King curatorial description of this work: http://collection.stormking.org/artist/maya-lin/.

   - Has your view of the image changed? With this new information, what would you add to or delete from your original description?
   - Based on your reading, what's the most significant aspect of this work?
   - Has the message shifted? What kind of a message do you believe Storm King Art Center wants *Wavefield* to convey to those who experience it?

3. Watch the *New York Times* video of Lin discussing her work. Take note of not only her descriptions of the work but also its inspiration. (Go to www.multimodalwritingcenter.org, Google *wavefield nytimes*, or visit http://www.nytimes.com/video/arts/design/1194832296918/maya -lin-s-wave-field.html to view this video.)

   - How does the artist's description of her work, her philosophy, and her goals shape the way you understand *Wavefield*?
   - What do you believe is Lin's message?
   - How do you reconcile your original take on this work with the layers of information provided by Storm King and Lin herself?

Figure 3.2. Maya Lin's Storm King Wavefield, *2007–2008, earth and grass, 240,000 square feet (11-acre site) (© Maya Lin Studio, courtesy Pace Gallery; photograph by Jerry L. Thompson, © Storm King Art Center, Mountainville, New York)*

CONCLUSION

Maya Lin is particularly good at talking about her work, its meaning, and how it communicates her interests and development as an artist. In the nytimes.com video, we actually get a number of artist statements in one concise video. Lin communicates the purposes, philosophies, politics, and methods that drive her work and her process as an artist. If we were to consider the most successful elements of how Lin explains her art, we might highlight many of the elements mentioned in the strategies for consultants earlier in this chapter. Lin's very good at assessing what her audience wants and needs to hear, and she has a confident and comfortable style and voice when it comes to discussing her work. But what's more, Lin can locate her work within philosophical and political frameworks that help viewers develop a meaningful appreciation of what she's created. This is the work of letting her statement help translate the visual to the verbal, fostering a dialogue about the significance of her work.

Effective artist statements take on these tasks, and as consultants, we can support artists in their efforts to focus these statements and to bring thoughtful and dynamic language to their visual work and artistic process. It's also important to keep in mind that writing the statement can be a vital part of an artist's learning process. As a tool for reflection, the statement is a powerful way to consider how new approaches and inspirations inform a creative individual's work or process. It's the consultant's job to help artists with this process and to help them find ways to promote their work and the concepts that drive their creativity.

RESOURCES

Describing and Appreciating Art

Smarthistory.org
> This website provides resources from glossaries to ways of observing and talking about art.

Elements and Principles of Art http://www2.oberlin.edu/amam/asia/sculpture/documents/vocabulary.pdf
> The Allen Memorial Art Museum at Oberlin College has created a useful handout on elements and principles of art.

Examples of Artists Discussing Their Work

"The Artist Is In"
> https://www.ted.com/playlists/3/the_artist_is_in
> This TED playlist offers a series of personal and entertaining talks by artists discussing their processes and perspectives.

Chris Jordan, "Turning Powerful Stats into Art"
> http://www.ted.com/talks/chris_jordan_pictures_some_shocking_stats
> Chris Jordan (2008) discusses his work, which represents statistical data through stunning and provocative visuals.

Further Reading

"How to Write An Artist Statement: Tips from the Art Experts." 2016. *Agora Gallery* (blog), July 23. http://www.agora-gallery.com/advice/blog/2016/07/23/how-to-write-artiststatement/.

Graham, Lisa. 2010. "Artist and Designer Statements." *International Journal of Humanities* 7 (11): 19–24.

KEY SEARCH TERMS

art and design statements; TED talks; art principles; art elements; artist bios; design philosophy

REFERENCES

Berger, John. 1973. *Ways of Seeing.* New York: Viking.

Dondis, Donis A. 1973. *A Primer of Visual Literacy.* Cambridge: MIT.

George, Diana. 2002. "From Analysis to Design: Visual Communication in the Teaching of Writing." *College Composition and Communication* 54 (1): 11–39.

Graham, Lisa. 2010. "Artist and Designer Statements" *International Journal of Humanities* 7 (11): 19–24.

Mendelsohn, Gael, and Michael Mendelsohn. 2000. *The Intuitive Eye: The Mendelsohn Collection*. New York: Ricco/Maresca Gallery.

"Maya Lin." Storm King Art Center. Accessed June 10, 2016. http://stormking.org/artist/maya-lin/.

Olsen, Erik. "Maya Lin's 'Wave Field.'" *New York Times*, November 7, 2008, accessed June 10, 2016. http://www.nytimes.com/video/arts/design/1194832296918/maya-lin-s-wave-field.html.

Van Gogh, Vincent. 1890. *Wheatfield with Crows*. Rijksmuseum Vincent Van Gogh, Amsterdam. In Van Gogh Museum. Accessed June 10, 2016. http://www.vangoghmuseum.nl/en/collection/s0149V1962.

Zucker, Steven, and Beth Harris. 2015. "Why Look at Art?" *Smarthistory*. http://smarthistory.org/why-look-at-art/.

4

BROCHURES
Helping Students Make Good Design Decisions

Sohui Lee
   California State University Channel Islands

Jarret Krone
   University of Colorado, Colorado Springs

CHAPTER OVERVIEW

Print brochures deliver brief, targeted information audiences can carry away and read quickly. The purpose of the brochure is not only to inform but also to advertise, persuade, or demand action. For instance, national-park brochures might inform individuals about locations of interest; however, brochures for nonprofit organizations might persuade readers to donate or volunteer. Whether to inform or persuade, effective brochure design does not merely display data or organize information: good design is tailored to engage readers, clarify complex ideas, or get readers to accept a point. This chapter introduces consultants to the brochure genre and provides strategies for how consultants can support students creating brochures and thinking rhetorically about them as three-dimensional print products. The chapter activity invites consultants to creatively explore how written, visual, and tactile modalities might be applied in brochures by addressing an enduring challenge: getting readers to turn the page.

ILLUSTRATIVE EXAMPLE: VISUAL HOOKS AND LAYOUT

In fall 2015, the Writing and Multiliteracy Center at California State University Channel Islands began to support faculty and students in creatively thinking about, analyzing, and composing written, oral, visual, multimodal, and digital forms of communication. In the first year, student "multiliteracy" projects tended to be oral speeches, slideshow presentations, and research posters.

DOI: 10.7330/9781607328469.c004

The first student to arrive at the Writing and Multiliteracy Center (WMC) with an assignment for making a brochure in spring 2016 was Lucas. He wasn't sure where to begin since he was unfamiliar with brochure design. Lucas brought the information he wanted to use, but he was not aware that he could not use it all. This dilemma was akin to writing an abstract of a ten-page paper. Second, he was unaware of the types of brochures he could create and how each type provides different options for displaying information. The visual strategy of a one-page brochure might engage readers like an infographic, offering a quick holistic view of the whole page—for more ideas on designing infographic's, see Alyse Knorr's chapter in this collection. A folded brochure, by contrast, depends on a visual hook to encourage audiences to open the cover and read the content. A WMC tutor explained to Lucas the genre and purpose of brochures and the various types he had to choose from. Through this process, Lucas realized designing and making a brochure isn't about "plug-and-play," that is, just finding the template to fill in with ready-made information. The session provided him with an opportunity to think more carefully about brochure types and about visual layout in terms of its persuasive impact on the viewer. Lucas learned strategies for effectively conveying the right amount and type of information.

BACKGROUND INFORMATION: WHAT CONSULTANTS NEED TO KNOW ABOUT BROCHURES

Brochures, typically used for advertising or distributing information, are printed in a portable format that ranges from a single sheet of paper printed on one or two pages (like a flyer) to "accordion" formats (z-fold arrangements) with multiple panels of images and/or information.

Brochures might come in different sizes and folds, but they share the following characteristics:

- *brief and portable:* Because brochures are usually portable and meant for casual reading, information in the brochure seeks to capture and retain audience attention through logical organization and easy-to-read text and visuals that carry few main points per page. For instance, a sales brochure advertising a new car is usually created for prospective buyers to take with them after they visit the dealership. By contrast, a brochure for national parks might provide lists of days and times of nature walks and campfire programs visitors might enjoy.
- *tactile and visual:* While students might think about the brochure as a visual product, they might not think about its dimensionality and how its "dimensional affordances" shape information or visual design (Lee 2014, 32–34). The brochure is a three-dimensional product that can

inform and/or advertise through touch and interactivity. Unlike flyers, brochures are usually printed on matte or glossy thick paper to suggest the quality of a document to keep for future reference. Because of the cost to print brochures, designers seek to maximize the rhetorical affordances, paying attention to a user's sense of touch or the size of the brochure (e.g., Should the brochure fit in the back pocket? Should it sit on the coffee table?). Designers also pay attention to the visual impact of a brochure to make the message more memorable or interesting. Regardless of approach, a well-designed brochure not only guides readers through the brochure but also actively engages readers to read further and remember the material.

- *targeted:* Brochures are usually targeted to specific audiences. An understanding of audiences informs how a student designer selects the format of the brochure, as well as the quality and quantity of information, graphics, and visuals the designer includes. Audiences might be narrowed down by region/nation, gender, age groups, cultural/ social interests, or politics.

Specifications of Brochure Formats

In general, brochures, like other forms of technical writing and communication, rely not only on delivering the right kind of information but also on providing good information design—that is, the way information is curated on the page to help people process information. Information design involves graphic-design strategies such as those discussed in the introduction of this book (e. g., grouping, use of color, font and font sizes); it also involves layout styles, use of columns, and spacing.

All these graphic-design choices are shaped in part by the size of the brochure itself or by page specifications of different brochure formats. Brochure formats set constraints for what designers can do: formats tell designers how much space they have for columns, size of font or images, and even how much information can be provided. However, the formats also shape viewers'/users' interaction with and understanding of the content. Student designers must ask themselves:

- Would the layout of a bifold be more interesting to readers hoping to get a range of quick visual and textual information?
- Does a trifold brochure make sense because of its narrow size and transportability?
- Or, is there another brochure format that would better engage an audience?

There are many different brochure templates student designers could use, but students must actively consider the reasoning behind choosing a particular template. Appendix 4.A provides detailed specifications of two basic brochure types: one-page brochure or pamphlet and folded brochure (bifold and trifold brochures). In addition, appendix 4.B offers suggestions for the type of software students might use to create brochures. This information can be used for training consultants or sharing with student designers.

Languages of Brochures: Visual, Verbal, and Tactile

Once students have selected the type of brochure they would like and set the specifications for brochure dimensions, they should consider how they would like to design their brochures and communicate the brochure information. The goal of the brochure design is not limited to communicating information or conveying a message. The objective might be to promote a brand or set a mood. For more information about creating a brand, see James Truman's chapter on personal branding. Brochures do all these things through a combination of visual, verbal, and tactile modal strategies (figure 4.1).

Visual Modality

Visuals are commonly employed in brochures to convey dense and critical information to readers through visualizations such as tables, graphs, or maps. Park brochures provide maps to identify hiking trails, areas for picnicking, and so forth. Bank brochures might show tables of interest rates for various savings programs. Visuals include use of images, pictures, and icons. Finally, graphic-design effects are important visuals: size and color of font might help highlight important points or convey important information content. Layout (for instance, use of columns, bullet points, whitespace) is important because it helps readers navigate through information, break up texts, and better grasp the tone of a brochure (serious, fun, informational, etc.).

Verbal/Written Modality

The importance of the verbal or written component of brochures (what designers call the *copy*) might be obvious: the written text often carries crucial information content intended for the reader to absorb and understand. However, consultants can help students use the written text to improve the clarity of the content by following the less-is-more rule (being concise and efficient with language). This rule is important because too much information might lead to information overload and result in the reader forgetting what they read. Written text can also help project brand personality or set a tone and mood. Paying attention to

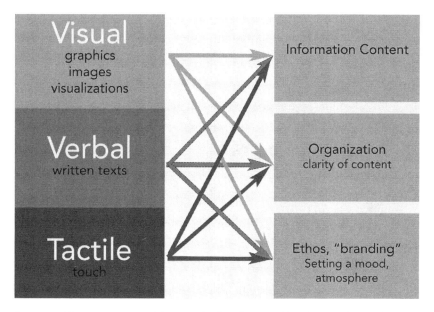

Figure 4.1. Three common modalities used in brochures and brochure goals (gray boxes on the right)

audience and carefully selecting language are important for producing a memorable copy.

Tactile Modality

Tactile modality is the touch sensor, which includes how the paper feels (texture of matte or glossy, thick or thin), as well as how readers interact with the brochure through touch (opening, folding, turning). One of the best ways to think about the power of touch is to reflect on how other print genres, such as greeting cards, use touch modality in memorable ways (humor, sadness, happiness, etc.) and, in general, invite readers to play with them and keep them on their shelves. For readers, touch can also organize information (e.g., joke on the cover of a card with the punchline inside the card) or set a tone through novel use of material. While brochures are more formal than greeting cards, a creative designer can borrow techniques to keep reading audiences engaged through tactile strategies.

CONSULTATION STRATEGIES FOR BROCHURES

This chapter previously listed content goals focusing on the delivery of the main message, organization of the content, and the mood or tone of the message. In addition to considering how much time the student has, and the student's level of technical skill in designing and creating print products, consultants' feedback on brochures should be shaped by the student's stage in the process of producing a brochure, a process that can be compared to the stages in writing. Here, we describe three stages of brochure production: the *ideation stage* involves brainstorming, prototyping, and invention; the *draft stage* involves outlining, drafting of content, and exploring options for design and layout; last, the *final revision stage* signals last-minute revision work on issues that can be resolved or improved quickly.

Engaging the Ideation Stage

The earliest stage of creating brochures is what we call the *ideation stage*, which includes brainstorming and prototyping. Unless students receive assignments that specify formats for brochures, students might need help in identifying the type of brochure that best suits the need of their assignment. Consultants can help students work through the design process by

- setting up a foundation for selecting and prioritizing information content (step 1),
- helping students explore the rhetorical aspects of their brochure design (step 2),
- encouraging students to sketch multiple design layouts or prototypes (step 3).

These three ideation stages are essential for students prior to their work on the visual design (color, font, layout, etc.) of brochures. Table 4.1 can help consultants walk students through this process.

Prioritize, Organize, and Focus in the Draft Stage

During the draft stage, student designers might present a digitally created draft of the brochure or share it as a printed copy. After reviewing the assignment and discussing the objectives of the brochure with the student designer, consultants have an opportunity to offer more substantial organizational, content-based, and design-oriented feedback. During this stage, consultants should look to offer feedback in the areas listed in table 4.2.

Table 4.1. Ways consultants can help with ideation stage of brochure making

Ideation Stage		
STEP 1 *Purpose, Audience,* *Content*	*STEP 2* *Foundations for Design*	*STEP 3* *Prototyping*
Ask questions regarding the purpose of the brochure and its audience. Help the student think about how to appeal to the audience. Facilitate discussion focusing on listing and prioritizing information content needed for the brochure.	Examine brochure templates with the student and discuss the potential formats. Help map a timeline for making the brochure (including due dates, student's other obligations, technical skills, acquiring info/data, printing). Play a role in helping the student recognize what the shape of the brochure can and should do.	Help the student sketch/storyboard two or more brochure layouts. Help the student prototype/test their layout template on Word or Google. Without focusing too much on the design details of the brochure, work with the student to figure out the information "flow" of the brochure. That is, what information will come first, second, last? Is key information conveyed memorably?

Table 4.2. Ways consultants can help with drafting stage of brochure making

Draft Stage		
STEP 1 *Review purpose,* *audience, and content*	*STEP 2* *Review brochure format*	*STEP 3* *Review strategies of* *information design*
Ask questions regarding the purpose of the brochure. Ask the student to explain the target audience of the brochure and why the audience will find it useful. Develop a prioritized list of must-have information. In what order should this information be "read"? How has the draft followed the order of prioritization?	Discuss the student's format. Has the student considered other options? Is this the best format for purpose, audience, and content?	Help the student take out interesting but irrelevant information in the brochure. Help the student identify information that could be visualized. For instance, could they use a map? Could they create a chart? Could they include relevant illustrations? Help the student provide visual prioritization of textual information, such as consistent larger font for subheadings and appropriately smaller font for detailed text.

Make Adjustments in the Final Revision Stage

The final revision stage is the moment in the brochure-development timeline in which last-minute minor adjustments can be made. This stage signals a rapidly approaching brochure due date; consequently, major changes cannot be made. Instead, the consultants might respond to the brochure in ways listed in table 4.3.

Table 4.3. Ways consultants help with final revision stage of brochure making

Final Revision Stage		
STEP 1 Review purpose, audience, and content	STEP 2 Review brochure format and information design	STEP 3 Review strategies of visual design
Ask questions regarding the purpose of the brochure and the target audience of the brochure. Discuss whether all the must-have information is included (review the syllabus with the student; consider basic information that might be left out, such as the student's name, title of the brochure, etc.). Check for clarity in the written text and flow of the brochure from start to finish. Check grammar, punctuation, and numbers.	Review the order of information provided and what information catches the eye (and what doesn't). Provide feedback on the visual effectiveness of the first thing the reader might see. Provide feedback on the visual effectiveness on the last thing a reader sees. Help the student take out interesting but irrelevant information that might clutter the brochure.	Check to see that icons used are consistent and appropriate in size. Check to see whether graphs and charts are clear and aligned on the page. They should have citations or references with labels that are legible. If possible, advise the student on the use of color (color palette, consistency, patterns) to make the brochure more visually interesting.

ACTIVITY: HOOKING A BROCHURE'S AUDIENCE

Description

In this activity, consultants will creatively explore the brochure as a three-dimensional print product and explore the interplay of visual-verbal-tactile modalities. Consultants will create a brochure prototype (any format) for their writing or multiliteracy center, focused on sketching the first page that will "hook" university or college students.

Greeting Cards as Creative Models

The birthday or greeting card might be a good model for how print products apply various modal strategies to engage readers. The extent of the meaning of the card is never fully conveyed on the cover alone. In some way, the cover works to capture the reader's initial interest, to persuade them to open the card and discover the rest of the message. The following are three strategies greeting cards might employ singly or in various combinations:

- creative use of visuals (graphic design, color, images that hook readers)
- creative use of words (words convey mood but also entice to read further for jokes, unfinished sentences, and so forth)
- creative use of interactivity (the card itself might be used for rhetorical effect)

Figure 4.2. Closed card reads "You are AWFUL."

Figure 4.3. Open accordion-style card reads "You are awesome & delightful."

An example of how visuals, words, and interactivity can be combined might be seen in the card in figures 4.2 and 4.3.

The card in figures 4.2 and 4.3 is inspired by card designer Heather Abbott and utilizes an effective combination of wordplay and interactivity strategies to engage and capture the interest of a potential reader. The front cover of the card reads "You are AWFUL." This statement is shocking and draws audience attention because the nature of message is in conflict with what one typically expects from greeting cards. However, the accordion-style format does the work of revealing the punchline—the statement ("You are awesome & delightful") that is the opposite of the initial message. The point of this card is to surprise the reader and make them laugh, and this reaction happens only when the reader opens the card.

The goal for the activity is to produce a prototype of a card like the one illustrated above. You will be analyzing and describing the strategies you notice in your favorite commercial greeting card and applying the same or similar strategies to your brochure for the writing or multiliteracy center.

Steps for Activity

1. *Select a commercial greeting card and analyze its rhetorical strategies using visual, verbal, tactile/interactive techniques.* Go to the student store on campus or a local drug store to buy or take a picture of a greeting card (inside and out). Consider the following questions:

   • How does the front cover of the card encourage or persuade you to open it and keep reading? What types of design techniques and rhetorical strategies does the card use?

   • Do you notice one or more applications of visual, verbal, or tactile/interactive strategies? Do you notice other unique strategies? If so, what are they?

   Take detailed notes on all the techniques you notice in terms of how the authors of the cards create "cues" or "bait" to get you to open it and keep reading.

2. *Apply one or two techniques from the greeting card to a mock-up of a brochure advertising your writing or multiliteracy center.* After you have finished sketching and folding the brochure paper, answer the following questions:

   • What type of brochure format have you chosen and why?

   • Given the context surrounding this brochure (why it was created, who the audience is, what needs to be achieved with the distribution of it), what might be the best ways to encourage students to pick up the brochure in the first place? What key elements could be added to the cover to ensure people notice it?

   • In addition to interactive choices, what tactile modalities will your brochure include? What texture and paper stock will the brochure be printed on?

   • Beyond the goal of creating a visually appealing cover, how does your new understanding of greeting cards influence your design choices for the brochure?

3. *Time to share and discuss.* Share your answers to question 2 with your fellow consultants and share your final prototype of the brochure. What was the response of your fellow consultants to the creativity and effectiveness of your brochure cover?

CONCLUSION: BRAVE NEW WORLD OF BROCHURES

As more students are asked in various courses to make rhetorical print products like brochures, consultants might be reminded of a powerful concept in Aristotelian rhetoric: strategic appeal. For Aristotle, rhetoric is about strategy and making choices that will be most persuasive to an audience, considering a variety of factors such as media, time, and one's own personality. Being a rhetorically effective communicator—whether through writing or through the design of a brochure—means considering all the modal and dimensional affordances one might have available with a medium and making a choice to maximize persuasive effect. Consultants can help students play with visuals and tactile modalities; they can help students consider the rhetorical implications of three-dimensional media that might have parts that move, that audiences can look through, or that readers interact with. In exploring their own creativity and composing process, consultants can encourage students to be innovative and embrace the brochure in 3D.

RESOURCES

The resources in this section focus on visual design principles, three-dimensional print products, technical brochures, and data visualization.

Further Reading

Lee, Sohui. 2014. "Situated Design for Multiliteracy Centers: A Rhetorical Approach for Visual Design." *SDC: A Journal of Multiliteracy and Innovation.* 19 (1): 26–40.

Palmquist, Mike. 2005. Designing Writing: A Practical Guide. Boston, MA: Bedford/St. Martin's. 20–23; 97–101.

Web Resources

https://www.ted.com/talks/david_mccandless_the_beauty_of_data_visualization
    In this TED talk, "The Beauty of Data Visualization," David McCandless provides information on visualization that could be used in a brochure.

http://extensionpublications.unl.edu/assets/pdf/g2028.pdf.
    University of Nebraska–Lincoln provides information on how to make a technical brochure.

http://www.webdesignerdepot.com/2009/06/50-great-examples-of-data-visualization/
    Webdesignerdepot.com's "50 Great Examples of Data Visualizations" provides creative examples of how data visualizations are used and the software tools used to cre-

ate them. Even if you don't want to get too deep into visualizations, you might find it helpful to peruse the website to get inspiration and ideas for ways you can represent information, networks, relationships, patterns, comparisons, and so forth.

KEY SEARCH TERMS

visual design; brochure; data visualization; tutoring strategies

REFERENCES

"50 Great Examples of Data Visualizations." 2009. webdesignerdepot.com. http://www.webdesignerdepot.com/2009/06/50-great-examples-of-data-visualization/.

Lee, Sohui. 2014. "Situated Design for Multiliteracy Centers: A Rhetorical Approach for Visual Design." *SDC: A Journal of Multiliteracy and Innovation* 19 (1): 26–40.

APPENDIX 4.A

These are two basic types of brochure formats with basic specifications for page sizes: the "magazine-style" brochures and bifold/trifold "accordion" brochures.

Magazine-Style Pamphlet/Brochure
One-page brochure
Printed on one or two sides
Design dimensions: 8.75" × 11.25"
Final trim size: 8.5" by 11"

If you want your background to print to the edge of your design, set the dimensions of your design about .25" beyond the final trim size. For instance, when working with your brochure design, set the dimensions of your page brochure to 8.75" × 11.25" with an inner trim line at 8.5" × 11". Extend your design beyond the trim line. When the brochure is ready to print, have it trimmed to 8.5" × 11".

Tabloid-size brochure (or "poster" size)
design dimensions: 11.25" × 17.25"
final trim size: 11" by 17" or 17" by 11"

Bifolds and Trifolds (Accordion Style)
Bifold brochures
Bifolds are typically the size of a sheet of paper, folded once (page size 5.5" by 8.5") and have four printed pages. The bifold is printed so the brochure can be viewed in the following order: page 1 for cover, pages 2 and 3 for inside information, and page 4 for the back. To accomplish

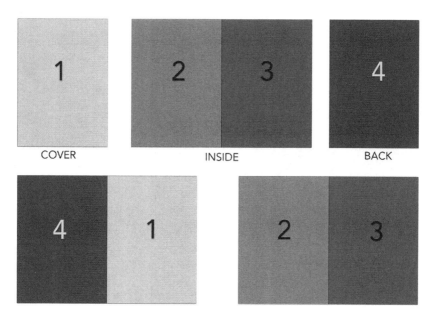

Figure 4.4. Bifold brochure pages. The bottom figure illustrates the sequence of one page (double-sided paper) that is folded.

Recommendation

> *Design dimensions: 11.25" × 8.75"*
> *final trim size: 11" × 8.5"*
> *folded size: 5.5" × 8.5"*

this, set up page 4 and page 1 (cover) information on one page in Word (landscape format, see recommended dimensions in figure 4.4) and the inside information on another page (landscape format, see recommended dimensions in figure 4.4). Print double sided.

Trifold brochure

The trifold brochure is typically a sheet of paper folded in three equal parts. It includes an "inside" section and the "outside" section (the flip side of the page).

APPENDIX 4.B

To best support students in creating print brochures, consultants should be aware that students might have a range of technical or digital literacy skills. Students might need as much help in understanding the basic formats of brochures as they do in considering the rhetorical questions when designing brochures.

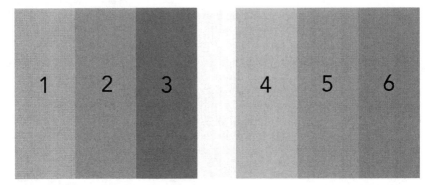

Figure 4.5. Trifold brochure pages. The figures illustrate the "page" sequence when one page of a double-sided paper is folded. The trifold might be folded with the "pages" appearing in different orders depending on the sequence of information and its organization.
Recommendation

design dimensions: 11.25" × 8.75"

final trim size: 11" × 8.5"

folded size: 3.67" × 8.5"

PowerPoint or Microsoft Word

PowerPoint or Microsoft Word can be used to design brochures. They share many of the same tools, but Word includes some templates for creating brochures and includes some designing tools that make it easier to design a brochure.

Microsoft Word

Microsoft Word has templates for brochures. To view these templates (using Word 2011):

Select File > New from Template, and under Publishing Layout View select Brochures. They offer templates for magazine-style one-page brochures, tabloid brochures, and several trifold brochure designs.

We recommend that you first run through our strategies for making a brochure before selecting any templates because these brochures offer designs that might limit how you think of your own brochure design and style.

While these brochures offer some color choices and layout designs to start, you might want to create your own custom brochure template using the basic dimensions we provide in this section of the chapter. To create a brochure template (using Word 2011), follow these steps:

1. Create a new blank document.
2. Select File > Page Setup > Paper Size.

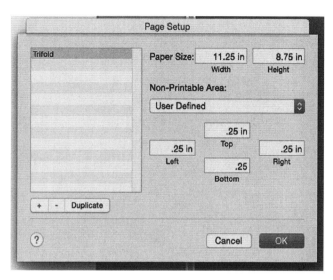

Figure 4.6. Microsoft Word page setup for customized trifold brochure

3. A drop-down menu will appear. Click on Manage Custom Sizes at the bottom.

4. On the left side of the box, click on the + sign. You can then change the name of the "page" from *untitled* to whatever you'd like. In the example in figure 4.6, below, I call it "Trifold." Then input paper size for width and height with margins (these are the trim lines).

PowerPoint

PowerPoint slides can also be customized in the brochure's dimensions. To set the dimensions for your brochure using PowerPoint 2011, follow these steps:

1. Create a New Slide and choose Blank, or delete the Title and Subtitle box, which opens as a default.

2. Go to File > Page Setup and select Custom (drop-down menu under Slides Sized For). Select the appropriate width and height.

3. *PowerPoint might state that the page size exceeds printable area in the paper. Rather than allowing it to Automatically Fit the page on the paper, click on OK to continue with the customized page size you requested.*

4. When you are ready to print, save as a PDF.

Google Docs

You can set the dimensions of your brochure, although Google docs currently provides only preset sizes. To set the dimensions, follow these steps:

1. Create a new document.

2. Go to File > Page Set Up and change paper size.

3. You can select only preset sizes of letter (8.5" × 11") or tabloid (11" × 17").

4. Adjust Orientation for bifolds and trifolds to Landscape.

5. Adjust margins to .25".

5

ACADEMIC RESEARCH POSTERS
Thinking Like a Designer

Russell Carpenter and Courtnie Morin

Eastern Kentucky University

CHAPTER OVERVIEW

Academic research posters provide students and scholars a multimodal outlet for sharing and displaying information, research, and scholarship. Drawing from the Noel Studio for Academic Creativity's tutoring program, this chapter provides academic research poster examples, strategies, and activities for designing tutorials to support student composers. Within the Noel Studio, students learn strategies for reading, consuming, discussing, and analyzing multimodal texts. Sessions are tailored to students' questions, goals, and communication projects while also considering the modalities with which they are composing. The chapter then concludes with applications for integrating academic research poster services into centers with a variety of different missions and goals.

ILLUSTRATIVE EXAMPLE: EXPERIMENTING WITH DESIGN OPTIONS

At Eastern Kentucky University (EKU), students in the parks and recreation department often visit for poster-design tutoring sessions. Students schedule one-on-one tutorials that guide them in the process of moving their poster design from low-tech prototypes on paper to digital projects on screen. Students and consultants refer to the paper prototype as they incorporate design decisions into the digital version, analyzing these possibilities throughout the revision process. The consultant opens the session with the student by discussing the rhetorical challenges and opportunities of presenting research posters.

During an individual session, Beth displayed a draft of her research poster—created in PowerPoint in this case—presenting data of how the addition of parks can lead to healthier communities. Beth explained to

DOI: 10.7330/9781607328469.c005

the consultant that the purpose was to inform her audience about the benefits of adding parks to her local community. In addition to presenting this research poster to her class, she also wanted to share it at a local city-council meeting. The consultant asked her about the audience's familiarity with the topic and her main takeaway message. Because her audience was the general public, they discussed the importance of simplicity and keeping the message direct.

Once the rhetorical situation was determined, the consultant asked Beth to *view* the poster simply by looking *at* it for nothing in particular, accepting the design elements as they appeared on the screen. Beth and the consultant then viewed the poster and discussed the first design elements that came to mind, focusing on the layout of her research, balance of text and graphical images, color choices, and the use of white space.

Next, the consultant reviewed basic design concepts—specifically figure-ground contrast, repetition, and alignment—and outlined broad definitions of these strategies with Beth. Now that she had an understanding of basic design concepts, Beth was encouraged to view her draft poster through the perspective of a designer, someone skilled and versed in the language of research-poster composing processes. Important to note, Beth discussed the poster by looking *through* it as a designer to consider it as a whole composition. Again, Beth examined the poster but this time discussed design decisions, ways the poster met the rhetorical expectations of the situation, and ways in which future revisions might enhance the research poster. In addition, Beth also analyzed decisions such as color, contrast, and line while addressing important global rhetorical issues like organization, coherence, audience, purpose, and context.

Once Beth and the consultant established the discourse of research posters together, the session focused on the development of a low-tech prototype as a way to visually inform the changes she would make to her digital research-poster draft. Beth and the consultant used butcher paper, colored markers, paper cutouts, and tape to create a conceptual version of the next research-poster revision before moving these updated concepts to the screen. Through this process, they discussed the organization and layout in order to create a path for the eye to follow on the page by using consistent stylized headings, images for demonstration, and colors to establish a theme and relationship with the data. Following a blended low-tech and high-tech process allowed the consultant and student to work through complex design decisions before committing to elements in a revised electronic version.

The consultant gave Beth the opportunity to work through global issues from the beginning and experiment with available design options; Beth felt more prepared to fully engage the electronic design process after working through ideas on paper in a low-tech and low-stakes space. Beth also realized that lower-order concerns such as spelling or grammar, as discussed in the introduction to this collection, are not a priority at this stage in the process if the organization or structure, for example, are not coherent and convincing.

BACKGROUND INFORMATION: RHETORICAL, DESIGN, AND MULTIMODAL PRINCIPLES

Students often visit the Noel Studio having had little or no experience designing research posters. Moreover, students can overlook important design principles as purely aesthetic rather than critical to the multimodal composing process. Several major programs and various courses at EKU frequently require students to create research posters. The increase in research-poster-design tutorial requests has allowed the Noel Studio to develop and hone the approaches our staff members employ.

The entry point into academic research-poster-design processes is a discussion and understanding of rhetoric, ensuring students are aware of the available means of persuasion in a given rhetorical situation. In research-poster tutorials, students must first understand the context within which they will present these projects.

- Posters are often delivered in large, high-traffic areas at conferences.
- Audience members will likely move quickly through the display space.
- Audience members might not know much about the topic.

Figure 5.1 illustrates academic research posters designed with this context in mind. Note the angle at which the viewer in figure 5.1 approaches the research posters. When posters are displayed in high-traffic areas and forced to compete with other posters in the area, designers need to find ways to grab their audience's attention. The posters in figure 5.1 demonstrate how designers use colors and visuals in an effort to draw viewers into the research. To view the figures in this chapter in color and to find other research-poster resources, visit www .multimodalwritingcenter.org.

Research-poster-design tutorials provide essential information to student composers and are based on studio pedagogy (Carpenter et al. 2013), which preferences creativity, information literacy, and collaboration among student learners. Moreover, tutoring sessions teach students

Figure 5.1. Noel Studio research posters displayed in EKU's Crabbe Library during Scholarship Week 2015

creative approaches to multimodal thinking (Lee and Carpenter 2015; 2016). They encourage students to interact with low- and high-tech resources as they navigate the multimodal (in this case, a focus on designing with alphabetic text, photos, graphics, tables, charts, colors, and lines, for example) composing process of research posters.

Given that many students will have their first research-poster-design experience in the Noel Studio and in your own centers, consultants must make sessions engaging and interactive. After a discussion of context, consultants can begin with an overview of basic design considerations, using memorable concepts such as Robin Williams's (2008) CRAP (contrast, repetition, alignment, and proximity) principles—these principles are outlined quite nicely in Shawn Apostel's chapter on visual aids for presentations. CRAP principles are an abbreviated version of the Gestalt principles discussed in the introduction to this collection.

Figure-ground contrast is highly important to grab the audience's attention. Creating a clear contrast between the background and text allows passersby to easily identify the main points. The text and images must be clearly legible from a distance. Repetition in style, headings, and layout can be used to create a path of information and help the audience easily navigate the content. Additionally, alignment and spacing can create a balance of information on the page and help the audience understand in what order to read each section. Proximity is also an

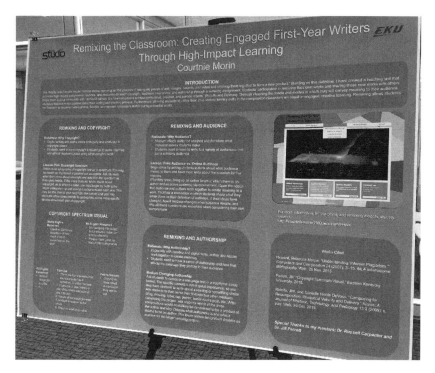

Figure 5.2. Display of research poster by Courtnie Morin that uses color to engage audience members (used with permission)

important layout tool to group information on the poster for the audience to easily understand the relationship between the text and images.

Consultants can expand on these basic concepts to discuss the following design principles: line, shape, color, and value ("The Principles" 2015). In addition, consultants might consider these related design features: layout, organization, and weight. The use of white space in a poster can be just as important as the content. Too much information on a poster can be overwhelming and create clutter. Effective posters are uncluttered and easy to follow, and the message is immediately clear.

Designing a research poster also involves exploring and discussing options regarding font type and character, the "type's personality" (White 1999, 26). Figures 5.2 and 5.3 offer a closer perspective (from about five feet) of sample research posters displayed to suggest the significance of design decisions when viewed through the eyes of audience members. In figure 5.2, the designer uses color to establish contrast and repetition throughout the research poster. Visit www.multimodalwritingcenter.org to view figure 5.2 in color, and then consider the following questions:

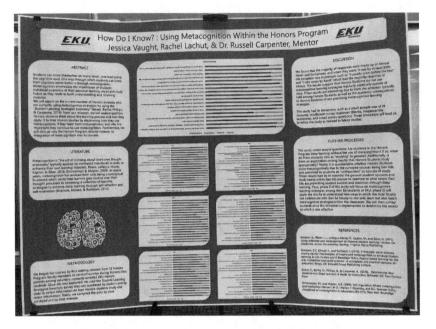

Figure 5.3. Display of research poster by Jessica Vaught and Rachel Lachut that uses color in data visualization (used with permission)

- What design elements do you notice first?
- How do the colors used in the research poster convey meaning to viewers?
- How do the colors contrast with other design elements?
- How is the designer using color to connect information for the viewer?

In figure 5.3, the designers are using color to present complex and large datasets in ways that allow viewers to access information quickly. In addition, the designers establish concepts such as repetition and alignment through the use of color. Again, a color version of figure 5.3 can be found at www.multimodalwritingcenter.org. Consider the following questions for figure 5.3:

- How are the designers using color to represent data visually?
- How are the colors chosen for borders, contributing to the overall organization of the research poster?
- How do the designers apply the color palette from the datasets meaningfully in other areas of the poster?
- In what ways are the designers using color to establish the design principle of proximity?
- How do the layout and color compare to the poster in figure 5.2? In what ways does that change the message?

Table 5.1. Common multimodal elements in chemistry research posters

Element	Modality	Affect
Photos	Visual	Shows visual context Deepens understanding of situations, scenarios, or operations Displays visuals and situations with emotional or aesthetic appeal
Tables	Visual/textual	Shows data and detail Combines basic visual elements—such as lines—with textual Organizes information to maximize readability
Figures	Visual	Displays complex information visually Employs multiple design elements Compares information visually

Table 5.2. Common multimodal elements in communication research posters

Element	Modality	Affect
Photos	Visual	Shows interpersonal elements such as human communication Displays discipline-related communication practices
Tables	Visual/Textual	Compares communication practices Displays qualitative research results
Figures	Visual	Provides data points Shows relationship between communication and communicators

Although students from across the disciplines participate in Noel Studio tutorials, some of the most vivid examples come from the sciences. Chemistry students arrive at tutorials with a general understanding of research posters, often having seen them in their department. These students bring research concepts to the session and have a strong command of methods and conventions in their discipline.

Tables 5.1 and 5.2 offer snapshots of common multimodal composing elements and considerations found in Noel Studio tutorials with students across the disciplines. Chemistry students offer an example, though, of disciplinary design conventions. Often, projects are complex and involve combinations of research and visual elements. Students must balance logical appeals with emotional appeals in their academic research posters, which provides students opportunities during the invention and design processes.

Students benefit from knowing and understanding how to use *affective* design elements. While they are not universal, many of these affective dimensions span disciplinary conventions and styles. Through the elements in these tables, students can explore how they work with modalities to produce affective dimensions.

Although consultants offer an overview of design theory, it need not consume a significant portion of the time during the session. Consultants can provide students with the basics and focus on helping them understand lenses through which we view research posters, which aids in the development of critical perspectives and acquisition of design language, with the goal of creating in students more informed, conscientious, and savvy designers.

CONSULTATION STRATEGIES FOR RESEARCH POSTERS

Tutoring students requires a solid foundation, to include an understanding of rhetorical appeals and canons of rhetoric. This section offers strategies that build on these understandings developed in the Noel Studio and applied in tutorial sessions with students from across the disciplines. Eric Hobson (1998) encourages designers to begin with "building bridges" between the written and verbal (10). In the spirit of Elizabeth Losh, Jonathan Alexander, Kevin Cannon, and Zander Cannon (2014), who advocate creating an approach to teaching rhetoric through visual, comic forms, we should encourage students to think in different ways about these same concepts and forms. Students should also explore depth cues in the visuals they select for use in their academic research poster: space, size, color, lighting, texture gradients, interposition, time, perspective, illusionary perspective, geometrical perspective, and conceptual perspective (35–38). These concepts apply to the research-poster design process. Ultimately, our role as consultants and facilitators is to help students see textual and visual compositions in new ways through six strategies: moving from low tech to high tech; interacting with the poster; focusing on design; prototyping; accessibility; and, critiquing designs.

Work from Low Tech to High Tech

Start with the low tech before the high tech. Students often jump straight to designing their poster within a program such as PowerPoint or InDesign. While the end product might be successful, in many cases we've seen students in the Noel Studio produce much more successful research posters when they've experienced a full, iterative design process. Developing a visual plan, or storyboard (see Brandy Ball Blake and Karen Head's chapter on storyboarding and planning), allows the student to consider all the elements when designing. Provide the student with low-tech resources such as butcher paper, colored pencils, colored scraps of paper, and paper cutouts. Noel Studio tutorials and workshops often incorporate paper-animal cutouts, for example. Allow the student to tape materials to the poster and to change ideas throughout the process. Model for the student ways in which to iterate through low-commitment, low-tech play with the poster-design process. Discuss ways, then, to remediate low-tech design elements for high-tech applications.

Make It Interactive

Students should interact with the poster, process, and each other. Passively observing research posters or discussing a sample can provide a good start or a strategy for understanding and analyzing finished products. Students learn research-poster design, however, by experiencing the process, including challenges, decisions, and even setbacks. Beyond posing open-ended questions to students, provide them with challenges to work through, and offer them real-time feedback from the perspective of an audience member. Give students a creative or fun design challenge and provide them with feedback as they talk through their choices.

Be Design Focused

View the tutoring process and product through the eyes of a designer. Many students have their first experience designing a research poster during this process. Teach students to think like a designer. Use design-focused terminology and explain to students what these concepts—and the terms—mean and how to implement them in their own process. Ask students to explain the concepts behind the design decisions they make. Appreciate design elements often taken for granted such as color (and color palette), alignment, and choice of photographs. Help students see how important each decision is and how design decisions relate to their writing style.

Drive Decisions with Prototyping

Create multiple iterations of the poster in low-tech and high-tech forms. Poster design requires the act of creating multiple visual and written ideas in combination with one another on multiple occasions over time. Provide the student designer with time during the tutoring session to create iterations of poster aspects. Seeing multiple

organizational and design options allows the student to consider layout and data representation from different perspectives. Encourage
the student to create while you look on, and discuss ways to implement
strategies such as contrast or repetition (Williams 2008). In addition,
provide time and space for students to explore concepts such as depth
or layers by designing and adjusting elements such as text boxes, shading, or callouts.

Design with Dynamism and Accessibility

Help students recognize the importance of making posters accessible
to all audiences. When designing posters, writers should make sure the
text can be read three to six feet from the poster and not place text
over images, as they become indistinguishable (for more information
on accessibility of font, image, or colors, refer to Lindsay Sabatino's
introduction). An option for writers is using augmented-reality software
to create a more dynamic experience for the audience. *Aurasma* and
Layar: Augment Reality are free apps that allow users to add graphic,
video, audio, and 3D content to a static object or "trigger." Writers can
record themselves explaining concepts presented on the poster, providing descriptions for images or charts, or they can include additional
research and resources for their audience. When the audience points
their phones or tablets at the trigger point, the connected video or
audio will play. This option allows audience members to view the content at their own pace, read transcripts for video or audio content, or
access the information if the writer is not standing at their poster or is
conversing with another person.

Create > Critique > Create

Generate ideas and critique them through multiple perspectives.
Drawing from the culture of the artist's critique, display the research-
poster draft (if electronic) or prototype (if in low-tech form) in a context similar to the one in which the poster will be displayed, such as a
high-traffic and public space within your center. At first, focus on what
you see when first when walking past the poster at a distance. Next, in
closer proximity, view the poster in quadrants beginning with the top,
which is often where the byline and affiliation are located. Then, follow
up with more specific questions about the student's choice of layout,
color, shading, lines, borders, and other design elements. With the
student, interrogate the poster prototype and the process or decisions

made. Stand and look from multiple angles and spend an exceedingly long time analyzing seemingly mundane and simple design decisions in the prototype. Dwell on design elements of the poster and pose questions to the student. View the poster in its entirety for global concerns or those that affect the poster as a whole. Then, view the details of the poster at the local level. Ask students questions such as, What was the designer's intent or goal? What design decisions did the student make that work well? What design decisions might be confusing or better delivered differently?

ACTIVITY: DESIGN A PROTOTYPE

This ten-step activity prepares consultants to provide feedback on academic research posters. Select a topic often discussed in your center with which you are familiar. The topic must benefit the center in some way. For example, you might select higher-order and lower-order concerns, effective collaboration, active listening, and so forth.

1. Research that topic thoroughly. Select up to five reliable resources to incorporate.

2. On a sheet of paper (butcher paper if possible, but 8.5 × 11 will work), sketch the outline of an academic poster that teaches students in your center about this concept. Consider the following design elements in your prototype:

   a. contrast

   b. repetition

   c. layout and organization

   d. color

   e. scannability

3. Consider the following questions as you design your prototype poster:

   a. How will students in your center navigate your poster?

   b. How will your poster make use of written and visual elements?

   c. How will visual and written elements complement one another?

   d. What would you like readers to think, know, or do?

   e. How will you incorporate the sources you selected above into your poster prototype?

4. Hang your prototype in a prominent, visible location in your center. Provide sticky notes for other consultants and students in your center to comment on your prototype.

5. Use the feedback to improve the design of your prototype.

6. Select an available design program that best fits your needs and composing project. Such programs might include PowerPoint, Keynote, or Publisher.

7. Transfer your low-tech prototype into an electronic format following a similar process, incorporating the feedback you received.

8. Show the newly designed poster to other consultants in your center or, if possible, leave the digital version on a public monitor.

9. Invite feedback, once again, on your poster. If possible, display your low-tech prototype beside it for comparison.

10. Reflect on the process of developing your poster. What feedback on your poster surprised you? What revisions did you make from your prototype to your digital poster that made it more effective? Based on the feedback you received, what types of questions would you ask a student designer?

CONCLUSION

Academic research posters represent an important multimodal composition genre in our center and their number will continue to increase in other centers as students and faculty seek new ways to show (rather than tell) the story of their research. The design process is time consuming. It is also enjoyable. Students should have the freedom in the design process to think creatively; that is, students should generate ideas original to them. This part of the process provides an important opportunity to remind our students that multimodal composing involves invention and thinking that begins with low-tech resources and tools. Serious thinking takes place before students remediate the poster on the screen.

Research-poster tutorials are not universal. That is, one tutorial might look different from the next. Each student will take a slightly different approach, which makes the design process exciting. As we consider the possible feedback we offer to students, however, tutors should focus on the individual ideas these students bring to this process. Academic research posters also present opportunities to engage students in different ways. For example, have students sketch, outline, map, and color as part of the tutorial. Encourage students to feel comfortable during this phase of the process. Help students understand and recognize the modal affordances available to them and what those options do for their academic research posters. Help students focus on multimodal composing that blends affordances with disciplinary research practices. Finally, help students realize that multimodal composing—low tech and high tech—and the process it requires is empowering. Through academic research posters, students learn to activate visual and textual elements in ways that will move audience members.

RESOURCES

Research Poster Examples and Templates

F1000posters: https://f1000research.com/browse/posters
> F1000posters provides a database of research posters submitted to their archives. Not all the samples submitted are exemplary, but this resource provides plenty of design and layout points of view to consider.

Noel Studio Research Poster Design Templates: http://studio.eku.edu/sites/studio.eku.edu /files/files/ResearchPosterTemplate.pdf
> This simple template allows designers to first fit academic topics into a traditional column-poster format—a trifold, column organization. Students can use the blank space on page 2 to break from the traditional, formal conventions of academic research-poster design and then compare the two versions.

Better Posters: http://betterposters.blogspot.com/
> This site provides perspectives on poster design with interesting insight into the decisions and processes.

KEY SEARCH TERMS

research posters; poster design; design principles; design strategies; multimodal thinking

REFERENCES

Carpenter, Russell, Leslie Valley, Trenia Napier, and Shawn Apostel. 2013. "Studio Pedagogy: A Model for Collaboration, Innovation, and Space Design." In *Cases on Higher Education Spaces: Innovation, Collaboration, and Technology*, edited by Russell Carpenter, 313–29. Hershey, PA: IGI Global.

Hobson, Eric H. 1998. "Seeing Writing in a Visual World." In *ARTiculating: Teaching Writing in a Visual World*, edited by Pamela B. Childers, Eric H. Hobson, and Joan A. Mullin, 1–15. Portsmouth, NH: Heinemann.

Lee, Sohui, and Russell Carpenter. 2015. "Creative Thinking for 21st Century Composing Practices: Creativity Pedagogies Across Disciplines." *Across the Disciplines: A Journal of Language, Learning, and Academic Writing* 12 (4). http://wac.colostate.edu/atd/perfor ming_arts/lee_carpenter2015.cfm.

Lee, Sohui, and Russell Carpenter. 2016. "Future Pedagogies of Applied Creative Thinking in Multiliteracy Centers: How Creative Thinking 'Opens the Ways' for Better Habits of Mind." In *The Future Scholar: Researching and Teaching the Frameworks for Writing and Information Literacy*, edited by Randall McClure and James P. Purdy, 223–48. Medford, NJ: Information Today.

Losh, Elizabeth, Jonathan Alexander, Kevin Cannon, and Zander Cannon. 2014. *Understanding Rhetoric: A Graphic Guide to Writing*. Boston, MA: Bedford St. Martin's.

Morin, Courtnie. 2016. "Remixing the Classroom: Creating Engaged First-Year Writers Through High-Impact Learning." Poster presented at University Poster Showcase, Scholarship Week, Richmond, KY, April 15.

"The Principles of Design." 2015. J6 Design. http://www.j6design.com.au/6-principles-of -design/.

Vaught, Jessica, and Rachel Lachut. 2016. "How Do I Know? Using Metacognition in the Honors Program." Poster presented at University Poster Showcase, Scholarship Week, Richmond, KY, April 15.

White, Alexander W. 1999. *Type in Use: Effective Typography for Electronic Publishing.* 2nd ed. New York: Norton.

Williams, Robin. 2008. *Non-Designer's Design Book: Design and Typographic Principles for the Visual Novice.* Berkeley, CA: Peachpit.

6

PREZI AND POWERPOINTS DESIGNED TO ENGAGE
Getting the Most Out of Quick-and-Dirty Pathos

Shawn Apostel

Bellarmine University

CHAPTER OVERVIEW

Visual presentation aids are often an expected addition to a verbal presentation. The two most popular programs for creating these visuals—PowerPoint and Prezi—have their strengths and weaknesses. Choosing which program to use can be a challenge. This chapter offers questions that will help students decide between the two. The chapter then outlines several design strategies, as well as common pitfalls users face while designing with PowerPoint and Prezi. Finally, the chapter offers easy ways to make a visual presentation aid composed on either program more compelling, what I term *quick-and-dirty pathos.*

ILLUSTRATIVE EXAMPLE: DESIGNING SLIDES WITH AUDIENCE IN MIND

Students frequently visit the studio requesting feedback on PowerPoint presentations, but I've learned that it's critical to first analyze the rhetorical context of the presentation before diving into design choices. Not only does this save time, it also offers students perspective on which programs to use and which design decisions are best for reaching particular audiences. Taking this approach was helpful when Jim, an accounting major, came to our studio to work on a PowerPoint for a five-minute persuasive-speech project. After conducting a quick rhetorical analysis with Jim, I understood that the primary audience was students of various disciplines in a public-speaking class. The purpose of his presentation was to encourage them to be part of the effort to clean up an area affected by a recent hurricane by volunteering during a spring-break service-learning trip, and the presentation was supposed to take place in an 8 a.m. class.

DOI: 10.7330/9781607328469.c006

Jim's PowerPoint featured twenty slides that outlined the facts of the situation: how many people were affected, the size of the area, the cost estimate of the damage, and the various ways students could take action. Each slide showcased charts and graphs comparing and contrasting this hurricane to others in history. Many slides contained clip-art images of a tornado-like graphic. The amount of information Jim had collected was impressive, but considering his 8 a.m. time slot, and the fact that his audience consisted of students in various disciplines—some of whom would appreciate his detailed charts outlining expenses of the storm and others who would find it hard to relate to the data—I suggested removing several slides of data and instead incorporating a video showing the destruction. I advised Jim to use the footage as a backdrop to his verbal presentation of the financial effects of the hurricane damage. By using the footage, I argued, Jim could help his audience feel empathy towards those affected; people are more motivated by how they feel than by the cold, hard facts of a situation.

The point of this story is not to dissuade people from ever using charts and graphs on PowerPoint; they have their uses. But, as we see in Jim's case, the PowerPoint standard-headline, bullet-points, clip-art slide design has become the go-to design template for a visual presentation. The problem with PowerPoint is that it is often approached with little thought: grab a template, plug in some text, add some clip art, and it's done. While templates might follow basic design principles, the visuals they provide can seem uninspired, and the slides might actually compete with the speaker as the audience struggles with the choice to read the slide or pay attention to the presenter. Templates also fail to recognize the rhetorical situation. An 8 a.m. class of students from various disciplines listening to ten back-to-back speeches is different than a class of Jim's accounting peers listening to one speech in an 11 a.m. class.

However, keep in mind that, given a choice, the audience might opt to tune out during either rhetorical situation. Remember, when people speak in public, they are competing against smartphones, and the phone is a tough competitor. So, like Jim, focus on what reaches the audience best from design principles to visual presentation aids. Instead of designing presentation aids the same way other people design theirs, be bold and stand apart, as Nancy Duarte recommends in her *Duarte Design's Five Rules for Presentations*. Students have many options for creating visual presentation aids—some of these options work better for different purposes such as collaboration, online connectivity, and design characteristics. The process I recommended for Jim in developing his presentation provided him an opportunity to think carefully about audience, design principles, and the tools available to presenters. The activity for this chapter is an opportunity for consultants to experience this process for themselves. So consultants will get the most out of this process, this chapter explores design choices for visual presentations and explains how to help students make choices, focusing on how and why these choices matter.

BACKGROUND INFORMATION: FROM CHOOSING A PROGRAM TO DESIGNING A SLIDE

Microsoft launched PowerPoint in 1990 as part of their office suite, and the program quickly revolutionized the use of visual presentation aids—which had been predominately relegated to handouts, overhead slides, and handwritten notes on transparencies and whiteboards. Once PowerPoint was introduced, the use of visuals proliferated, as audience members were dazzled by the use of color, whiz-bang dissolves, and clip art. However, over the years, PowerPoint has become ubiquitous with public speaking. Google *death by PowerPoint* for some examples of people's exasperation with the program. While there are ways to design PowerPoints that are strategically compelling, it is more common for people frustrated with PowerPoint to abandon the software entirely in favor of a newer, primarily cloud-based program: Prezi.

Prezi was founded in 2009 and quickly became a popular option for those seeking an alternative to PowerPoint. Today, Prezi has more than eighty-five million users around the world ("Visualizing"). Prezi users predominantly design with an online version of the program, giving them cloud access to their slides when they log into a computer connected to the internet. Unlike the slide-based approach PowerPoint offers, Prezi allows people to zoom in and around a large screen—think PowerPoint meets Google Maps. While this feature offers a wider range of creative expressions, audiences are often subjected to Prezilepsy: the feeling of motion sickness caused by an aggressive use of Prezi's zooming and flipping options (see the resources section at the end of this chapter for a link, or Google "Avoiding Prezilepsy by Shawn Apostel"). It is also important to note that while this chapter focuses on Prezi Classic, many of the principles also apply to Prezi Next.

PowerPoint or Prezi? Making the Right Choice

Many people I work with do not know whether to use PowerPoint or Prezi to create their visual presentation aid. Google Slides is another excellent option that has similar features to both PowerPoint and Prezi,

Table 6.1. Choosing a program: a quick reference guide

	PowerPoint	Prezi	Google Slides
Are you offering handouts of your slides?	Favor		Favor
Do you want to share your slides online?		Favor	Favor
Is internet connectivity not provided?	Favor		
Will the audience have connected computers?		Favor	Favor
Is this a collaborative presentation?		Favor	Favor
Is the deadline soon?	Favor		
Is this a linear, step-by-step presentation?	Favor		Favor
Should your slides to be ADA compliant?	Favor		
Are you showing how things are connected?		Favor	

but Slides offers limited flexibility when it comes to design, which is why this chapter focuses primarily on PowerPoint and Prezi. For many projects, either program will work fine; however, there are some reasons to favor one program over the other. Table 6.1 provides a list of some questions consultants can help students consider when choosing the best program for a presentation.

If presenters are using handouts, PowerPoint is a better option. While presenters can print each stop of their Prezi as a page, PowerPoint allows users to create a handout that features a small image of the slide along with lines for the audience to take notes on.

When it comes to sharing or collaborative work, Prezi is a great option for sharing because it is primarily cloud based (unless using a downloaded desktop copy). Since the slides are already online, sharing a presentation is as easy as emailing the link. Google Slides is another option for sharing slides online. Unlike PowerPoint, Google Slides is cloud based and can be easily downloaded as a PowerPoint file format or PDF document. While uploading or creating a PowerPoint on Google Drive or Microsoft One does allow presenters to share and edit a visual presentation aid with a large audience, Prezi replaces cursers with little happy faces as users navigate on a screen, editing and adding their information to a presentation. However, Prezi only allows up to ten users to edit a presentation at any given time. If a presenter is crowdsourcing a visual presentation aid or is one of many coauthors, Google Slides allows the creator to share an editable version of the slide show, allowing multiple people to edit and upload information onto the slide show at the same time.

While Prezi presentations can be downloaded and presented offline, users might prefer the comfort of a standard PowerPoint file rather than risk downloading a zip file of a Prezi, opening it, and storing it on a USB drive for a later presentation. There are fewer steps to dragging a PowerPoint onto a USB drive.

PowerPoints work really well for a step-by-step, linear presentation. Since one slide disappears when presenters transition to the next, it's easy for the audience to move on to the next step. Prezi works well when a presentation must show how things are connected. For example, discussing how the liver works in the human body can begin with a slide showing the entire human body. The next stop could zoom in to the torso, and the next stop could show the entire liver. By connecting the discussion visually, the audience is encouraged to consider the connections among the discussion items, not to move on from one topic to the next.

Finally, if time is short, suggest a software the student is most comfortable with. Research shows it's harder to learn something when people are experiencing stress. If a person wants to learn Prezi, suggest a project they have time to work on (and mess up on) so they'll be comfortable and ready to present when the time comes.

Slide-Design Pitfalls

Avoid Designs That Do Not Reach Your Entire Audience—Be More ADA Compliant

It's important to note that Prezi is not currently ADA compliant and therefore has a significant limitation in terms of reaching all audiences. There are some strategies slide designers can use to make their work more accessible.

- Use alternative text to describe the images being used in the slide show.
- Be sure the text being used is actually text, not an image.
- If using a link in the slide, add text that describes where the link will take the person.
- Do not rely on color alone to communicate information.
- Add audio to the slide stops that describes what is being shown on the screen.
- Provide PDF versions of the Prezi to audience members who use PDF reading software.
- Prepare a script of your presentation to handout to audience members.

Avoid Preselected Layout Patterns

It might be tempting to use PowerPoint's layout patterns, but there are always creative approaches to designing slides. Not every slide needs a title, image, and words. Some slides might just need one word, number, or image. Presenters should be encouraged to resist the urge to repeat everything they are going to say on the slide. Slides function best as stage decoration. Presenters are the stars; the audience should focus on them.

Avoid Stock Photography and Clip Art If Possible

Encourage presenters to take their own photos and to design their own images (or have a friend help). An audience can smell stock photography a mile away, and audiences crave authenticity. Having original images in the PowerPoint is a good way to let the audience know of the speaker's experience with the subject matter.

Avoid Disorienting Audiences

PowerPoint is linear, so each slide means a new set of information appears. Prezi is special. The zooming and panning movement Prezi offers can be easily overused. Be mindful of how often the Prezi stops move from one area to another. Prezi offers the ability to move around on the screen, but doing so too quickly or across long distances can make people motion sick, causing them to feel what I referred to as *Prezilepsy* earlier. The audience should be able to anticipate where the next movement will go (more on this later). Move in and out only when needed.

Consider the examples below to see how I embedded information in the Prezi I created for Bellarmine University.

Notice how the landing page, or first stop, seen in figure 6.1, offers an overview of the three topics the presentation will discuss.

After the introduction (which offered an overview of the three topics being discussed), the Prezi zooms into the first point. Notice how the points in figure 6.2 are blurry. We can tell there are a few circles with information inside them, but we can't see all the information. That's okay. The audience knows where we are going next: to the circles. Knowing which way to go helps the audience anticipate the next move and avoids disorienting the audience.

The next stops focus on individual points of interest. The text in figure 6.3 encourages a bit of reading. While I normally advise against so much text on a screen, this Prezi's secondary audience was people who missed the presentation and needed to read the slides to be informed. The lines of texts are kept short enough so that they can be read quickly. The speech that accompanied this presentation offered more details.

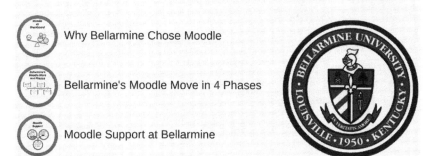

Figure 6.1. Bellarmine University's move to Moodle landing page slide

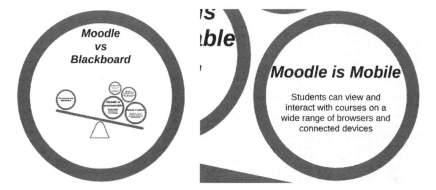

Figure 6.2. Bellarmine University "Moodle versus Blackboard" slide

Figure 6.3. Bellarmine University "Moodle is Mobile" slide

Designing with PowerPoint and Prezi: A Few Things to Consider

Since presentation aids like PowerPoint have been highly utilized, many students feel comfortable creating one. But, just because students are familiar with the software and have created PowerPoints before does not mean they know how to do so effectively. Consultants can help students explore designing presentations and doing so in new, innovative ways. Whether students use PowerPoint or Prezi to show information, be sure they remember the audience and their needs in a presentation design. Consider how close the audience will be to the projector. If the room is large, make sure the information can be clearly seen at the back of the room. If color is an important part of the slide, be sure colors contrast enough so people who have trouble distinguishing colors can read and see each image. As mentioned in the introduction, use colors readable by all audiences; make sure the colors are on the opposite ends of the spectrum, and avoid using colors with green and red pigment together. And be sure each image has a logical resting place for the eye. Ask students, What do you see first? Second? Third? The best designs draw the eye to where it's needed, when it's needed. US audiences tend to "enter" a slide from the top left. They then tend to move right and down. Use this tendency rhetorically.

Furthermore, creating ADA-compliant PowerPoints requires designers to utilize the features built into the software, like alt tags and comment boxes, among other best practices. However, Prezi's classic, online software requires more action if it is to be useful for those who cannot see the presentation. Prezi allows designers to import audio into each slide, which can be useful if the audio adequately describes the visuals in each Prezi stop. For audiences who cannot hear the presentation, text must be added to each stop. Since this addition of text affects the design of the presentation, I recommend having the text downloadable via a link in the Prezi description. The text can then be referenced during each stop in the Prezi.

As mentioned in the introduction of this collection, designers use Gestalt principles to help audiences make quick sense of information. Four of these are discussed by Robin Williams's CRAP principles. The *C* stands for *contrast*. One can see that principle right here on this page. The text stands out from the paper. It's easier to read. Imagine how hard it would be to read this chapter if the words were yellow instead of black. The *R* stands for *repetition*. For instance, the chapter headings and font sizes remain consistent throughout this book. When things remain consistent, readers associate them as working together. The same is true with visuals. Presenters should repeat the same fonts, color, and image styles throughout their slides. The *A* stands for *alignment*. Notice the clear line for the text to start along the left side of this page. When bullet points or numbered lists are used, they are usually indented and lined up top to bottom. When things line up, readers and viewers know they belong. And, finally, the *P* stands for *proximity*. Our eye tends to group items together that are closest to one another. This happens for every paragraph in this book. They are visually separated from each other to break up the text into information clusters.

Figures 6.4 and 6.5 show how the CRAP principles apply to a PowerPoint slide.

To examine color versions of figures 6.4 and 6.5, visit www.multi modalwritingcenter.org. The *contrast* in Design B is really evident.

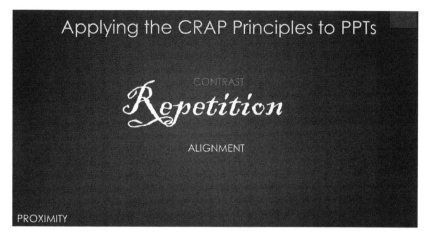

Figure 6.4. Design A

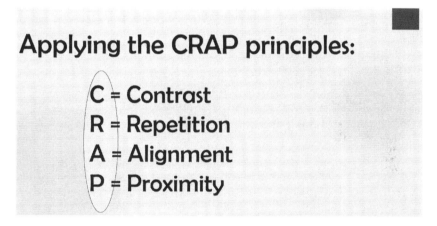

Figure 6.5. Design B

Notice how the letters *CRAP* stand out. Design A has some light-colored text; it's hard to see with that dark background. Viewers need colors that contrast more with the background, as seen in Design B.

Repetition is being used effectively in Design B. Notice how the same font is being used for the body of the text. Notice also how the color red is being repeated on the slide template and the oval behind the letters *CRAP*.

There seems to be no *alignment* in Design A. The text is all over the page. Notice how Design B has text that all lines up? By lining words up, we let the audience know the words belong together. It also helps us showcase the word that makes these principles so easy to remember.

Chunking together related information is how *proximity* is being used in Design B. It's hard to tell what information is related on Design A because it's all over the place.

As noted in the illustrative example, before jumping into any visual presentation aid project, help the student take a step back and think about all the choices they'll need to make to meet the audience's expectations. In this next section, I offer tips for making effective presentations and using slide-design techniques that engage audiences.

CONSULTATION STRATEGIES FOR SLIDE DESIGN: USING QUICK-AND-DIRTY PATHOS TO ENGAGE AN AUDIENCE

Any given audience has people who process information best when it's given verbally or when it's given visually. A successful presentation makes a bridge that connects the two. Public speakers should use their visuals to support, illustrate, and/or make an emotional connection between the content being provided and the audience being reached. Anyone can get up and say something; a successful presenter gets up and moves someone to take action. Visuals can help in this process. So, once consultants help students navigate the presentation choices available, they can help students think about designing presentations that capture an audience's attention. When tutoring a student who has a pretty strong presentation to start, these strategies can help push a good presentation into strong presentation territory. They allow the presenter to harness the power of the audience's emotions, which is where decision-making occurs. Use these strategies ethically!

Make Use of Movement

Instead of static images, encourage students to embed moving images as a background to their presentation. Nothing catches the attention of a human eye like movement, so presenters should use this to their advantage. For example, a student talking about the devastation of a tsunami shows a video of the event taking place while he explains the need for the audience to send financial aid to those affected. Or a professor talking about classroom activities has videos of students involved in small-group discussions projected on the screen behind her. Video works really well for information that's not too detailed. Just make sure the sound is turned off on the computer.

The Presenter Should Be the Focus

Don't let the visual presentation aid tell the presenter what to do. When a speaker looks at the slide to remember what to say next, the audience looks at the slide as well. Keep the attention on the presenter. Text-heavy slides also draw the attention away from the presenter. An audience typically reads and makes sense of a slide first before listening; the time spent reading the slide means the audience is not listening to what the speaker has to say. Have the students mark in their notes when they want to transition, and then have them click as they talk. When using Prezi, make sure students have their line ready to begin before making a long transition (like moving to another part of the screen). Silence during these transitions can take the energy out of a speech.

Use Keyboard Shortcuts

Teaching students about basic keyboard shortcuts can improve the impact of their presentations. PowerPoint has three helpful keyboard shortcuts that can help a speaker gain the audience's attention. Selecting the B key in presentation mode turns the screen black. Selecting the W key turns the screen white. For instance, consultants can recommend presenters use the B key to hide opening slides. It's also nice to use when the light from the projector is hitting the presenter's face when they are walking around the room. Using the W key gets the attention of the audience. Consultants can discuss tricks to keep an audience focused. For instance, when people begin to lose focus, having the screen turn white jolts them back to attention because they think something is broken. The third shortcut is the ctrl + P option. Using this turns the curser into a pen tool. Presenters can use this tool to point or draw on the screen; however, the point is hard to see from across the room. The drawing is easy to see.

Use a Clicker Tool

While many people use a tool like a clicker on their PowerPoints, using one on a Prezi is possible but not commonly done. To do this, presenters should have a clicker with a mouse option. They must place the curser on the arrow below the Prezi and use the mouse option to transition from one stop to the next. Consultants should advise students that this takes practice, but it allows a speaker the option of moving around the room instead of hugging the podium.

Help the Audience Focus Their Attention

Consultants can help presenters determine where the audience will enter and exit a visual with their eyes. If there is more than one item on the screen, consultants can suggest that one thing stand out more than the others. Presenters should be sure there's something to focus on first, then second, and then, if applicable, third. The audience needs to have a place to begin. They normally don't want to look around a Where's Waldo slide. They want to know what's important right away. If there's a chart, presenters should be sure it's clear what is important. As an example, consultants can provide feedback on whether or not the audience is asking What's that? in their thoughts before the presenter begins to explain the sudden uptick shown in the graphic.

Use Gravity to Your Advantage

While we all know projected images have no physical weight, human eyes still perceive projected objects as having physical weight. Don't believe me? Compare the word **ARMY** to *Army*. Which one looks tougher? It's the same word, but the first word looks heavy. It looks hard to push over. It looks as if it will stand its ground. The second one looks wispy, like an aroma. Explaining the power of gravity to presenters is important because it affects how we see everything.

Remember We All Have Bodies

Having a body means we favor some environments over others. Consultants can explain how long horizontal lines create stability, rolling lines denote calmness, and sharp angles denote pain or anxiety. Even if those lines are in the background, the audience will feel the way the speaker would like them to during the presentation.

Use the Slide Wisely

A centered slide is a boring slide, and that can be okay if the speaker is talking about stable subjects, like interest rates at a local bank. Think of someone balancing across a rope over a high location. That person wants to be right in the middle of the rope. However, if the subject is designed to inspire and excite an audience, items can move around on the screen. Think figure skating. They stay upright on the ice, but their arms and legs and bodies stretch out and create visual interest. Slides can do the same thing.

ACTIVITY

Good Design, Bad Design: A Visual-Communication Activity

PowerPoint offers a wide range of design options, which is exciting or perhaps frightening to someone who doesn't feel qualified to work with visuals. These activities can help consultants feel better equipped to design and discuss the designs of a wide range of visual presentation aids like PowerPoints, Prezis, and research posters.

Step 1: Collect poorly designed PowerPoint examples from the internet.

Conduct an image search for bad PowerPoint presentation and then collect the ones that need the most work and place them in a PowerPoint slide show. Next, look for good PowerPoint slides and insert in the slide show as well. After these images are collected, go through each image and talk about what you notice with a partner or a group of other consultants. Here are some guiding questions:

1. Which slides grab your attention?
2. Which slides lose your interest?
3. What's the difference between these two?

Step 2: Separate the best slides from the worst.

There might be some debate at this point. One person might really like one slide while another might dislike it. Move those sides to the side. Pick the slides that are clearly the best and worst (by group consensus) and arrange them on a single slide. Discuss what techniques are being used in the effective slide, and slowly weave in the CRAP principles. Remember, CRAP stands for

- **C**ontrast: the eye needs to know what to look at first;
- **R**epetition: the eye tends to group elements that are repeated;
- **A**lignment: the eye tends to group elements that flow into or align themselves together;
- **P**roximity: the eye tends to group elements together that are physically closest to one another.

Step 3: Taking CRAP into account, redesign the worst slides.

Once you've discussed the CRAP principles, select one of the worst slides and redesign it with these principles in mind using PowerPoint. Once you are done, present the new slide to your peers, explaining how the CRAP principles are being applied.

Move the Discussion from PowerPoint to Prezi

Now that you have a working PowerPoint, discuss ways to reinterpret the visual display on a Prezi.[1] Discuss how the elements of Prezi, such as movement, change the presentation of the content. Redesign the PowerPoint into a short Prezi presentation. Share both the Prezi and PowerPoint with your peers. Discuss what you noticed about the difference between the two presentations. What did PowerPoint allow you to do that Prezi didn't? What did Prezi allow you to do that PowerPoint didn't? Based on your topic, which was most effective and why?

Made You Look: A Design Exercise

Prezi and PowerPoint allow designers to add a tremendous amount of content to any given stop or slide. While this might be helpful to someone who cannot be around for a presentation and is getting the information without a speaker, too much information can disrupt the speaker's ability to communicate effectively with an audience because the audience will have a difficult time knowing what to focus on. This exercise can help illustrate this concept.

Step 1: Open a Recent Visual Presentation

Any visual presentation aid will do, but it's best if this is a presentation you created personally.

Step 2: Start Cutting

Remove any words, images, shapes, and/or dots that do not add information to the slide. Shorten sentences to key words. Move images to the sides so only half the image is showing. Do whatever you can to reduce the amount of data on the screen. You might need to make two or three slides from the one slide you started with. That's okay!

Step 3: Make a Path for the Eye

What do you want the audience to see first, second, and third? Design the visual to facilitate that action. We tend to notice bigger things first, things that are higher, things that are brighter. Play around with the design until you think you've got something that works. Then ask someone else to look at your design. Ask them to point where they are looking first, second, and third. If it works, congratulations! If not, try something different.

CONCLUSION

Both PowerPoint and Prezi can be used to create memorable and engaging visual presentation aids if students use the programs rhetorically—always keeping in mind the primary audience, the purpose of the presentation, and the context in which it will be delivered. We began this chapter with some information to guide students in choosing the best software for their situation. Once a program is selected, be sure visuals are being used to their full rhetorical power. Discuss the CRAP principles, and share the common pitfalls of PowerPoint and Prezi. Finally, guide that visual to a more effective level by considering *quick-and-dirty pathos*. Visuals are an easy way to engage with your audience emotionally. Use that to your advantage.

NOTE

1.   This is a technique I learned in a course at Clemson University taught by Kathleen Blake Yancey. To learn more about that experience, read this short article I published on *Kairos*: http://kairos.technorhetoric.net/18.1/disputatio/apostel/.

RESOURCES

Slide-Design Guides

Apostel, Shawn. 2017. "Avoiding Prezilepsy: Organization Strategies to Reduce Motion Sickness caused by Prezis." Prezi. https://prezi.com/-a3q9q7qxn2a/avoiding-prezilepsy-organization-strategies-to-reduce-motion-sickness-caused-by-prezis/.
   Prezi's zoom capabilities can create a sense of motion sickness. This Prezi discusses strategies that reduce this sickness—which I call *Prezilepsy*.
Apostel, Shawn. 2017. "Prezi Design Strategies." Prezi. https://prezi.com/bm9alx1pbtmc/prezi-design-strategies/.
   This Prezi shows how to apply concepts used in video production to Prezi design.

Further Reading

Arola, Kristin L., Jennifer Sheppard, and Cheryl E. Ball. 2014. *Writer/Designer: A Guide to Making Multimodal Projects.* New York: Bedford/St. Martin's.
Earnest, William. 2007. *Save Our Slides: PowerPoint Design That Works.* Dubuque, IA: St. Edward's University.
Williams, Robin. 1994. *The Non-Designers Design Book: Design and Typography Principles for the Visual Novice.* Berkeley, CA: Peachpit.

KEY SEARCH TERMS

PowerPoint; Prezi; Google Slides; presentation slide design; ADA compliant presentations

REFERENCES

Duarte, Nancy. 2009. "Duarte Design's Five Rules for Presentations." YouTube video, 4:28. Posted December 16. https://www.youtube.com/watch?v=hT9GGmundag.

"Visualizing Great Things." N.d. Prezi. Accessed June 06, 2017. https://prezi.com/about/.

Williams, Robin. 1994. *The Non-Designers Design Book: Design and Typography Principles for the Visual Novice.* Berkeley, CA: Peachpit.

7

INFOGRAPHICS
A Powerful Combination of Word, Image, and Data

Alyse Knorr
Regis University

CHAPTER OVERVIEW

Infographics are multimodal texts that combine words, visuals, and data to convey complex data. This chapter outlines the basic design principles of infographics and offers tips for consultants working with beginning infographic designers, as well as resources for planning, creating, and revising infographics. Key topics include rhetorical awareness, working with data, organization, typography, and color. By focusing on the rhetorical situation and the story behind the data, consultants help student designers create powerful, communicative infographics.

ILLUSTRATIVE EXAMPLE: VISUALIZING
READER-RESPONSE CRITICISM

At Regis University, all English majors take a 300-level "boot-camp" course called Literary Analysis, which is paired each semester with a one-credit Digital Writing Lab. One of the students' lab assignments is to take a challenging concept they learned in Literary Analysis and simplify it using an infographic. The goals of this assignment are for students to develop their rhetorical awareness and their ability to tell a story through visuals. For "word people" like English majors, who are often more comfortable writing about a topic than representing it visually, this task can be challenging.

One semester, I worked with a student named Meghan, who was designing an infographic to explain gender studies and queer theory. The first draft of Meghan's infographic consisted mostly of text, with a few visuals included as illustrations rather than as a means of conveying information. It also wasn't clear from Meghan's first draft what queer theory actually is or how it's used. I asked Meghan what she envisioned as her audience and purpose for the infographic, and she told me she wanted

DOI: 10.7330/9781607328469.c007

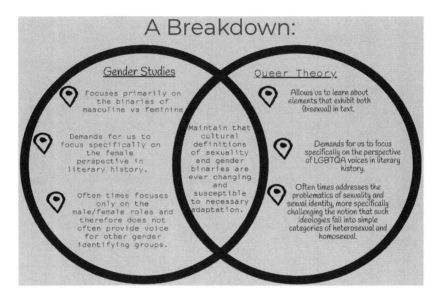

Figure 7.1. "A Breakdown," an infographic by Meghan Burklund (2017)

to create a very basic introduction to gender studies and queer theory for new college students. I then asked her what design choices she should make to ensure her infographic achieved this purpose for this audience.

With this rhetorical framework in mind, Meghan then realized exactly what she needed to add to her infographic: a clarification of the major similarities and differences between gender studies and queer theory. In the final draft of her infographic, Meghan took advantage of the spatial mode's affordances and incorporated a Venn diagram to clarify those differences (figure 7.1).

Meghan's story provides a powerful example of why it's important to start the design process with an awareness of the rhetorical situation. As noted in Lindsay Sabatino's introduction to this collection, a designer's choices of everything from content to color to size should flow from an understanding of the designer's purpose, audience, and context. Once the designer has a firm grasp of their rhetorical situation, the rest of the process often seems to fall into place naturally.

BACKGROUND INFORMATION: WHAT YOU NEED TO KNOW ABOUT INFOGRAPHICS

An infographic is a visual multimodal text that combines still images, words, and/or numbers to inform, persuade, or entertain. Infographics visualize complex data and ideas into a simpler, clearer form an audience can grasp quickly and easily. Infographics use the affordances of the linguistic, visual, and spatial modes in conjunction with one another to create a multimodal message.

Infographics can take many forms, including flow charts, maps, diagrams, graphs, or some combination of these. They can incorporate photographs or stick to basic symbols, icons, and illustrations (Parkinson 2016). Infographics are usually not only informative but also aesthetically pleasing, leading scholars Michelle Borkin, Azalea A. Vo, Zoya Bylinskii, Phillip Isola, Shashank Sunkavalli, Aude Oliva, and Hanspeter Pfister to term them a type of "Functional Art" (2013, 2314).

The visual language systems of ancient Egypt and Sumeria may be considered the world's first infographics. Maps, however, were the first "true" infographics—the first examples of pairing language with images to easily communicate information. Historical timelines followed in the 1700s, then tables, pie charts, and graphs in the early 1800s. Today, a countless number of companies, media outlets, libraries, educators, medical professionals, and even the White House create and disseminate infographics. The introduction to this book notes that writers evolve with technology to find new communication methods, and infographics provide a fantastic example of this evolution. Infographics help readers make sense of the "age of Big Data" we currently live in (Thompson 2016, 24), and they are just one of the many new tools changing the way we define literacy.

The core assumption behind infographic design is that by marrying text and visual representations of data, a designer can create an informative graphic that is greater than the sum of its parts (Occa and Suggs 2016). Research on how the brain processes visual input tends to back up this concept. Visuals grab our attention (Knobloch et al. 2003; Sargent 2007) and help us remember information better (Borkin et al. 2013) and faster (Evans 2016).

But infographics aren't all about speed of processing. They can also provide a way to wrestle with problems more deeply by synthesizing and comparing information in a format that appeals to "multiple literacies" (Abilock and Williams 2014, 47). Political scientist Robert Horn goes so far as to claim that "Visual Language is one of the more promising avenues to the improvement of human performance in the short run. . . . When words and visual elements are closely intertwined, we create something new and we augment our communal intelligence" (2001, 1). Horn maintains that visual languages can aid with key challenges like cross-cultural communication and the comprehension of increasingly difficult concepts. In this way, infographics are just one of the many types of new communication media that are, as the New London Group states, "reshaping the way we use language" (Cazden et al. 1996, 64).

Consider figure 7.2 for an example of these infographic-design principles in action. All infographics must have a clear purpose or argument and focus on one main topic or story (Davis and Quinn 2014; Evans 2016; "Infographic Design Guide" 2016), and this graphic is no exception. The purpose of "The Banning of Books" infographic is to introduce to a viewer some of the basic concepts behind book banning.

Like any strong infographic, this one showcases multiple types of data from multiple sources, cited at the bottom left-hand side of the image. An infographic wouldn't be an *info*-graphic without information. "The Banning of Books" displays complex information from its sources using an easy-to-comprehend pie chart, pull-quote statistic, and book-cover images. The infographic's visuals don't exist as mere decoration or illustration—they exist to clarify the data and convey key concepts.

"The Banning of Books" also has a clear organization designed to guide the viewer through its argument. Strong infographics usually have a focal point, visible title, or dominant image on which the eye lands first. Through the placement of its large title in the top left corner, "The Banning of Books" infographic provides viewers with a hierarchical dominant image from which to start. The graphic then leads the viewer's eye through a clear trajectory around the information. As noted in Sabatino's introduction, Western audiences always move from top to bottom and left to right (Balliett 2011; Evans 2016; "Infographic Design" 2016; "Infographic Design Guide" 2016; Johnson 2011; Smith 2012). In this example, the pie chart at the top left provides a brief overview of who bans books before the infographic proceeds into the reasons these groups ban books, which books they ban, and how others respond to book censorship.

Furthermore, in successful infographics, typography plays a key role in communicating information. Differences in font type, size, weight, hue, saturation, and value can convey meaning and organize a document by creating visual hierarchies ("Infographic Design Guide" 2016). Note how "The Banning of Books" creates a visual organization by using one font for headings and another for body text. The bold font and larger sizes of the section headings neatly structure the content and allow the viewer to move through the argument smoothly. At the same time, the infographic achieves unity because it uses *only* two fonts and stays consistent about when and how those fonts are used. You can access a color version of this photo at www.multimodalwritingcenter.org.

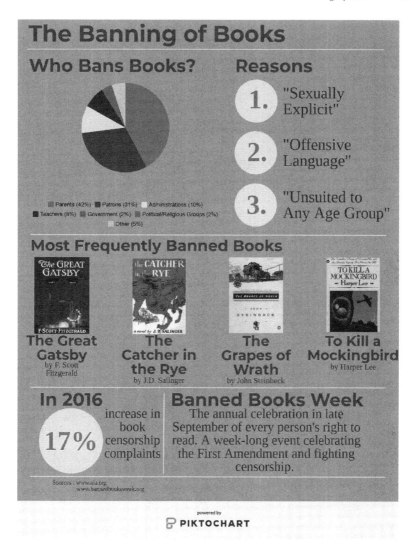

Figure 7.2. "The Banning of Books," an infographic by Michelle Hart (2017)

CONSULTATION STRATEGIES FOR INFOGRAPHICS

Analyze the Rhetorical Situation

As in Meghan's case, and as noted in this book's introduction, it's very beneficial to begin a tutoring session with a conversation about the student designer's rhetorical situation—especially about the purpose, audience, and context of the project. What prompt has the student been assigned? What is the purpose of this infographic, and who is its audience? In what context will this graphic be presented or published? The answers to all these questions should influence the choices the student makes throughout their entire design process, so try to encourage the student to keep returning to these points again and again.

If the designer gets stuck on a tough decision about colors, size, content, font—anything!—ask them to consider what would be best suited for their specific audience, purpose, and context. For example, a diagram for fourth graders about how to recycle likely needs to use a very different set of colors, font, and language than an organizational flow chart for a corporate office.

Another way to frame this conversation with infographic designers is to ask them what story they want their infographic to tell. With all the data and visuals to consider, it can be easy to forget that infographics must communicate a central, clear message (Balliett 2011; Johnson 2011; Smith 2012). As graphics expert Mike Parkinson (2016) writes, "Most educational infographics fail because they are a collection of random content, data, and icons with no clear message or story" (26). Help the student avoid this problem by keeping them focused on their rhetorical situation.

Start with the Data

One of the most challenging steps in creating an infographic is determining how to visualize the data. Ask the student what exactly they want to highlight about their data. Are they trying to make a comparison? To show differences geographically? To show a change over time? Answering these questions will help them determine what type of visual to use.

Here's a brief overview of options:

- Use a line graph to show a change over time (Archambault 2016; "Infographic Design Guide" 2016).
- Use a pie chart to demonstrate percentages compared to the whole (Archambault 2016; "Infographic Design Guide" 2016).
- Use a bar graph to show how items rank, compare, or distribute (Archambault 2016; "Infographic Design Guide" 2016).
- Consider other methods such as timelines, maps, alphabetical order, compare/contrast charts ("Infographic Design" 2016).

Not all infographics must incorporate numerical data. For instance, a diagram of the parts of a cell phone or a chart with step-by-step instructions on how to change one's oil might not incorporate any numerical figures (Parkinson 2016). If the infographic does contain numerical data, however, it should fairly and accurately represent that data. Review the charts or the scale of any charts or graphs with the student and help them locate any misrepresentations. Finally, remind the designer to cite where their data comes from somewhere on the infographic; see Molly Schoen and Sarah Blazer's chapter on copyright and citations for more information.

Make a Plan

Before the student opens up their design software, encourage them to sketch a mock-up of their infographic on paper. Sticky notes and lined graph paper are useful for this step. Ask the designer what content they plan to use and which pieces of information are most important, and guide their mock-up accordingly. Remind the student that their goal is to simplify the information for the viewer and tell a story. Finally, set the designer's mind at ease by reassuring them that this step can and should be messy! It's where the creativity happens (Balliett 2011; Parkinson 2016). For more ideas on using storyboarding in a session, refer to Brandy Ball Blake and Karen Head's chapter.

Organize the Image

Sara McGuire (2018), writing for the online infographic tool Venngage, identifies seven ways of organizing an infographic: statistics, information, timeline, process, geography, comparison, or hierarchy. As the student designer sketches up their infographic mock-up, it might help to show them examples of these organization schemes and to explain the purposes of each.

A *statistical infographic* communicates a message primarily through data and numbers, often visualized as charts or graphs. *Informational infographics* tell a story using text formatted with icons, bullet points, and sections that divide the content up into logical categories. *Timelines* represent how a process or event unfolded or will unfold over time. *Process infographics* break complicated tasks down into smaller steps. *Geographically organized infographics* use maps to convey information about a place or group of places. *Comparison infographics* are used to show pros versus cons or similarities and/or differences; they can also provide advice about what to choose among several entities. Finally, *hierarchical infographics*, such as organizational flow charts or pyramids, show the relationship of different entities to each other using levels in various orders.

Consider Color and Typography Carefully

As the student makes design choices about color and typography, use the Gestalt visual principles to guide them. Remind the designer that to create a structural contrast, they should use at least two different fonts, but to maintain unity, they shouldn't use more than three ("Infographic Design" 2016; "Infographic Design Guide" 2016). Incorporating bold, italics, underlining, all caps, and different sizes and colors can create variety in how fonts look while maintaining cohesion and unity.

Likewise, encourage the student to limit their infographic to two or three main colors, including one background color, to achieve a cohesive and consistent appearance (Balliett 2011; "Infographic Design" 2016; "Infographic Design Guide" 2016). Using different shades of the same color can help achieve variety without overkill (Archambault 2016). When the student is ready to choose colors, consult color wheels to determine what colors look best together; see the "Resources" section below for links to some online color wheels. Subtle differences in hue, saturation, or value can create useful contrast that draws the viewer's attention to certain areas (Archambault 2016).

Remind the designer that font and color selections should always be based on the rhetorical situation of the infographic; for instance, Comic Sans isn't best for a professional document, but it would work for an infographic about comic books. All colors in the document should serve a clear purpose. Bright colors work best for fun, entertaining topics, while a more subdued palette might appear more professional. Finally, certain text and background color combinations, such as green and red or blue and yellow, are not visible to those who are color blind (Archambault 2016).

ACTIVITY

Analyzing and creating infographics provide a great foundation for helping students contextualize, develop, and organize as they work to visualize their data. The questions and advice offered in the two following activities provide an opportunity to experience firsthand the strategies discussed for tutoring infographics in this chapter.

1. Analyzing Infographics

Examine the infographic in figure 7.3. With a partner, discuss the following questions:

A. Consider the *rhetorical situation* of this graphic.
- What story is being told?
- What problem is being explored?
- What is this infographic's argument?
- Who is the audience and what is the purpose of this infographic?

B. Identify the *text, images, and data* displayed here.
- What kinds of data are provided, and in what formats are they presented?
- How are text, image, and data working together in this graphic to achieve the purpose you identified in step A?

C. Reflect on this graphic's *organization.*
- What is the focal point?
- What are the sections, and how are they organized?
- What trajectory does the designer set up for your eye to travel through the image?
- Which of the seven types of infographic organization does the designer use, and why?

D. Analyze the *typography.*
- How many font styles does this image use?
- How is typography used to organize the information, convey meaning, and create contrast?

E. Examine the use of color. (You can access a color version of this photo at www.multimodalwritingcenter.org.)
- How many colors does this image use?
- How is color used to organize the information, convey meaning, and create contrast?

2. Creating an Infographic

A. *Find a story to tell.* Explore your school's website for data. Many schools have a Facts page under their About section. You could look at student demographic data, tuition changes over time, faculty/staff structure, history of your school, writing center statistics, and so forth. Find some information you think would be better conveyed visually.

B. *Consider your rhetorical situation.* What is the purpose of your infographic? Who is the audience? What story, problem, or argument do you want to convey? How will your rhetorical situation affect your design choices?

C. *Plan your graphic.* Decide which methods would work best for displaying the information visually. A map? A pie chart? A bar graph?

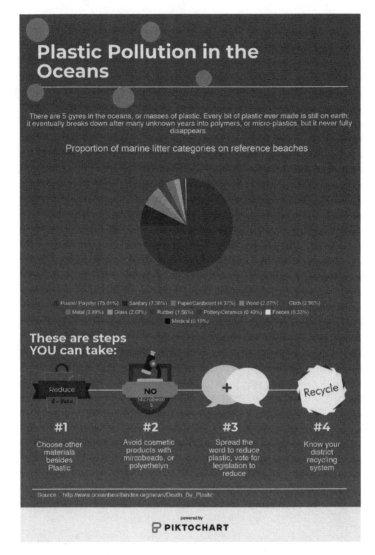

Figure 7.3. "Plastic Pollution in the Oceans," an infographic by Hannah Creasman (2017)

Illustrations? You might need a combination of methods, as in figures 7.2 and 7.3.

D. *Sketch a mock-up* of your infographic on paper. Determine your organization. Choose a focal point, sections, and a flow trajectory for the viewer's eye. Decide where to use text, images, and data. Don't forget a title!

E. *Create your infographic.* Use one of the free web-based software tools mentioned below in the "Resources" section.

F. *Revise* your infographic based on the design principles discussed above.

CONCLUSION

Good infographics often look so simple and effortless it's hard to anticipate how difficult they really are to make. To design a successful infographic, one must juggle an understanding of complex data, compelling narrative, and effective design—in other words, one must be a "numbers person," a "word person," and a "visual person" all at once.

This makes it all the more important for beginning infographic designers to get feedback and guidance from tutors. Thanks to the incredible free software available today for infographic design (see below), with practice, attention to detail, and careful attention to rhetorical situation, anyone can make an excellent infographic. If knowledge is power, infographics are a powerful tool indeed.

RESOURCES

The following resources provide examples and software for infographics, as well as tools to assist with color and graphic choices.

Infographic Examples

informationisbeautiful.net
    A data journalist and information designer runs this blog, which displays fantastic
    infographics and other data visualizations. The site's aesthetic is sleek, minimalist,
    and professional.
infographicsshowcase.com
    This site collects and displays colorful, icon-heavy infographics.
coolinfographics.com
    Browse through this site for a collection of fascinating infographics, all of which are
    timely and some of which are animated or interactive. The infographics here tend
    to be heavier on the hard data than those on infographicsshowcase.com.

Creation Software

Piktochart.com, Easel.ly, Canva.com, and Venngage.com
    These sites are free, cloud-based infographic-design software tools. They're easy to
    use, flexible, and versatile. Paid accounts open up more template options, but you
    can do a lot from scratch with any of these tools.
Infogram.com
    This site is a great piece of cloud software that's heavier on the data side of the
    design process.

Design Support Tools

color.adobe.com

   Color swatches can be intimidating. Luckily, Adobe's color wheel lets designers
   easily build a color palette with colors that pair perfectly. Simply start with one color
   and then the program will provide complementary, analogous, monochromatic,
   shaded, triad, or compound palettes of colors that look great together. You can also
   use a sliding scale to slightly adjust how bright or dark the color palette is—adjust
   one color and the whole palette stays updated. Once you've found the perfect colors, copy down their HEX, CMYK, or RGB values to use these colors in any digital-
   design program.

paletton.com

   Similar to Adobe's color selector, Paletton provides assistance in choosing colors for
   an infographic. After you select a color on the wheel, Paletton displays the complementary color or a whole palette based on adjacent, triad, or tetrad schemes. It also
   lets you view varying shades of each color selection and provides all the info for each
   color choice—RGB, hue, and luminosity values—so you can use that color in any
   digital-design program that allows for RGB input value.

billiondollargraphics.com/graphic-cheat-sheet

   This interactive web page can help designers determine which type of graph is best
   for their infographic, based on the type of data available and the aspects of the data
   that need to be highlighted.

KEY SEARCH TERMS

infographics; infographic design; multimodal texts; multimodal design;
data visualization; information design; graphic-design principles; typography; rhetorical awareness

REFERENCES

Abilock, Debbie, and Connie Williams. 2014. "Recipe for an Infographic." *Knowledge Quest*
   43 (2): 46–55.

Archambault, Susan Gardner. 2016. "Telling Your Story: Using Dashboards and Infographics for Data Visualization." *Computers in Libraries* 36 (3): 4–7.

Balliett, Amy. 2011. "The Do's and Don'ts of Infographic Design." Smashing Magazine. https://www.smashingmagazine.com/2011/10/the-dos-and-donts-of-infographic
   -design/.

Borkin, Michelle A., Azalea A. Vo, Zoya Bylinskii, Phillip Isola, Shashank Sunkavalli, Aude
   Oliva, and Hanspeter Pfister. 2013. "What Makes a Visualization Memorable?" *IEEE
   Transactions on Visualization and Computer Graphics* 19 (12): 2306–15.

Burklund, Meghan. 2017. "A Breakdown."

Cazden, Courtney, Bill Cope, Norman Fairclough, and Jim Gee. 1996. "A Pedagogy of
   Multiliteracies: Designing Social Futures." *Harvard Educational Review* 66 (1): 60–92.

Creasman, Hannah. 2017. "Plastic Pollution in the Oceans."

Davis, Mark, and David Quinn. 2014. "Visualizing Text: The New Literacy of Infographics."
   Reading Today 31 (3): 16–18.

Evans, Rachel. 2016. "Infographics on the Brain." *Computers in Literature* 36 (6): 4–8.

Hart, Michelle. 2017. "The Banning of Books."

Horn, Robert E. 2001. "Visual Language and Converging Technologies in the Next 10–15 Years (and Beyond)." Paper presented at the National Science Foundation Conference on Converging Technologies for Improving Human Performance, December 3–4.

"Infographic Design." N.d. *Canva*. Accessed August 29, 2016. https://designschool.canva.com/how-to-design-infographics/.

"Infographic Design Guide." N.d. *Venngage*. Accessed August 29, 2016. https://venngage.com/blog/infographic-design/.

Johnson, Joshua. 2011. "10 Tips for Designing Better Infographics." *Design Shack*. https://designshack.net/articles/graphics/10-tips-for-designing-better-infographics/.

Knobloch, Silvia, Matthias Hastall, Dolf Zillman, and Coy Callison. 2003. "Imagery Effects on the Selective Reading of Internet Newspapers." *Communication Research* 30 (1): 3–29.

McGuire, Sara. 2018. "The Top 9 Infographic Template Types." *Venngage*. Accessed November 29, 2016. https://venngage.com/blog/9-types-of-infographic-template/.

Occa, Aurora, and L. Suzanne Suggs. 2016. "Communicating Breast Cancer Screening with Young Women: An Experimental Test of Didactic and Narrative Messages Using Video and Infographics." *Journal of Health Communication* 21 (1): 1–11.

Parkinson, Mike. 2016. "Infographic Tips and Tools." *TD: Talent Development* 70 (5): 26–28.

Sargent, Stephanie Lee. 2007. "Image Effects on Selective Exposure to Computer-Mediated News Stories." *Computers in Human Behavior* 23 (1): 705–26.

Smith, Josh. 2012. "10 Steps to Designing an Amazing Infographic." *Fast Company*. https://www.fastcodesign.com/1670019/10-steps-to-designing-an-amazing-infographic.

Thompson, Clive. 2016. "How Data Won the West." *Smithsonian* 47 (4): 23–27.

8

ePORTFOLIOS
Collect, Select, Reflect

Lauri Dietz
Stanford University

Kate Flom Derrick
Northwestern University

CHAPTER OVERVIEW

This chapter offers an overview of ePortfolios and provides tutoring strategies for helping writers across disciplines showcase, reflect on, and assess their accomplishments and learning through media, design, and text. Consultants can help writers creating ePortfolios identify underlying themes across their work and learning and select media to illustrate and support those themes.

ILLUSTRATIVE EXAMPLE: USING EPORTFOLIOS FOR A VARIETY OF PURPOSES

Like many institutions, DePaul University adopted ePortfolios as a part of its curriculum, and students are often asked to create different types of ePortfolios throughout their education. For example, during her first year at DePaul, Sarah T., a creative writing major, created an ePortfolio[1] for a required first-year writing course. Sarah built her ePortfolio with her professor as her target audience and without feedback from a peer writing consultant. Sarah's composing process focused primarily on the content of the ePortfolio, with minimal consideration of the aesthetic and organizational design. At the time, Sarah did not see her ePortfolio as much more than an electronic filing system. Looking back, Sarah saw how connecting her content with a visual theme might have helped her to write a reflection that more explicitly connected her artifacts to the learning she felt she experienced.

DOI: 10.7330/9781607328469.c008

At the end of Sarah's sophomore year, Sarah created a new ePortfolio.[2] This time, Sarah was composing an ePortfolio for a much different audience and purpose. As a new peer writing consultant within DePaul's University Center for Writing-based Learning (UCWbL), she created an ePortfolio within a required Writing Center Theory and Pedagogy course to demonstrate her professional development and individual goal accomplishments. Each year Sarah worked at the UCWbL, she continued to update and revise this professional ePortfolio and even used it to apply for a leadership position as a head writing fellow. Her audience was now her supervisors at the UCWbL and the DePaul community, who could view her ePortfolio through her staff profile on the UCWbL website.

In addition to thoughtfully selecting artifacts that demonstrated Sarah's growth as a peer writing consultant and curating them with reflections about her composing process, Sarah also spent time considering the aesthetic and organizational design of her ePortfolio. This time, Sarah made an appointment with peer writing consultant Theresa B. to talk about ways to integrate content and design. In Theresa's consultant log reflecting on the appointment, she explains,

> Sarah was having a lot of trouble thinking of different [visual] abstractions, so I asked her to name some authors or literary characters who she would want to be tutored by. I then asked her what about those tutors made them good tutors. This helped Sarah grasp the concept. We then moved on to integrating her theme.

Theresa asked Sarah questions related to types of visual metaphors, which helped Sarah make the move from content to design. As a result of this session, Sarah chose a theme based on *Alice's Adventures in Wonderland* and made explicit connections among her memories, feelings, and thoughts about Alice and her work throughout her first year as a peer writing tutor. Sarah explains in her ePortfolio why she chose Alice:

> Through her adventures, Alice realizes that people are always changing and growing, that there are millions of ways to view the same situation, that there are countless paths that will get you to the same place, and that every person you meet can teach you something new. I believe that these ideas are important and are especially applicable to the work we do at the Writing Center.

Additionally, most pages of her ePortfolio featured quotations and media related to *Alice's Adventures in Wonderland* that reinforced her reasons for choosing it. Sarah's ePortfolio was successful in helping her get the job of head writing fellow and is consistently used at the UCWbL as an example of an effective *assessment* ePortfolio.

BACKGROUND INFORMATION: WHAT YOU
NEED TO KNOW ABOUT EPORTFOLIOS

In the most basic terms, an ePortfolio is "a digitized collection of artifacts including demonstrations, resources, and accomplishments" that can document, represent, and reflect on a writer's experiences, development, and/or work (Lorenzo and Ittelson 2005, 2).

The *artifacts* are the elements on display within the ePortfolio that give the ePortfolio shape and purpose. A distinct advantage of ePortfolios (in contrast to hard-copy portfolios) is the ability to incorporate a wide array of media; an ePortfolio can contain videos, GIFs, PDFs, a gallery of images, and audio files. In Sarah's first-year writing ePortfolios, her artifacts included scanned images of newspaper articles and essay drafts with comments on them and text from drafts copied and pasted directly into modules. As she grew more aware of and comfortable with the genre and working with DePaul's ePortfolio platform, her variety of artifacts increased. In her peer writing tutor ePortfolio, her artifacts became more dynamic, as she included excerpts from and links to blog posts, PDFs of workshop materials, and GIFs and JPEGs.

Regardless of the types of artifacts included, they should be accompanied by *curator's notes.* Much like artifacts in a museum, each artifact within an ePortfolio benefits from an explanation—or curator's note—providing the context and purpose for inclusion. Depending on the type and purpose, a curator's note can be reflective, making explicit connections between experiences and learning, or more factually based to clearly illustrate specific accomplishments.

As Sarah's various experiences creating ePortfolios demonstrate, ePortfolios can be used for a variety of purposes. The three main types of ePortfolios are

- developmental ePortfolios,
- assessment ePortfolios,
- showcase ePortfolios.

Developmental ePortfolios are primarily used in academic contexts. As the name suggests, developmental ePortfolios aim to illustrate, through the pairing of artifacts and reflections, how the composer is learning. Sarah's first-year writing ePortfolio is an example of a developmental ePortfolio, as her goal was to show how she accomplished specific learning outcomes related to writing and revision through her engagement with course material. Developmental ePortfolios can often focus on the "messy" side of learning, pointing out challenges, missteps, and other elements that illustrate the recursive nature of learning.

Assessment ePortfolios can be used both academically and professionally to demonstrate the composer has accomplished a specific goal or task. Assessment ePortfolios tend to display artifacts that represent experiences and completed projects (as opposed to process-based artifacts found in developmental ePortfolios) and include reflections throughout. In Sarah's case, she created an assessment ePortfolio to be used in her application to become a head writing fellow, making the case throughout that she was a capable applicant. At DePaul University, several programs, including the master's of English and master's of communication, have adopted assessment ePortfolios as a graduation requirement. Students must complete the required elements of the ePortfolio by the end of their program, and their ePortfolios are then assessed by a panel of professors to determine whether or not the students have successfully completed the program.

Showcase ePortfolios are primarily used professionally and might be what comes to mind most readily for someone unfamiliar with ePortfolios. A showcase ePortfolio is a selection of the creator's best work, whether it be artwork, writing, or other projects. Reflection is typically not included in a showcase ePortfolio; instead, brief curatorial information is provided for each artifact to establish context.

CONSULTATION STRATEGIES FOR EPORTFOLIOS

All peer writing tutors at DePaul's UCWbL maintain professional-development ePortfolios using the university's official ePortfolio platform. Each consultant profile on our website links to a public version of their ePortfolio. Having experience with both the technical and rhetorical aspects of ePortfolios helps consultants, such as Sarah T., show writers how interconnected the technical and the rhetorical are. If a writer asks the consultant how to embed a video, the consultant can help them learn the mechanics of the platform while asking them reflective questions such as:

- Why video?
- Why *this* video?
- Why this video *here*?

Portfolios combined with reflective writing have a well-established link to metacognition, which is why they have been an increasingly popular pedagogical tool. The great news about ePortfolios is that they expand and diversify the opportunities for metacognition because the process for choosing, integrating, and organizing new media also promotes metacognition (Wozniak and Zagal 2013). Consequently, when consultants approach conversations with writers working on ePortfolios, they should be prepared to encourage writers to reflect on all elements.

Collaboratively Set an Agenda with the Writer

ePortfolios can be challenging for consultants to work with because they tend to have layered content that can take multiple sessions to cover. To that end, consultants can encourage writers to set up recurring appointments throughout an ePortfolio project to help manage the workload of each session. This allows the consultant and writer to go more in depth with feedback and revisions for each component.

Regardless of the project, consultants should start any relationship with a writer by collaboratively setting the agenda with them. Agenda setting helps focus the work and manage time within an appointment or over a series of appointments. Conversations about agendas can also help manage writers' expectations about what can be accomplished in any given appointment. For example, while there might not be time to focus on every artifact in the ePortfolio, there might be time to focus on one artifact that can serve as a model for revising other artifacts.

At the start of a synchronous appointment, consultants should work with writers to set an agenda by talking about

- whether the ePortfolio is a developmental, assessment, or showcase;
- the writer's goals for the project;
- deadlines or due dates;
- materials related to the ePortfolio (e.g., the assignment, application prompt, or job description);
- where the writer is in the ePortfolio-creation process;
- possible ways of representing the writer's ideas (e.g., discussing the different user experience with video versus text and image);
- any feedback the writer has received to date on this project; and
- patterns of feedback (both praise and criticism) the writer has received in the past on any projects.

Based on this information, the consultant should work with the writer to decide on up to three goals for the appointment; however, consultants might find they need to revisit or revise the agenda as the work of the appointment progresses.

Organization

Organization can be one of the biggest challenges in designing an effective ePortfolio. Similar to website creators, ePortfolio creators can't assume viewers will experience their ePortfolio linearly—a set path from start to finish. When consultants work with writers on organization for an individual paper, the specific sequence of paragraphs typically matters, as argument or meaning is developed from one paragraph to the next. For an ePortfolio, the most a writer can assume is that the home page will be most viewers' starting point. Thus, if an ePortfolio creator wants to encourage viewers to read sections in a specific order, they need to provide a road map for the viewer on the home page and create headings and subheadings that signal the desired order. This can happen through numbering, temporal cues (e.g., September, October, November), process signals (e.g., first draft, revised draft, final draft), or thematic metaphors (e.g., seed, sapling, oak tree). For information about structural layout of websites, see Clint Gardner, Joe McCormick, and Jarrod Barben's chapter on web design.

Discussing organization can be helpful at any stage of an ePortfolio. However, depending on the ePortfolio platform, revising organization could be rather labor intensive. In those cases, consultants should recommend the writer create an organizational plan before creating an ePortfolio.

There are a number of assistive technology tools, both analogue and digital, that can be an ePortfolio creator's best friend when tackling organization. One of our favorite digital tools at DePaul's UCWbL is Trello.[3] Trello is a free project-management tool with which the user creates a "board" to organize "cards" (essentially digital sticky notes) on "lists." The user can add images and attachments, drag and drop cards and lists, set due dates, and add collaborators. Trello allows ePortfolio creators to storyboard their ePortfolios before they start constructing within the targeted platform.

In a face-to-face appointment, consultants can incorporate sticky notes into a conversation about organization. The consultant can have the writer write down a different potential artifact on each sticky note to think about grouping and sequencing. The consultant can also have the writer use separate sticky notes to identify the different potential sections. The writer can even snap a photo of the sticky-note organizational scheme to refer to later and to potentially incorporate into an ePortfolio as evidence of process.

Figure 8.1. The left image is a Trello board used to organize and communicate about revisions and changes to DePaul's Digication Get Help Guide *(right). Each ePortfolio page has its own card and stickers (i.e., green check marks) to indicate when a page is ready to be published. (Trello is not affiliated with this collection in any way and does not endorse this book.)*

Breaking Up Walls of Text

One of the potential downfalls of developmental and assessment ePortfolios is that they can feel like digital file cabinets where writers post essays exactly as they would format them for traditional paper-based MLA/APA/CMS projects. The potential problem with that approach is that it can create ePortfolio pages that are just walls of text. Online viewers often do not have much patience for giant walls of text, and important content can be lost if ePortfolio creators do not adapt their approach to incorporate online-content-development best practices, such as using headings, breaking up text into small chunks, using larger fonts, incorporating complementary graphics through images and typography, using a color scheme that aids in readability, and so forth. In addition, design choices like these lend themselves to accessibility. For more information, see Gardner, McCormick, and Barben's chapter on web design.

Yet, writers might find a challenge in deciding how to best to incorporate essays into their ePortfolios. One option, which many DePaul UCWbL tutors use when formatting their tutoring philosophies in their ePortfolios, is to use the navigation menu to create separate subsections for each part of their philosophies. So, instead of having headers on one page to break up content, they use the headers to create separate pages. One of the bonuses to breaking up essays into separate subsections is that it creates more space to incorporate visual elements too.

Consultants can talk with writers about how they might divide an essay into sections and brainstorm potential headings and complementary imagery for each subsection.

Figure 8.2. In Sarah's WRD103 ePortfolio (left), she pasted her text directly from a Word file without adding any additional elements. For her Writing Center ePortfolio (right), she added hyperlinks and images and included a brief introductory curator's note.

First Contact Points

In a multimodal world, first impressions can make or break an ePortfolio creator's ethos. For almost all ePortfolios, the first impression happens with the home page. To prepare for a discussion about the home page, consultants should ask writers to explain the tone and voice they want to capture in the ePortfolio. Tone is the attitude the writer has towards the material, and voice is the personality that shapes that attitude. For example, two ePortfolio creators could have an attitude that they are proud of the accomplishments included in their ePortfolios, but one might want to represent that pride through a cooperative personality and the other might want to represent it through a scholarly personality, so each writer must choose language, color, and images that reinforce and complement the intended tone and personality. The consultant plays an important role in this process by reflecting back to the writer which elements of the ePortfolio work towards that aim and which might undercut it. The Ideonomy Project at MIT has a helpful list of 112 positive personality traits[4] that could help a writer brainstorm a specific and focused personality for their ePortfolio.

The consultant's role can be to perform a miniusability test for the ePortfolio creator by providing real-time feedback about those first impressions.

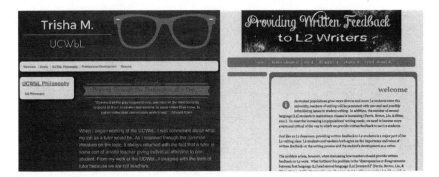

Figure 8.3. Trisha's ePortfolio (left) is an example of her cooperative personality, demonstrated through her conversational tone and emphasis on peerness. "Providing Written Feedback to L2 Writers" (right) emphasizes a scholarly personality, as it leads with cited research and uses a formal, academic tone throughout.

- Where does the eye go first on the page?
- What initial assumptions did you make about the writer?
- What do you expect to find in each section?
- To what extent was the text easy to read and understand?
- To what extent were the images easy to understand?
- Where would you navigate next and why?

In developmental and assessment ePortfolios, cover letters or other reflective components might also be important first-contact points for evaluators and assessors of the ePortfolios. Consequently, taking time in an appointment or devoting an entire appointment to this particular component might be a particularly valuable use of time. In many ways, consultants can approach the reflective piece as they would any other paper-based appointment. However, there are some extra points to consider as consultants discuss the reflective artifact with the writer.

- To what extent is the writer backing claims about learning with evidence from the ePortfolio?
- Where within the cover letter could the writer link to specific artifacts?
- To what extent does the writer address the rationale and decision-making for aesthetic choices throughout the ePortfolio?

Visuals
As illustrated by Sarah T.'s first ePortfolios, without visuals, an ePortfolio is not much more than a zip file. To build a true ePortfolio, especially

a showcase ePortfolio, the creator must attend to design, images, and overall aesthetics to develop visual, spatial, and multimodal meaning in addition to linguistic meaning. In essence, every ePortfolio benefits from branding. A consultant can play an important role in helping writers develop and refine branding to complement the rhetorical purposes of any given ePortfolio.

Building on the concepts of design principles outlined in Lindsay Sabatino's introduction, ePortfolios can also benefit from cohesive visual branding. In marketing, the language of a visual brand is comprised of four components: brand personality, personal attributes, design principles, and signature elements. Each component works together and builds on each other to create a cohesive visual brand language.

Brand personality refers to the human characteristics of the writer's brand and serves to create an emotional connection with their audience. *Example: Sarah's use of* Alice's Adventures in Wonderland *connects her tutoring personality to curiosity and adventure.*

Questions for tutorials:

- What are the most important characteristics you'd like your audience to know?
- Is there a mantra or motto you can develop to quickly communicate these traits?

Personal attributes are the elements that distinguish the writer from someone else, based on the characteristics of their brand personality. *Example: Sarah distinguishes herself from other tutors by using whimsical images and quotations from* Alice's Adventures in Wonderland *to highlight her curiosity.*

Questions for tutorials:

- What can you offer the audience that is unique to you?
- How does this unique offering connect to your brand personality?

Design principles are visual concepts based on identified characteristics and attributes that guide the expression of the brand. As brand principles become more defined, the characteristics of the brand become more tangible and actionable. *Example: Alice is a personification of a curiosity and whimsy that Sarah wants to convey to writers who might want to work with her.*

Question for tutorials:

- What visual elements can you incorporate into your portfolio to communicate your brand personality and personal attributes?

Signature elements are the sensory tools used to create and communicate a visual brand, including color schemes, logos, and other media.

Example: The Cheshire Cat, John Tenniel's wood engravings, and Animation from Disney's Alice in Wonderland *are all recognizable signature elements from* Alice's Adventures in Wonderland.

Questions for tutorials:

- What color scheme will create the desired sensory experience?
- How can the banner function as a logo for the ePortfolio?
- What supporting media, such as images, video clips and animation, and audio elements, will reinforce your branding and messaging?

As consultants coach writers to choose signature elements, they should encourage writers to first consider the connotations and implications of each element—What are the potential cultural associations with the colors? Do the images need explanation to be understood widely? How might different groupings of particular images change their meaning? For a more in-depth discussion on creating a personal brand, see James Truman's chapter.

ACTIVITY: GENERATIVE KNOWLEDGE INTERVIEWING

Because of the particularly strong connections among ePortfolios, reflection, and metacognition, we have found that developing consultants' ePortfolio expertise requires contextualizing ePortfolios within a metacognitive-focused curriculum. A cornerstone of that curriculum is generative knowledge interviewing (GKI).[5] GKI is a small-group activity developed by Melissa Peet (2010) that draws on structured interviewing techniques to help participants uncover and discuss tacit knowledge, skills, abilities, and themes. Especially for developmental and assessment ePortfolios, the writer's chief educational task is to surface that tacit knowledge. When consultants adapt GKI strategies while working with writers, they support writers in creating more substantive, reflective, and evidence-based ePortfolios.

As with Sarah's experience, abstracting visual themes and metaphors from text-based content can be challenging. By modifying the GKI process for a one-on-one tutorial, peer writing consultants like Theresa can be instrumental in helping ePortfolio creators uncover the visual possibilities within and related to their content. One of the best ways for consultants to learn how to guide writers through this process is to experience it for themselves. In the following activity, you will engage this process to develop a foundation for your own ePortfolio.

This activity involves five steps and is best completed with a fellow consultant as a partner:

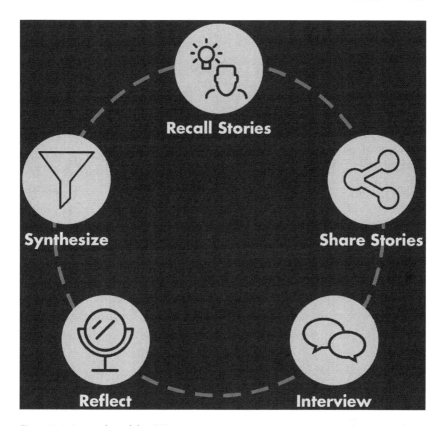

Figure 8.4. A snapshot of the GKI process

1. Recall stories.
2. Share stories.
3. Interview the storyteller to learn more and identify patterns.
4. Reflect themes and tacit connections between the stories.
5. Affirm the storyteller (optional).

Step 1: Recall Stories

Recall three specific stories related to the scope and purpose of your ePortfolio. For example, for a developmental portfolio in a writing course, you might freewrite about the first story that comes to mind for each prompt:

1. Describe a time you successfully accomplished a course learning objective.

2. Describe a time you were challenged meeting a course learning objective.

3. Describe a favorite experience in this course so far.

The goal is to identify your existing knowledge, skills, and attitudes.

Step 2: Share Stories

Share the stories with a fellow consultant, being as detailed as possible. During this process, your partner should listen without interruption and take notes on details, language, and images that stand out to them, confuse them, and have potential for multimodal representations.

The process of listening to stories requires your partner to practice generative listening. Generative listening is a process of listening deeply, of paying attention to what is below the surface and often not said. The generative listener listens for patterns, connections, and future possibilities.

Step 3: Interview

After fully listening to the story, your partner asks follow-up questions with the goal to uncover and identify patterns, themes, and audio-visual attributes.

Here are some interviewing best practices:

- Ask open-ended questions.
- Ask questions about the narrative trajectory.
- Ask questions about the types of characters in the stories.
- Ask questions about the contexts for the stories.
- Ask questions about how the storyteller defines keywords.

Step 4: Reflection and Artifact Generation

After the interview, your partner shares with you what tacit knowledge, skills, abilities, and attitudes they noticed in the stories and responses to the interview questions. Together, you should determine whether the experiences and story would best be represented through a developmental, assessment, or showcase ePortfolio. Discuss what artifacts would represent your different experiences, tacit knowledge, skills, abilities, and attitudes. This list can be developed through engaging in a conversation about the patterns, themes, and insights that emerged, especially in terms of how you might translate them into visual representations.

Your partner can reflect back to you what they learned and help you recognize imagery, color schemes, color-based words, or striking metaphors you used.

Step 5: Synthesize

Collaborate to synthesize the key takeaways from the story and experiences. The synthesis can be in the form of an affirmation, question, statement, or list. The synthesis should give you a clear action plan for how to move forward with the design and creation of the ePortfolio.

CONCLUSION

ePortfolios provide writers the opportunity to collect their work, select specific, significant artifacts, and reflect on and connect their learning experiences. Unlike paper portfolios, ePortfolios allow writers to connect their reflections to their work through hyperlinks, images, videos, audio files, and other kinds of media.

When done well, an ePortfolio can be a visual representation of the writer's personal brand, revealing characteristics and values they want to impart to their viewers. When working with writers on their ePortfolios, consultants can provide a sounding board for helping writers identify these characteristics and values.

RESOURCES

The following resources can be helpful for creating effective and well-designed ePortfolios:

Design-Support Tools

https://color.adobe.com/
 Adobe Color CC allows users to create color schemes and browse thousands of colors.
   It is a free graphic-design-tool website that makes design simple and easy for users.
Canva.com
   Canva provides users access to images and fonts.
creativecommons.org
   Creative Commons is a nonprofit organization that enables others to share their
   own work or find somebody else's work to use royalty free.
Pixlr.com
   PIXLR is a cloud-based set of image tools and utilities that allow for simple to advanced photo editing.

Content-Development Technique

generative knowledge interviewing (GKI): https://www.youtube.com/watch?v=2uLKlWPpTCg
   This video from the DePaul Teaching Commons explains how students can uncover
   and reflect on their tacit knowledge by using a teaching technique called *generative
   knowledge interviewing.*

KEY SEARCH TERMS

artifacts; curator's notes; developmental portfolio; assessment portfolio; showcase portfolio; generative knowledge interviewing; ePortfolio;
personal branding; brand personality; personal attributes; design principles; signature elements

NOTES

1.   Sarah T.'s first year ePortfolio: https://depaul.digication.com/sarah_tierneys_wrd
     _104_portfolio/Welcome/published.
2.   Sarah T.'s ePortfolio for DePaul's University Center for Writing-based Learning:
     https://depaul.digication.com/sarahs_ucwbland_adventures/Welcome/published.
3.   Trello, free project-management tool: www.trello.com.
4.   Personality traits: http://ideonomy.mit.edu/essays/traits.html.
5.   Generative knowledge interviewing: https://youtu.be/2uLKlWPpTCg.

REFERENCES

Lorenzo, George, and John Ittelson. 2005. *An Overview of E-portfolios.* https://net.educause
   .edu/ir/library/pdf/eli3001.pdf.
Peet, Melissa R. 2010. *The Integrative Knowledge Portfolio Process: A Guide for Educating Reflective Practitioners and Lifelong Learner.* MedEdPORTAL.
Wozniak, Kathryn, and Jose Zagal. 2013. "Finding Evidence of Metacognition in an ePortfolio Community: Beyond Text, Across New Media." DePaul University, *School for New
   Learning Faculty.* Paper 36. http://via.library.depaul.edu/snl-faculty-pubs/36.

9

WEB-DESIGN TUTORING
Responding as a User

Clint Gardner and Joe McCormick
Salt Lake Community College

Jarrod Barben
Salt Lake Community College/University of Utah

CHAPTER OVERVIEW

Effective tutoring and response strategies for assisting with web design allow consultants and web designers to focus on the writing/design as opposed to the technological aspects that can so easily overcome discussions of design. Web design entails many skills and abilities a *writer* might not possess. For that reason, we call the *writer* a *web designer* to reflect the full range of what they are doing. Likewise, we use the term *user* rather than *reader* when referring to a web-design project's target audience, simply because a website *user* does much more—and sometimes much less—than the typical *reader*. As with technological expertise, however, the effective consultant does not have to be a top-notch visual artist to give an effective response. Being an experienced *user* of web content goes a long way in building a response and giving feedback to the *web designer*. As with other computer media, the *user* is engaging with a site in a variety of ways, and the effective web designer must be familiar with all of them.

ILLUSTRATIVE EXAMPLE: CONTENT MANAGEMENT

With the increase of assignments asking students to create websites and ePortfolios, Salt Lake Community College (SLCC) has worked with designers at all experience levels from novice to expert. Students who come to the SLCC Student Writing Center with ePortfolios or other web-design projects work on both the textual elements of their site and its design. With students who have more expertise, as Joe

DOI: 10.7330/9781607328469.c009

describes below, we recognize that the designer has a great deal of knowledge about web design already and is well equipped to implement our suggestions into their design. We help such students figure out what questions they want to ask about their design, if they don't already have them. We then give them feedback on our experience using their sites.

Like many other colleges and universities (Kahn 2014), SLCC has implemented a web-based ePortfolio for students to demonstrate learning (Clark and Eynon 2009), and students are required to use web-based content-management systems (CMSs) such as WordPress. Each year, there is a series of awards given to students who have demonstrated creativity in designing their ePortfolio. One of the first ePortfolios to win the annual award was developed by one of the coauthors of this chapter, Joe McCormick. Students, like Joe, are encouraged to be creative with the overall design of the ePortfolio but must use a CMS to implement it, as they would for a website. Here's a description of Joe's project in his own words:

> Web development has always been a hobby of mine, so I took on the ePortfolio as a labor of love. I chose WordPress as the development framework, because I had created other sites with it before. However, this would be the first time I had made such a large project; the entire site comprised of more than 20 pages. When composing my ePortfolio, I considered the design, user experience, and the flow of my content. WordPress has thousands of themes to choose from, and the popular ones become popular because they already exhibit uses of strong web design. Personally, this gave me an opportunity to go beyond the requirements of the project and build custom designed pages. I selected a theme I liked and thought was simple, and went from there.
>
> The simplicity of WordPress, as far as the actual development of the site (pages, menus, image inclusion, etc.), opens up a lot of time for users to play with other site settings, like colors, fonts, etc. Blogging platforms these days have collapsed the novice web design experience down to making a few higher-order choices that will go a very long way for the average user. A lot of the actual work that is done in making sites on these platforms is toward the goal of making the site attractive and legible. (pers. comm.)

We also conduct tutoring sessions with students who have less experience with web design. For example, Isabella, a student working on a WixBlog for her English 2010 course, had a really cluttered website that tried to incorporate too many visual elements and had very confusing and often perplexing links. She seemed to have all the elements required by her assignment, but it was hard for her users to find them. She knew how to use her chosen CMS almost too well since she wanted to incorporate all its bells and whistles. Consultants working with Isabella had to caution her about how users would experience her site to ensure it would be easy to navigate, more visually appealing, and match her rhetorical situation.

We also encounter students who have absolutely no familiarity with web design, nor with the resources they can use. One student we recently worked with, Jimmy, was given, like Joe, the task to create an ePortfolio. Unlike Joe or Isabella, however, Jimmy had never published anything on the web—not even on social media. As he told us, he knew "squat about web stuff."

With students who are complete novices at web design like Jimmy, we show them various SLCC resources we've developed for web designers. Next, we discuss how to choose a CMS to implement the site and the various stages of planning and drafting their design. After helping them visually outline or storyboard their web page, we discuss moving from the written page to placing the elements in the student's chosen CMS. This tutoring is done in concert with our ePortfolio Lab. The ePortfolio Lab focuses on the basics of choosing the appropriate CMS, creating an account, and getting materials up on that site. Once they actually have a site, we in the SLCC Student Writing Center can then offer more effective rhetorical feedback to the designer, discussing the impact of their color, font, and media choices. Overall, using a CMS and putting in hard work, Jimmy was able to create an ePortfolio that represented his studies at SLCC.

Our experience has shown us that asking designers about their experience with web design and the various tools they might use is a crucial starting point. In that way, we can determine what level of writing/design/technical assistance they need in order to implement their designs.

BACKGROUND INFORMATION: WHAT YOU NEED TO KNOW ABOUT WEB DESIGN

We contend that in order to provide feedback on web design, a consultant need not be a tech expert. We must admit, however, that there is a bit of disagreement in the multiliteracy center field about this topic. Dave Sheridan argues in his essay "All Things to All People: Multiliteracy Consulting and the Materiality of Rhetoric," from *Multiliteracy Centers: Writing Center Work, New Media, and Multimodal Rhetoric*, that consultants in multiliteracy centers might necessarily need to learn specific technical knowledge, such as working with programs or particular devices, in order to conduct a session. He realizes, however, that such tech help can often reduce what a consultant is doing to "something even worse than a grammar lab: a tech lab where students come not to engage in critical conversations about communication, but to perform mindless technical procedures" (2010, 271) and states that there are probably better technical-support resources for web designers to use. However, we think critical conversation about design is what tutoring web design is about, and if the consultant just happens to have some technical knowledge, that might be useful, but it is not necessary to the type of feedback a consultant gives.

A conversation about web design is complicated by several key factors.

- The web is *media* rather than a specific genre within a medium.
- *Fashionable trends* that often masquerade as good design principles shape the advice writers are given about the development of websites.
- *Content management*, or how web developers put their work onto the web, has changed drastically over the years and continues to change and develop in the present.
- Usability, accessibility, and readability work together in creating a *user experience* of a website.
- Developing for the web is not really a *technological concern*, but it *is* a *rhetorical* one.

An informed consultant should be aware of resources web designers can use to address these complications—including technical-help resources. With years of experience, a consultant of web design will, no doubt, pick up a great deal of technical expertise, but in such situations, a consultant must ask themself what is appropriate "help" in the circumstance. A rhetorical approach to tutoring rather than a technocratic one is key. As Sheridan argues, a tutor should teach *design* rather than "silly rules" (2010, 278). He goes on to suggest that consultants should "map the terrain . . . seek out heuristic rules instead of algorithmic ones" (278–80). A storyboard or low-tech mock-up for a website helps designers consider the rhetorical and design elements of a website without focusing on the technological platform. Consultants encourage designers to draft a visual plan in order to focus on effective ways to incorporate the content and brainstorm layout options.

Ultimately, an informed web-design consultant must take into consideration what, exactly, good web design entails. Based upon how much the web has changed over the past twenty years, it is fairly clear that principles of good web design are mutable and often follow *fashionable trends* rather than design principles. For example, most web pages nowadays seem to follow the fashion of being more *scalable*, or "pad like," in their appearance and usage, most likely because of the innovation of pad devices and smartphones to access websites. An effective consultant for web design must be a well-versed web-page user rather than a *demagogue* of design principles. A *demagogue* spouts rules and demands adherence to them, while a well-versed consultant gives the designer feedback on *how* the website is working for the user. For example, if the user is having difficulty navigating the website, that is a key rhetorical issue the designer must address. Demanding that navigation panes and so forth appear in certain locations or in certain ways does not keep in mind that each designer is guiding users toward the critical content available on the site, urging them to continue to click. Good web design is a rhetorical consideration and typically follows more basic design principles, as outlined in Lindsay Sabatino's introduction to this collection.

Nevertheless, as Janice Fernheimer (2014) states, "Recognizing that users will draw on past experiences, the designer needs to build on familiar conventions for usability—orienting users, making things easy, and keeping things consistent." The web designer must be flexible in their approach but realize there are rhetorical conventions at play. Such rhetorical conventions often relate specifically to how users interact with web pages. Kathryn Whitenton (2013) argues that designers should avoid visual clutter, build on existing mental models, and offload tasks. Avoiding visual clutter includes removing "redundant links, irrelevant images, and meaningless typography flourishes [that] slow users down." Having repetitive links on a page often creates a click crisis for the user: they are uncertain as to where to click or end up clicking on repetitive links without purpose, which can lead to frustration on the user's part. Additionally, web designers can resolve visual clutter by making use of white space, which allows important elements to stand out, and by effectively grouping items on the page through proximity or similarity—see Sabatino's introduction for a discussion of proximity and similarity. Images that have no relation to the purpose of the page can impair usability by causing the user to spend inordinate amounts of time trying to figure out an image's relevance. Web designers should also avoid using an image or patterned background, as it "substantially reduce[s] the figure-ground contrast of text" (Hilligoss and Howard 2001, 99) and distracts from the purpose of any additional images on the page.

To build on existing mental models, the designer should rely on how users are already experiencing websites or the genre of the website. Eye-tracking studies of how users read websites show two common tracks: F-shaped and Z-shaped (Jones 2010; Nielsen 2006). For the F-shaped pattern, users whose language tracks from left to right "first read in a horizontal movement, usually across the upper part of the content area. . . . Next, users move down the page a bit and then read across in a second horizontal movement. . . . Finally, users scan the content's left side in a vertical movement" (Nielsen 2006).

The Z-shaped pattern works in a similar fashion, with the user's eyes tracking across the top of the page forming the letter Z. Designers can make use of these basic patterns by placing important features where the user's eye is most likely to first land: across the top, along the side, or at the bottom (if following the F-shaped pattern), or along the top and bottom if following the Z-shaped pattern. In both these layouts, the top left portion of the page is the single most-looked-at spot on a web page, so a designer should treat it with special reverence, as a place to convey specific information about the site. This is why web pages typically have navigation bars across the top or down the left side of the screen. Additionally, it is usually the location of the home button, which the user clicks to go to the primary page of a site, or where companies place their logos. For more information and examples of F-shaped and Z-shaped layouts, see the "Resources" section of this chapter.

Offloading tasks means to simplify making decisions, performing a task, or even reading text for the user. A design that permits the user to quickly see where they need to click on the page to do a specific action generally provides the user with a smoother experience. Having the design do the mental work for the user is important. For example, a user can quickly spot a home button and know exactly where that will take them. Since users don't read design elements the way they do other texts (Nielsen 1997), the designer helps the user to actually read what matters on the page rather than trying to read and interpret the design elements of the page. Design principles are also why CMSs are becoming the preferred method of delivering web pages: they provide a consistent package that takes into account how design should facilitate page usability. A CMS allows anyone to produce an effective website without substantial training in web design. These days, CMSs are generally *de facto* for web page/site implementation ("CMS Distribution"). Novice web designers working with HTML directly are rare. Usually, only students going into web design as a career still learn HTML coding.

Accessibility

An essential question web designers need to ask is whether or not their web design meets accessibility standards for people with disabilities. Creating an accessible design is not just a sideline activity designers take on: accessibility should be integrated into web design from the start. In other words, accessible design is *standard design.*

Designers should adhere to the Web Content Accessibility Guidelines (WCAG) established by the World Wide Web Consortium ("Essential Components"). When those guidelines are followed, web browsers and assistive technologies work together to create an accessible experience for the user ("Essential Components"; "Web Content"). Assistive technologies are devices or programs through which a user with disabilities accesses content ("Essential Components"). A screen reader that reads web pages audibly is an example of an assistive technology.

WCAG is broken down into four principles, with several guidelines under those principles:

1. All information must be **perceivable** to users.
2. Interface components and navigation must be **operable**.
3. The user interface must be **understandable**.
4. Content must be **robust** enough for assistive technologies to interpret. ("How to Meet")

In terms of web design, **perceivable** means a user can readily discern the contents of a web page, such as text, images, or other media. Distinguishing these elements is important because it allows users to perceive the information on the page through assistive technologies. Most assistive technologies for websites make use of <alt> tags in the HTML in order to adequately describe page contents, such as images or operable elements like "buttons." Access to <alt> tags is readily available in most CMS interfaces. Designers can consult the documentation for their CMS to find out more about how to access tags and about accessibility features in general. As far as the actual content of the <alt> tag, however, Web Accessibility in Mind (WebAIM) advises that content should be determined by the context of where the visual element being used.

> The first step when determining appropriate alternative text for an image is to decide if the image presents content and if the image has a function. In most cases, an image will only have a function if it is contained within a link. . . . Determining if the image presents content and what that content is can be much more difficult. If the content that the image conveys is presented within text in the surrounding context of the image, then an empty alt attribute may suffice. ("Alternative Text")

WebAIM explains that <alt> tags should be "accurate" and "succinct" and should "not be redundant;" therefore, tagging images with "image of" is unnecessary since it is usually perceivable that the element is an image, and the user only needs to know what the image consists of.

For example, an image of Maya Angelou could be tagged <alt="Maya Angelou"> in the context of a biography page about Angelou to be clearly perceived as an image of the poet and not mistaken for an operable element on the page, such as navigation button. Decorative image elements also need not be tagged since they do not perform informative or operable functions.

Most effective CMSs automatically include other assistive tags, such as those that demark menus using either the standard HTML tag of <label> or specialized accessible rich internet application (ARIA) landmark tags such as <main>, <nav>, and <header> ("Using ARIA Landmarks"). These tags make your web design not only **perceivable** and **understandable** but also **operable** in that the user with an assistive technology will be able to determine navigation elements on the page itself ("Designing for Screen Reader Compatibility"). Having all page elements clearly designated provides all users with a **robust** experience.

The careful web designer should be aware of how their design is being perceived by users with assistive technologies. In order to do this, it is best to test the design for accessibility by making use of web-accessibility page testers. There are several accessibility checkers freely available on the web, such as one provided by WebAIM (see "Resources" section).

Finally, while most CMS providers diligently attempt to ensure their themes and templates have accessible elements, accessibility is not universally adhered to, and some CMS templates are not very accessible. We suggest you examine carefully the description of the templates/themes you are considering to see if they adhere to accessibility standards.

CONSULTATION STRATEGIES FOR WEB DESIGN

Be Upfront about Experiences and Abilities

First, consultants must be upfront with the designer about their experiences with web design. If a consultant lacks experience creating web projects or has never worked with the system or program the designer is using to publish their design, they should let the designer know. It is only fair for the designer to know who is giving them feedback. However, the consultant should let the designer know about their experience in giving feedback to writers working on different types of projects, and that expertise in web design, or technological competence, does not always translate to the ability to give a designer effective feedback on their work.

Know Other Tech-Support Services

Whatever the consultant's level of experience with web design, they should be familiar with various tech-support resources available. If they are working at a school, college, or university, they can familiarize themselves with campus resources devoted to helping students with baffling tech-support issues. They might also want to explore, with the designer, the support services the designer's chosen CMS or computer program has to offer.

Know the Tools Available

For the sake of a truly fledgling web designer—one who doesn't have the first clue about creating websites—consultants should familiarize themselves with various online tools designers can use to manage their web projects. CMSs such as WordPress, Weebly, Wix, Blogger, and so forth all present easy-to-use interfaces for developing websites. While some are extremely limited in what they offer, others are extremely complicated. The consultant might wish to play around with various providers and understand their limitations and benefits. Understanding the features and functions of the different CMSs allows a consultant to help the designer identify the appropriate CMS based on the designer's goals and ideas for designing the website.

Let the Designer Call the Shots

As with any other tutoring session, the designer should be fully engaged in the session and in charge. Basically, this means the designer is the one calling the shots. Since web design is often conflated with technology, which often has black-and-white solutions, the novice designer might be more apt to believe in an expertise model, and that there are decidedly right and wrong answers to everything, and will turn to the consultant for those answers. Consultants must be careful that their experiences working with web design do not lead them to bully or overwhelm the designer into making another bad decision: just doing something because an authority figure said so. The designer should make an informed decision based upon the reasons the consultant as user offers.

Establish the Rhetorical Context

Like most other writing tutoring sessions, consultants begin by exploring the rhetorical context of the designer's project. If it is an academic assignment, the web designer usually has some sort of guidelines and/ or grading rubric. These guidelines will establish much of the rhetorical situation. If the designer is working outside an academic setting on a project for which they need to establish their own guidelines, the consultant and designer can spend time exploring that context and seeing what other designers have done when addressing that particular context. Whether the writer is working in an academic or non-academic context, it is easy to skip over this important information; sometimes the designer wants to skip over it and pushes the consultant to do so. The consultant should ask questions about the purpose of the website, whether the site is meant to inform, persuade, and/or request a call to action. Based on the designer's goals, the consultant can help the designer match the language and media to the purpose. Don't fall into the temptation of overlooking the context, as knowing the parameters of what the designer is working on not only helps establish the focus of the session but also helps the consultant give the most effective feedback.

Map, Plan, and Mock-up

Web designers might want a consulting session when they are starting out on a project. Such a designer might have no idea where to even begin or what options are available to them. Often designers in these situations are looking for options as to how to deliver their content to users and what elements to include. While consultants might need to talk about delivery options or CMSs with a designer in such a situation, delivery is not the only thing to be concerned with. Consultants also must focus on what is going to be delivered, and making a map, plan, or mock-up of web pages is a good way for the designer to see the scope of the project. Designers benefit from drawing a map/plan that connects their various pages and resources together. During this brainstorming stage, consultants and designers consider layout options, color choices, content, and complementary media (e.g., image, videos, podcasts, infographics). Together, the designer and consultant can create a storyboard or visual plan for the website—refer to Brandy Ball Blake and Karen Head's storyboard chapter for suggestions. Since many CMSs are drag and drop, having a plan mocked up allows the designer to easily put the elements in place and can help them avoid wasting design time in needless repetition on the various site pages/resources.

Be a Test Audience for the Web Designer

No matter the goals mutually set in a session, it is a good idea for the consultant to cast themself in the role of a test audience or test user for the designer. Consultants can navigate the designer's site and give feedback in context while the designer watches. Consultants should specifically point out elements of the pages that might not be working for a user. Likewise, pointing out elements of the page that make it easy to use, navigate, and read provides vital information to the designer. With the designer, the consultant should also test the site for accessibility. As previously mentioned, there are several accessibility checkers the consultant and designer can use together in order to ensure the site is accessible for all users (see "Resources" section).

ACTIVITY

With a team or individually, create a new writing center website. The goal is to create an interactive website that provides information not only about location and services but also about how writing consulting works at your institution. This is also an opportunity to create resources about writing and designing that students will find useful. The target audience is students at your institution, but you should also keep in mind that instructors will also use the site to learn about the writing center and find useful resources to help their students with writing.

Things to consider:
- What is the mission of your center? How will that mission impact the design of your website? How can you best represent that mission to site users?
- What critical information will students need?
- How can students get to see a writing tutor? Does your center offer appointments? How can a student make an appointment?
- Does your center offer workshops or other services?
- What resources about writing would students at your institution find useful?
- What accessibility needs will students have?
- What information will instructors find useful about your center?

Explore and Analyze

The first step in creating your website is to see what other writing centers have done. Search the web for *writing center* to see what comes up.

You might also try to search for *writing tutoring* or *help with writing*. Try to find websites at different types of institutions (high schools, community colleges, large research institutions, small liberal arts colleges, art institutions, or vocational schools), not only ones that mirror your own institution. Once you have found two or three useful writing center sites, analyze them. Imagine yourself as a student at their institution. What do you need to know from the site? Does the site provide what you need, and does it allow you to find it quickly? What is the mission of the center, and how is that demonstrated throughout the website?

Map and Plan

Your next step is to map out the various pages you will need to accomplish your ends. What content is most important to deliver your message? What images represent the story you are trying to tell? For ease of use, we recommend you dedicate one page for each specific purpose in order to avoid confusion. Draw your map of pages or resources on a separate document. Think of it as a storyboard for your website.

Next, determine how you are going to implement your project on the web. Which CMSs (content-management systems) are out there available for your use? Which management system are you most comfortable with? Do these systems meet accessibility standards for people with disabilities? Once you have chosen your CMS, you can see whether there is a template that will work best for your situation.

Mock-up

Next, make a mock-up of the site with the various pages you will need. Create a visual representation of the elements for your web page (layout, color, images, font, text, etc.). You can draw them on paper or actually create the mock-up in a CMS, depending on the resources you have available. Consider the navigation of the page and how the user can easily find what they need. You might find it helpful to create a storyboard that maps your ideas.

Test Users

Finally, develop tasks and questions to give test users. Observe users as they engage the site, and ask questions to see users' processes. Use your observations and users' responses to revise your work.

CONCLUSION

Websites create an opportunity for writers to directly interact with a live audience. The key factor to remember when working with web designers is that they are working in a rhetorical situation just like any other writer. Conversations and feedback on web design must start with the rhetorical choices of the designer and the basic design principles that best represent the designer's ideas before moving into any conversations about technical support. Using the strategies discussed in this chapter, consultants can provide designers open, transparent feedback that helps determine the impact their work has on a user.

RESOURCES

The resources listed below provide a review of CMSs, rhetorical principles for web design, tutorials, and accessibility.

Content-Management Systems

http://www.makeuseof.com/tag/10-popular-content-management-systems-online/
    Christian Cawley reviews some of the most common CMSs.
http://www.business2community.com/web-design/should-you-redesign-your-website
    -01609968#GuAc6lSVck2ChUoI.97
    Jon-Mikel Bailey gives a sense of the amorphous nature of web design and how it
    quickly changes.

Web Design

https://www.smashingmagazine.com/2008/01/10-principles-of-effective-web-design/
    In this article, Vitaly Friedman takes a practical approach to web design but empha-
    sizes rhetorical principles similar to those we discuss in this chapter.
https://webdesign.tutsplus.com/articles/understanding-the-z-layout-in-web-design–web
    design-28
    Brandon Jones explains Z-layout, provides examples, and discusses how to accom-
    plish the format when designing a website.
https://webdesign.tutsplus.com/articles/understanding-the-f-layout-in-web-design–web
    design-687
    Brandon Jones describes F-shaped layout, includes examples, and discusses how the
    F-pattern format works.

HTML and CSS

https://www.w3.org/standards/webdesign/htmlcss
    W3C, or the World Wide Web Consortium, offers specific information on the basic
    guts of web pages.
https://www.w3.org/2002/03/tutorials.html#webdesign_htmlcss
    W3C also offers a variety of useful tutorials.

Accessibility

https://www.w3.org/standards/webdesign/accessibility
    An important consideration in designing any website is accessibility for people with
    disabilities. W3C also provides guidelines.
http://wave.webaim.org/
    WebAIM provides a web-testing tool to determine whether a website is accessible.

KEY SEARCH TERMS

authoring tools; CMS; CSS; HTML; usability; user experience (UX);
user-interface design (UI); visual-design principles; web accessibility;
web-accessibility evaluation tools; web design; web development; web-
page layout; web-safe fonts; web usability

REFERENCES

"Alternative Text." N.d. WebAIM. Accessed October 25, 2017. https://webaim.org/tech
    niques/alttext/.
Clark, J. Elizabeth, and Bret Eynon. 2009. "E-portfolios at 2.0—Surveying the Field." *Peer
    Review* 11 (1). https://www.aacu.org/publications-research/periodicals/e-portfolios
    -20—surveying-field.
"CMS Distribution in the Top 1 Million Sites." N.d. Built With. Accessed October 25, 2017.
    https://trends.builtwith.com/cms.
"Designing for Screen Reader Compatibility." N.d. WebAIM. Accessed October 25, 2017.
    https://webaim.org/techniques/screenreader/.
"Essential Components of Web Accessibility." N.d. W3C: Web Accessibility Initiative.
    Last modified February 17, 2018. https://www.w3.org/WAI/intro/components.php
    #guidelines.
Fernheimer, Janice W. 2014. "Principle 2: Design for Usability." In *Design for User Engage-
    ment on the Web*, edited by Cheryl Geisler. New York: Routledge.
Hilligoss, Susan, and Tharon Howard. 2002. *Visual Communication: A Writer's Guide*. New
    York: Longman.
"How to Meet WCAG 2." N.d. W3C: Web Accessibility Initiative. Last modified Septem-
    ber 13, 2018. https://www.w3.org/WAI/WCAG20/quickref/.
Jones, Brandon. 2010. "Understanding the Z-Layout in Web Design." Envato Tuts. https://
    webdesign.tutsplus.com/articles/understanding-the-z-layout-in-web-design-webdesign
    -28.
Kahn, Susan. 2014. "E-Portfolios: A Look at Where We've Been, Where We Are Now, and
    Where We're (Possibly) Going." *Peer Review* 16 (1). https://www.aacu.org/publications
    research/periodicals/eportfolios-look-where-weve-been-where-we-are-now-andwhere
    -were.
Nielsen, Jakob 1997. "How Users Read on the Web." NN/g: Nielsen Norman Group.
    https://www.nngroup.com/articles/how-users-read-on-the-web/.
Nielsen, Jakob. 2006. "F-Shaped Pattern for Reading Web Content." NN/g: Nielsen Norman
    Group. https://www.nngroup.com/articles/f-shaped-pattern-reading-web-content/.
Sheridan, David M. 2010. "All Things to All People: Multiliteracy Consulting and the
    Materiality of Rhetoric." In *Multiliteracy Centers: Writing Center Work, New Media, and
    Multimodal Rhetoric*, edited by David Sheridan and James A. Inman, 75–107. Cresskill,
    NJ: Hampton.

"Using ARIA Landmarks to Identify Regions of a Page." N.d. W3C. Last modified January 3, 2014. https://www.w3.org/WAI/GL/wiki/Using_ARIA_landmarks_to_identify _regions_of_a_page. "Web Content Accessibility Guidelines." N.d. W3C: Web Accessibility Initiative. Last modified June 22, 2018. https://www.w3.org/WAI/intro/wcag .php.

Whitenton, Kathryn. 2013. "Minimize Cognitive Load to Maximize Usability." NN/g: Nielsen Norman Group. https://www.nngroup.com/articles/minimize-cognitive-load/.

10

PODCASTS
Sound Strategies for Sonic Literacy

Brenta Blevins

University of Mary Washington

CHAPTER OVERVIEW

This chapter offers an overview of podcasts and provides writing consultants with strategies for developing and working with sonic literacy. A podcast is a digital audio recording made of such auditory elements as speech, music, and sounds and can be listened to via computer, media player, or smartphone.

Podcasts often run online as a series, with the creators releasing them in routine installments. By contrast, classroom podcasts are often one-time audio assignments in which students conduct interviews, present "sound essays," share oral histories, or otherwise speak about their research. When students receive their first podcast assignments, they often respond with anxiety. Consultants can help podcasters apply knowledge they already have to succeed in this new medium.

Note: Some individuals use the terms *video podcast* and *audio podcast* to distinguish between audio-only podcasts and podcasts that incorporate visual or video elements. Video podcasts are series of short video clips with audio components. Video podcasts sometimes use traditional video clips, while others use primarily audio elements and include only some visuals. This chapter discusses audio podcasts and hereafter refers to them as *podcasts*. For more information on video projects, see Patrick Anderson and Florence Davies's chapter in this collection.

ILLUSTRATIVE EXAMPLE: USING AUDIENCE AND
PURPOSE TO EFFECTIVELY SYNTHESIZE INTERVIEWS

Many universities have courses across their curricula that focus on written and spoken communication. To address oral-communication components, instructors increasingly assign podcast compositions in a

DOI: 10.7330/9781607328469.c010

variety of different classes. Classes that require primary research that involves interviewing others, such as experts in the field or individuals with personal experience, might require the creation of an audio recording of the interview. The assignment might then call for the recording to be edited and to be released as an audio podcast to share with the class or with others.

During one such assignment, I worked with a student, Carla, who went above the minimum assignment requirement of interviewing at least one subject-matter expert about their work. Ambitiously, she assembled a panel of three such individuals, resulting in a recording lasting over forty-five minutes. Although she had hoped to use her recording as-is, like a radio interview, and to add a podcast-style introduction and conclusion, the podcast assignment specified a time range of five to seven minutes. Carla didn't know how to proceed. She did not want to delete any of her interviewees' comments, as she felt it might be disrespectful to the individuals who had given her their time for the interview.

Acknowledging her concern, I asked Carla for more details about her assignment. Carla shared that this assignment was for a speaking-intensive introductory research class for which individuals conducted primary research, such as interviewing or surveying, and secondary research that investigated others' findings. The podcast was an early assignment in the class. Later, the class required students to create an informative essay on the topic for which they had conducted the interview and then do a presentation about the research they had performed.

It is important for creators to think about audience, purpose, and context. Asking Carla, an individual majoring in consumer apparel, about her audience—her classmates of different majors—helped her think about which content she could, should, or must include. Because her audience did not have her experience with apparel and fashion, she knew more about consumer apparel than did her classmates. Carla realized some sections of the interview might be hard for other students to understand. Thinking about her audience helped Carla make decisions about her podcast. She decided to keep some parts of the interview because the discussion was clear and likely more interesting to a general audience. At other points, Carla chose to narrate a summary and offer more general explanation for her audience.

Next, we talked about the purpose of this research. While the podcast was Carla's first opportunity to present her primary research, it was not her last. I asked Carla for more information about the purpose of her research in this course. She identified that she was conducting research from a variety of different sources to learn how to use evidence to support her claims. In that discussion, Carla recalled that her class had talked about the importance of using quotes when they are most effective. Carla decided to apply this idea to her podcast, choosing to use several specific sections of her recorded interviews rather than taking the entirety of one longer clipped section.

We also discussed whether some information might be better represented in writing. For example, when listening to her interviewees talk about a series of numbers and statistics, I asked whether it might be easier to understand that information as presented in a chart. By considering how audiences might respond to information presented in different media, Carla began identifying sections to keep in the podcast and sections that might work better in her later assignments.

As Carla's story shows, some decisions about podcasts include the medium—when sound might work better than words, or vice versa—the audience and what information they might be confused by and need, the context in which the audience receives the text, and the purpose, which is often identified in school on the assignment requirements.

BACKGROUND INFORMATION: PODCASTING AND THE ELEMENTS OF SOUND

Podcasts engage the audio aspect of multiliteracy. As Cheryl Ball and Byron Hawk note, however, in discussing *Multiliteracies*, "The entry on audio design is the shortest," including simply music, sound effects, and so forth (2006, 263). Still, this brief definition initiates a starting point for composition studies to include audio (263).

Podcasts make meaning through audio. As this book's introduction indicates, that meaning can be made through "noise, music, and sound effects." While students have routinely been assigned speeches and other presentations, some students react with anxiety to primarily audio assignments. Indeed, Cynthia Selfe reminds us that it is "unusual . . . to deliver an oral presentation without a written text" (2009, 627). However, the audio form of multiliteracy offers us the opportunity to explore how, "barring hearing loss, we live immersed in sounds" (McKee 2006, 335). An audio-focused assignment provides an opportunity for engaging in critical thinking about the audio environment around us, as well as how central sound is to human communication. Indeed, Theo van Leeuwen argues that while the visual is a solitary activity, hearing and listening are social, as both involve communion and connection through speech (1999, 197). Assignments focused on conveying meaning through audio provide an opportunity for active listening to spoken conversation and to other audio elements. Audio compositions possess, as Lindsay Sabatino's introduction discusses, a foreground, middle ground, and background. Sound is intentional and unintentional, all of which must be considered in terms of the rhetorical effect upon the audience.

Rob Walch and Mur Lafferty identify eighteen different genres of podcasts—including news, music, education, and gaming—even while noting most podcasts "don't fit into any pigeonhole" (2006, 43). Instructors use podcasts in speaking-intensive classes, in classes that require primary research and oral-history research, and for opportunities to extend beyond the traditional essay assignment with a writing-with-sound podcast project. Podcast assignments might include a persuasive public service announcement—for more information specifically about PSAs see Alice Johnston Myatt's chapter—an oral history interview, an audio portrait of a place, a review of a performance, a performative demonstration of different musical styles, and even an ecological study of a natural environment through the recording of local noise.

Regardless of the genre or assignment particulars, podcasts rely on the audio-design principles outlined in the introduction, as well as on the voice and delivery of any podcast speakers. In discussing how to analyze and to produce compositions that use sound, McKee focuses on four elements of sound: vocal delivery, music, special effects, and silence. McKee's discussion of vocal delivery combines eighteenth-century elocution with van Leeuwen's discussion of delivery. Music, she notes, is the element most often associated with movie soundtracks and songs to create evoke particular "moods" (2006, 343). Theater and video games use sound effects to evoke action, settings, and proximity or distance, for example. McKee further suggests that we pay attention to "silence, the almost sound of no sound, [which] also needs to be part of any rhetorical considerations of sound" (337). Paying attention to silence is challenging and necessitates "listening for an absent presence, what is there and not there" (351). When we attend to sound, we should remember that the "sound envelope includes not only the moments when a sound is present but also the moments before and after as well" (352). McKee's four elements of sound—speech, music, special effects, and "not sound"—offer approaches to auditory creation and analysis.

Classroom podcast-assignment instruction might begin by having students listen to a range of podcasts. Students might even self-select podcasts to listen to. In doing so, students can identify the different features of the podcast medium and their particular podcast's genre. For example, students can observe how the elements of podcasts are usually structured. Jennifer L. Bowie (2012) identifies a typical arrangement of a podcast in addition to its main body:

- **preintro:** offers episode-specific information such as date and episode title
- **intro:** provides a quick (approximately forty-five second) introduction to "hook" the listeners and otherwise introduce the topic
- **outro:** concludes with a routine podcast standard closing, including perhaps contact information, website URL, Creative Commons license or other citation information, closing saying, source and transcript information, and so forth (Episode 4)

Becoming familiar with podcasts can equip creators and consultants with multiple different rhetorically effective ways of writing with sound.

CONSULTATION STRATEGIES FOR PODCASTS

While students generally have fewer formal spoken assignments than written ones, consultants might help students recognize class participation as a familiar speaking assignment. Providing that link can help students build on their prior experience and knowledge. Students routinely engage in critical thinking about the listening they do; for example, in class, students choose which notes to take and which not to take. They choose when to speak in class discussions and when to respond to particular sounds, such as cell-phone calls or computer notifications.

Likewise, consultants themselves are familiar with the importance of the auditory in many tutorial interactions. In much the same way that writing-assignment tutoring involves both reading aloud a piece of writing and a conversation between writer and consultant, the podcast tutoring session entails listening to both the podcast and its creator. In discussion, consultants can help students with a framework for thinking about their encounters with sound, speech, and music within the classroom.

Communicating in a Nonvisual Medium

While many multimodal texts link words and images, the podcast links words with sound to convey meaning. Audio podcasts include only voice, sound (music and/or effects), and silence. Podcasters must consider how their audience will receive information through only the auditory mode, particularly considering that listeners have a harder time rewinding audio than readers have rereading.

Consultants can help podcasters consider such questions as:

- How should the delivery of wording be adjusted for hearing: shorter sentences, explanation of vocabulary, and so forth?
- How can verbal delivery be improved for memorability?
- What might the audience have trouble understanding without additional narration or sound effects?

The podcaster uses the available means of speech, sound effects, music, volume, and even silence to help convey the people, places, or other material that might not be comprehensible to the listening audience. By considering the means available to podcasts, consultants and the podcaster can brainstorm multiple ways of conveying audio meaning.

Understanding the Purpose of the Podcast

The podcast is a broad medium capable of communicating for a wide range of purposes and topics. Purposes include storytelling of real-life or fictional events, journalistic reporting, informative interviews, debates on matters serious and trivial, and persuasive arguments. Even when several podcasts have the same topic, such as politics, those podcasts might have different purposes and audiences. As we see with Carla's project, thinking about the purpose of the podcast—such as being an informative presentation of primary research—can help students make decisions about which auditory information to include. Podcasters might choose to include an interview with a subject-matter expert rather than simply summarizing research as a means of informing their audience about a topic.

Understanding the Role of Editing

Interview-based podcasts often involve the podcaster first recording an interview with another person or group of people before they create the final edited file for sharing with an audience. Just as writers often research and make notes on more material than could ever fit into an essay assignment, podcasters often record more material than can fit under the assignment's maximum limit. As we saw in Carla's podcast, consultants prompt podcasters to consider what content from the interview can best serve as evidence for their intended purpose. Consultants can also help podcasters develop reverse outlines of the content, combined with the audio logs Sylvia Church and Elizabeth Powell describe as having timelines (in minutes and seconds), track-layer identifiers, and editing actions for the podcaster to take (2007, 137). The purpose of the podcast directly guides the content that is included and how it is delivered.

Link Tone, Style, and Voice

The concepts of tone, style, and voice are all linked. *Tone* is the mood or attitude of a piece. Tone might, for example, be serious or humorous, formal or informal. The tone for a presentation that memorializes a recently deceased person and their life likely should have a different mood than a presentation of someone's successful venture, whether climbing a mountain or performing well in a recent on-campus play.

Style relates to how a message is delivered, including word choice and devices such as metaphors and similes. The words and devices should support the intended tone; a joke might go well with an informal, storytelling podcast, but likely it would not suit a serious memorial audio presentation.

Voice is an individual's personality expressed through unique wording. Consider, for example, how different friends use particular phrases or wording unique to each person. Even within considerations of tone and style, your voice can lend uniqueness to the podcast and you can become recognizable as the podcaster.

As McKee (2006) reminds us, music can powerfully evoke moods—in movies, dramatic performances, and podcasts. Likewise, sound effects can accomplish something similar. As with the spoken words included in the podcast, podcasters must consider whether the tone is consistent among music, sound, silence, and vocal delivery to ensure a unified comprehensive message.

Building Ethos

While students might be familiar with creating citations for written assignments, they might not be familiar with oral citations that credit the creators and creation dates for work or research the students cite or include. Further, students might not be familiar with what is legal or ethical to include as a sound within their podcasts. Consultants should ask the podcaster about how they ensured that any music or sound effects they downloaded were ones licensed for download—such as through Creative Commons; for more information, see the "Resources" section at the end of this chapter—and that the student had consent to record individuals, if the podcast does not specify. Consultants can ask about whether the podcast is providing appropriate in-text citations for any cited material and whether the podcast provides all the citations for the podcast music or sound effects that might be included in the project. For more detailed information about copyright and proper citation for multimedia sources, please refer to Molly Schoen and Sarah Blazer's chapter.

Developing Transcripts

In order to make audio podcasts accessible for all audiences, students should provide a transcript for their audio file. Consultants can help students develop a script before recording the audio and then revisit the script for accuracy after recording. The transcript provides a textual representation of the podcast, allowing the audience to follow along at their own pace and providing access to anyone who is hearing impaired.

Troubleshooting the Technical

While some tutoring sessions might involve only rhetorical concerns, students might also have questions about assignment problems. Church and Powell review how technology itself might need troubleshooting (2007, 135). In order to help students determine all the possibilities of their podcast, consultants need some familiarity with recording and editing software, such as Audacity, as well with as sites that include sound and music that can be used freely (see the "Resources" list for more information about these). Church and Powell suggest that audio editors keep multiple file backups of edited and unedited files, save files often, consult program documentation, keep detailed editing notes, and be prepared to rerecord, among other recommendations (136–41). Before proceeding with a session, consultants should ensure that the podcaster has made a backup copy of materials prior to making any additional changes. Consultants might need to refer students to additional resources for help on campus.

ACTIVITY: ANALYZING SOUND

Many of us have listened to radio and heard—in addition to music—interviews, commercials, speeches, narrated sports, and public service announcements (PSAs), among other programs and messages. Podcasts often include interviews and clips from performances, or they might be informative, like a PSA. While we might have familiarity with interviews and certain other forms of audio performance, we might not have as great an awareness of the role different types of sounds play.

One good way of paying attention to sound is to think about our expectations of our aural environments. The twentieth-century American composer and music theorist John Cage provides a perfect opportunity for one such thought experiment. Although he composed, among other works, dance and concert pieces, he is probably best known for his 1952 composition *4'33"* (pronounced "four minutes, thirty-three seconds" or "four thirty-three"). This composition of three movements (that is, three self-contained units in a piece of music) calls for the musicians to sit with their instruments and musical scores but not play their instruments for the specified four minutes and thirty-three seconds. Instead, the musicians sit as if they were performing, turn the sheet music, and then indicate when the four minutes and thirty-three seconds have passed.

Although some refer to *4'33"* as over four and a half minutes of silence, Cage wanted the audience to think about music in a new way. Cage is often credited as saying, "Wherever we are, what we hear mostly is noise." Since the piece's initial composition in 1952, it has been performed by orchestras and individual musicians such as pianists and drummers. Performers have even created dubstep and death-metal versions of this composition.

This activity asks you to locate a version of *4'33"* and to listen to it. This activity should be performed multiple times—first by yourself and then with a group. The goal is to become more aware of how noise is all around us and to provide an opportunity to think about what music is and how we can meaningfully incorporate sound into recordings.

1. When you are by yourself with no people and no pets around, access YouTube.com and search for John Cage's *4'33"*. Listen to any performance of *4'33"* you wish to.
   - As you listen, what stands out to you during the performance?
   - How would you describe the relationship between sound and no-sound (or silence)?
   - Is this recording of *4'33"* an audio performance? Music? Why or why not?

2. Next, listen to *4'33"* with a group.
   - As you listen, what stands out to you during the performance?
   - Notice if the performance seems different in comparison with your solitary listening.

- Listen to at least one other performance of *4'33"* and observe whether you discern anything different from prior listenings to *4'33"*.

3. Next, sit in a quiet space, such as a library.
   - What do you observe from an auditory standpoint?
   - How would you create a podcast that conveys the quiet setting?

4. Next, go to a noisier space, such as a coffee shop.
   - What do you observe from an auditory standpoint?
   - What do you *not* observe that you noticed in the quiet space?
   - What would you use in a podcast to convey this setting without uttering the name of the location?

ACTIVITY: ANALYZING AND THEN CREATING A PODCAST

This next activity is a multipart activity in which you create a podcast.

Analyze

The first phase of this activity focuses on analyzing podcasts. This part of the activity enables you to become familiar with the wide range of choices podcasters have and the relationship of those choices to audience, context, and purpose. Structured podcast analysis reveals the flexibility podcasters have in creating their recordings. Talking with other consultants about their own analyses reveals there is no one way to create a successful podcast, but instead podcasters have multiple choices and can create a variety of podcasts for a variety of purposes, audiences, and contexts. Such awareness can guide discussion with students who come into a tutoring session needing feedback or planning assistance.

1. Identify the purpose of the podcast you want to make. Will it be primarily for entertainment? For sharing information? Will it present research or an interview? Will it be for persuasion?

2. Find a podcast you might use as a model for your own work. See the resources at the end of this chapter or conduct a web search for *best podcasts* and find a reputable listing of recommended podcasts corresponding to your particular purpose.

3. Listen to the podcast. Take notes on what you notice.

4. Relisten to the podcast and create a reverse outline of the way it structures the sounds and spoken words. In general, note how podcasts begin and end: Do they use music? Is the music the same at the beginning and the end? Do they use sound effects (like the sound of

doors opening or closing? applause?) In general, what makes up the podcast's foreground, middle ground, and background? What sound is intentional and unintentional?

5. Take notes on the podcast's information organization. If the podcast presents an interview, notice how the podcast narrator/interviewer introduces the interviewee. Notice when the interviewer asks questions and the interviewee answers them or when the interviewer summarizes the responses. When does it seem as if a longer interview has been shortened for the podcast? When is spoken word chosen in lieu of sound and vice versa?

Create

After you analyze the elements of a successful podcast, the creation part of this podcast activity enables you not only to become familiar with making podcasts but also to become more experienced with the range of choices available to podcast makers. While this activity guides you in making a podcast, it also provides you with opportunities to experiment with the different effects and purposes of the speech, music, and sound options available to podcasters using podcasting software and resources. For example, after first creating a podcast, you can create different versions of that same podcast by changing effects and music and listen to how different choices result in different outcomes. Such familiarity can assist in discussions with podcasters during consulting sessions.

1. Create an outline of speech and sound for the podcast you wish to create. Consider how you will layer sound, establish a tone and style, build ethos, and evoke visual images.

2. Use a microphone (for best results) plugged into a computer and audio-capture software, such as Audacity, to record spoken materials for your podcast. Save a backup copy of this recording.

3. Using additional Tracks in Audacity, add any music (or sound effects) you have the rights to use (such as through Creative Commons permissions or sounds you have created or recorded). Keep backup copies of these music or sound-effects files.

4. Move the Tracks around and adjust timings as appropriate.

5. Save the Audacity project.

6. Next, export the podcast in a format compatible with most audio players, such as .mp3.

7. Listen to your podcast and determine whether there are changes you wish to make. In what ways does your podcast follow your outline? Pay attention to any unwanted background noises, like the ticking of a clock.

8. Create a backup copy of the Audacity project, then experiment with different sound effects, such as fading sound in and out, trying alternative music or sound, or volume levelling across tracks.

CONCLUSION

Like other rhetorically effective texts, successful podcasts engage the thoughtful consideration of audience, purpose, and context, but through audio. Rather than simply record a conversation, podcasters engage in number of decisions around invention, arrangement, style, and delivery. The means available to podcasters include deciding whether and when to use speech, music, sound effects, and even silence. Podcasters make numerous choices about whether, when, and how to edit dialogue, how quickly to pace the sounds, how many different layers of sound to include, and even when to narrate and summarize versus having an interviewee speak. Working on podcasts even provides opportunities for continued thought about writing assignments; for example, a writer might link podcast decisions with similar choices made in essays, such as when to use quotations as evidence and when to paraphrase. Lest there be any doubt about the power of audio, the narrator of *RadioLab*'s "The Heartbeat" episode (Webster 2016) discusses how during a live performance, the listening audience had strong responses to the audio sounds of heartbeats, including people who fainted from the sound effects alone. While podcasters might not strive to elicit such strong physical responses from their audiences, sound in its many forms can be a powerful available means of communication.

RESOURCES

The resources in this section include examples of podcasts and tools for outlining, creating, and editing podcasts.

Example Podcasts

http://www.radiolab.org/
  RadioLab describes itself as "a radio show and podcast weaving stories and science into sound and music-rich documentaries."
https://storycorps.org/listen/
  StoryCorps focuses on recording the stories of "everyday lives."

Other Podcasting Tools

http://www.audacityteam.org/
  Audacity is a freely available open-source audio-editing software.

https://search.creativecommons.org/
  Creative Commons Sounds provides a search tool for looking for items available for
  reuse under a CC license (which should also be verified when viewing the work a
  sound is used in).
https://www.freesound.org/
  Freesound is a collaborative database of audio snippets, samples, recordings, bleeps,
  and more released under Creative Commons licenses that allow reuse.
http://writingcenter.unc.edu/handouts/reverse-outline/
  The writing center of the University of North Carolina at Chapel Hill provides this
  helpful tool for creating reverse outlines.
https://storycorps.org/great-questions/
  StoryCorps provides Great Questions for Anyone.

KEY SEARCH TERMS

podcasts; podcasting; sonic; digital ethos; transcripts; interviews; audacity; audio editing; Creative Commons

REFERENCES

Ball, Cheryl, and Byron Hawk, eds. 2006. "Sound in/as Compositional Space: A Next Step in Multiliteracies." Special issue, *Computers and Composition* 23 (3): 263–65.

Bowie, Jennifer L. 2012. "Rhetorical Roots and Media Future: How Podcasting Fits into the Computers and Writing Classroom." *Kairos: A Journal of Rhetoric, Technology, and Pedagogy* 16 (2).

Church, Sylvia, and Elizabeth Powell. 2007. "When Things Go Wrong." *Multimodal Composition: Resources for Teachers,* edited by Cynthia L. Selfe, 133–52. Cresskill, NJ: Hampton.

McKee, Heidi. 2006. "Sound Matters: Notes towards the Analysis and Design of Sound in Multimodal Web Texts." *Computers and Composition* 23 (3): 335–54.

Selfe, Cynthia L. 2009. "The Movement of Air, the Breath of Meaning: Aurality and Multimodal Composing." *College Composition and Communication* 60 (4): 616–63.

Van Leeuwen, Theo. 1999. *Speech, Music, Sound.* Houndmills: Palgrave Macmillan.

Walch, Rob, and Mur Lafferty. 2006. *Tricks of the Podcasting Masters.* Indianapolis, IA: Que.

Webster, Molly. 2015. "*The Heartbeat.*" *RadioLab.* Podcast audio, May 12. http://www.radiolab.org/story/heartbeat/.

11

MULTIMODAL VIDEO PROJECTS
Video — Doing by Example

Patrick Anderson
Grand Valley State University

Florence Davies
Texas A&M University

INTRODUCTION

This chapter offers an overview of multimodal video projects by bridging connections between writing conventions and video production. By creating their own video compositions, consultants develop a vocabulary for assisting students with multimodal video projects. We encourage consultants to focus on the developmental process of their compositions as a way of creating a workable language for their intuitions about visual rhetoric. In the process, writing centers benefit from having their consultants create promotional or instructional digital content for their centers. Rather than present consultants with an algorithmic understanding of video production, which seeks precision and certainty, we present what Mike Rose (1980) has called a "heuristic understanding," which provides a flexible, pragmatic framework for helping students get to the next stage in their creative process.

ILLUSTRATIVE EXAMPLE: ENGINEERING A MULTIMODAL FUTURE

At the Texas A&M University Writing Center (TAMUWC), we are always seeking new ways to reach our students. While we often inform students about our services through informative workshops and resource fairs, we recently forged new ground. In the spring of 2016, the TAMUWC media team assisted with an on-campus informational session for the Engineering for You video contest hosted by the National Academy of Engineering. Participating students were to create a short video demonstrating how a concept of mega-engineering (large-scale projects

DOI: 10.7330/9781607328469.c011

engaging a cross-disciplinary engineering approach) could address and solve various global problems. The winning video was to receive a $25,000 cash prize and recognition for its respective university. This contest was of particular importance to the requesters, faculty within TAMU's College of Engineering, given that past Texas A&M students have placed well in the video competition. TAMUWC's contribution to the meeting involved offering tips and suggestions to students for their final video submissions.

To prepare for the informational session, our team viewed past winning video-contest submissions. And despite having won or ranked highly, some of the winning videos had significant flaws. Some had text competing with captions; others ignored the rule of thirds. Some misused sound and musical elements; others included disorientating editing. We sought to address these elements and general video production in our session and encourage the students' creativity. The experience was enlightening for us because it showed us how students view video production. Of particular interest to the students was the collaborative do's-and-don'ts list that stemmed from our review of past contest submissions. Having that specific framework allowed them to rethink some of the ideas they were already generating.

Video-project assignments are currently limited to particular courses and departments at our university, but the growing trend of multimodal inclusion will continue to creep into the curriculum. Thus, our consultants must be able to understand and address these audiences using language with which they are already familiar, and we have started preparing our consultants to help students navigate the multimodal landscape. As our media team has come to understand, the best way to teach someone multimodal practice is to experientially engage in these practices themselves.

BACKGROUND INFORMATION

From art and entertainment to sales and advertising, from politics and news to home movies and YouTube shorts, video is probably the most important mode of communication in the twenty-first century. As video technology has become more accessible, elite filmmaking institutions no longer have a monopoly on video production. As Iain Alexander (2012), founder of Film Industry Network, recently observed, "We are witnessing a digital revolution with millions of web users watching short films as they become the standard communication tool promoting values, culture and business ethics." The current generation of students increasingly relies on digital content for information, often using sites like YouTube the way some might use search engines. To keep up with the changes in communication technology, universities in general, and writing centers specifically, must adapt to meet the needs of students communicating in a visual-media world. Thus, writing centers should use multimodal communication to provide students with an understanding of what we do.

In meeting student needs, some of the most successful TAMUWC productions have been our grammar rap videos. We wanted to engage with our new intuitively multimodal generation of students through videos posted to our social media platforms. Originally, we envisioned the star of these videos, MC Grammar Punch, as giving instructional advice through song. But realizing that he could be used to promote the writing center and encourage students to use our services, we decided to use MC Grammar to change misconceptions about our center. TAMUWC could exist as a knowledgeable service to students, but in a manner unafraid to poke fun at itself. Despite our intentions, we soon discovered that the true value in the project did not stem from why we were creating the videos, but *how*.

Though we were already recording presentations and creating screencasts for our YouTube channel, creating the grammar raps posed new challenges. We did not consider ourselves film auteurs, yet we happened upon several of the guiding principles that inform most film compositions anyway. When gaps in our video-production knowledge materialized, we were able to call upon the expertise of our staff. But we were also creating a connection between the language ingrained in our familiar writing backgrounds and the newly discovered language of video and film. In the end, we had given ourselves a language for our intuitions, making new meaning from the already known.

Writing centers can use videos to promote their services in a multimodal world, and they can also help students with multimodal projects. While making the grammar rap videos, we learned that *writing* consultants should not feel limited by the adjective *writing*, for writing and video production are similar. As William Costanzo (1986) reminds us, "Films are compositions, too" (79). Some film theorists and moviemakers have analogized novelists and directors, arguing that film directors are the authors of their films just as novelists are the authors of their books. Other film theorists have presented the notion of film grammar as a metaphor for understanding the construction of visual meaning. Frank Manchel (1990) explains that understanding film as a language allows us to develop a grammatical understanding of meaning in film:

"Metaphorically, the 'grammar' of the film refers to theories that describe visual forms and sound combinations and their functions as they appear and are heard in a significant relationship during the projection of a film. Thus, film grammar includes the elements of motion, sound, picture, color, film punctuation, editing, and montage. . . . Print can do things that film cannot. But the reverse is also true" (96). In other words, just as the elements of language are combined to create meanings for a reading audience, the visual elements of film are combined to create meanings for a viewing audience.

To provide consultants with a basic vocabulary for working with students on film projects, in this chapter we introduce some concepts from film theory and film production—see the YouTube channels listed in the "Resources" section for examples and explanations of each of the italicized terms below. The two dominant traditions of film theory are realism and formalism. *Realism* emphasizes film's ability to capture natural movement and space just as it is, unmediated by the technical apparatus of the filmmaking equipment itself, with the goal of letting as much raw reality as possible come through to the audience. *Formalism* emphasizes the medium-specific aspects of film as a mode of communication, relying on filmmaking equipment and technology—especially editing—to create and convey ideas, concepts, and meanings not contained in any single shot. Of course, realist and formalist strategies are not mutually exclusive; they can be and should be combined to produce a number of creative possibilities.

There are three basic stages of the filmmaking process: preproduction, production, and postproduction. In the *preproduction* stage, filmmakers write a script, create a storyboard (a visual outline of the scenes), plan potential camera angles and lighting, select the cast and crew, and decide the locations, props, and costumes that will be used in the film. While changes might be made during later stages, the preproduction process allows filmmakers to have enough details planned for an efficient start.

In the *production* stage, filmmakers create the first building block of film: the shot (Kolker 2006). The *shot* is the outcome of the interplay between the set (staging and lighting) and the camera (framing and camera/lens movement).

Staging refers to the arrangement of people and objects against a background (also called *blocking set*). There is no one correct way to stage the actors and objects in a shot, but decisions about staging are crucial because they affect all the other aspects of a shot. *Lighting* refers to how bright (high key) or dark (low key) the shot will be. Sometimes, different objects in the same shot require different lighting keys to create contrast. Other times, three-point lighting is required for filming a human subject: a key light placed near the camera to illuminate the face, a fill light to remove undesired shadows, and a backlight to distinguish the subject from the set, creating a three-dimensional look. Three-point lighting is typically used for staged interviews. Color can also affect the mood of a shot: red tones usually convey a sense of danger or conflict and are used to light villains, while blue tones usually convey a sense of safety or calm and are used to light heroes.

Framing refers to the positioning of the camera in relation to the staging. The camera angle can be high, middle, or low, and the camera distance can be long, medium, or close-up. Different camera angles create different relationships of power between the audience and the subject. A high camera angle makes the subject appear vulnerable in relation to the audience, while a low camera angle makes the subject appear powerful in relation to the audience. A midlevel camera angle is used for a neutral, eye-level shot. Similarly, different camera distances establish different levels of intimacy between the audience and the subject. A long-distance camera shot places the subject far away from the camera, providing a wide view of the set and reducing intimacy between the audience and the subject. A close-up shot (usually of a human subject's face) places the subject close to the camera, providing a detailed view of the subject's emotions and increasing intimacy between the audience and the subject. A medium-distance shot allows the audience to see the whole subject in detail while providing a balanced level of intimacy.

When deciding how and where to position the camera, two rules are helpful. First, the rule of thirds: imagine a tic-tac-toe grid dividing the shot into nine sections, and position the most important objects where the lines intersect to produce a compelling visual dynamic. The subject or point of interest should appear along the lines of the grid, especially at the intersections but not in the center. As shown in figure 11.1, the bottom right corner of the sign is anchored at the bottom right intersection on the grid, making the focal point of the image where the sign and the human subject meet. Placing the subject off-center gives the shot a clear focal point, improves the composition, and balances the shot. Second, the 180-degree rule: imagine there is a line down the center of the set (the *axis*), and make sure the camera does not cross it. As shown in figure 11.2, when the camera remains on the same side of the action, the characters maintain their left-right organization. When the camera crosses the axis, however, the characters' positions are reversed, and this could disorient the audience.

Figure 11.1. Example of the rule of thirds: image of a man near a No Parking sign (by Brenden S. Murphy. Used with permission)

In addition to decisions about angle and distance, filmmakers must also make decisions about movement. *Camera movement* refers to panning (turning the camera side to side), tilting (moving the camera up and down), and tracking (moving the whole camera forward, backward, or sideways). Cameras are sometimes attached to a tripod or a dolly to help make the camera more stable or to make the camera movements more fluid, but some shots require the use of a handheld camera, which can help the shot express discomfort, uncertainty, or urgency. *Lens movement* refers to zoom and focus. The focus setting that most closely resembles the natural focus of the human eyes is soft focus, with which the main object of attention in the shot is in clear focus but the background is slightly out of focus. Once a shot is composed by staging, lighting, framing, and camera/lens movements, the last thing to decide is *shot duration,* or how long the entire shot will be from start to finish.

In the *postproduction* stage, filmmakers create the second building block of film: the cut (Kolker 2006). The *cut* is the visual interaction between two shots created during *editing.* The two basic approaches to cutting are continuity editing and montage editing. The goal of *continuity editing* is to reduce the conflict between two shots, producing a "natural" transition and attracting as little attention as possible to the cut. The goal of *montage editing* is just the opposite: to increase or highlight the conflict between two shots and call attention to the cut.

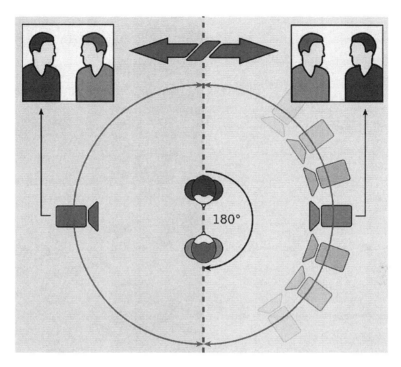

Figure 11.2. Diagram of the 180-degree rule (image by grm_wnr; used under the GNU Free Documentation License, https://commons.wikimedia.org/wiki/File:180 _degree_rule.svg#)

When deciding how to edit two shots together, it is important to know what their relationship is in the overall narrative of the film. A *sequence* is a set of shots that makes up one segment of a scene, and a *scene* makes up one segment of the *narrative*, or the whole story. If a cut is between two shots in a sequence, they should be edited to demonstrate that close relationship. If a cut is between two scenes, the editing should demonstrate to the audience that the storyline is progressing from one scene to the next.

Finally, audio elements are just as important as the visual elements of film. The filmmaker must determine which sounds should be *diegetic sound*, sound filmed live alongside the film, or *nondiegetic sound*, which can include a musical soundtrack, voice-overs, or sound effects that might be added during the editing stage. For more information on the layers and planes of sound, the process of narrative creation, and effective uses of voice and delivery, please refer to Lindsay Sabatino's introduction and Brenta Blevins's chapter on podcasting in this collection.

Accessibility

In order to make videos accessible to all audiences, they should include captions, transcripts, and audio descriptions. *Captions* provide an on-screen textual representation of the audio, allowing the viewer to absorb the visuals and the text simultaneously. Filmmakers can choose between open captions, which cannot be turned off by the viewer, and closed captions, which can be toggled on and off at the viewer's discretion. While there are free tools available to create captions, filmmakers should rely on their final script or use a caption editor to guarantee the most accurate presentation of the dialogue and other important audio elements. *Transcripts* provide a static textual representation of the spoken words and the visual actions of the video, allowing the viewer to read descriptions of the dialogue and important visual elements. Transcripts can accompany the video in a downloadable file or on a website. Filmmakers can produce a transcript quickly and accurately by adding descriptions of important visual elements to their final script. *Audio descriptions* appear during natural pauses in dialogue in a separate audio track. Audio descriptions offer verbal representations of important visual content not already conveyed by the dialogue, including set details and character costumes, actions, locations, body language, and facial expressions. Audio descriptions should also include verbalization of all on-screen text.

While captions and transcripts assist viewers who might have difficulty hearing or processing auditory information and viewers who might not be proficient in the language(s) used in the video, audio descriptions assist viewers who either have difficulty seeing or are unable to see the video. By including captions, transcripts, and audio descriptions, students can make their videos accessible to all viewers—see the "Resources" section for more information.

CONSULTATION STRATEGIES FOR MULTIMODAL VIDEO PROJECTS

Composition as Process, Not Product

Though we usually think composition is about the product we produce, Donald M. Murray (2003) reminds us that composition is a *process* with three basic stages. Just as written composition consists of prewriting, writing, and rewriting, video composition consists of preproduction, production, and postproduction.

Preproduction

The preproduction stage of filmmaking is similar to the prewriting stage. At this stage, students might still be in the research phase, determining the who (cast and crew), what (props and costumes), where (filming locations), when (production schedule), why (topic and audience), and how (audio/video equipment) of their video project. More important, students might need help developing a storyboard or drafting a script. During a brainstorming session, consultants help students generate ideas for a storyboard, the visual plan for the video narrative; watching short clips from Hollywood films or short videos in the same genre as the student's assignment can help jump-start the brainstorming process. For more information on visually planning with writers, please refer to Brandy Ball Blake and Karen Head's chapter on storyboarding. Consultants can also provide feedback and suggestions on drafts of scripts. If the student is developing a script, consultants can help the student outline scenes or dialogue; if the student has a working script, consultants can offer to read through it with them and provide feedback. The actors might not perform dialogue word for word, but a script not only supplements the storyboard, providing further guidance during the film shoot, but also makes it easier to add captioning and transcripts in the postproduction stage.

In addition to providing feedback on the narrative of the story, consultants can help students set realistic goals based on their time frame and available materials. They should also encourage students to film extra footage before moving to the production stage; after all, it is much easier to shoot more footage when they are already filming than to reshoot scenes because they missed something important. During the preproduction stage, helping students generate, develop, and organize ideas should be the focus.

Production

The production stage of filmmaking is similar to the writing stage. Students might be looking for feedback on individual shots, the construction of a sequence or a scene, or the relationship among multiple scenes. Students should be encouraged to shoot multiple takes of every shot and to review those shots while on the set since shot-composition quality is not always clear until it is viewed on screen. If a shot seems poorly lit or awkwardly framed, consultants can offer some suggestions on the lighting key or introduce the student to the rule of thirds if they are not already familiar with it. If a scene contains a cut from a long-range shot with low-key lighting to a close-up shot with high-key lighting, the effect is dramatic and will possibly disorient the audience.

Consultants can ask students whether the angles and lighting choices are intentional; if not, students might reshoot the scene with a more consistent lighting key and/or transition between long, medium, and close-up shots more gradually. If one scene mentions a character, event, or idea that has not been properly introduced in previous scenes, consultants can suggest that the student find a place to introduce this earlier in the video.

Continuity can also be an issue: if a character is wearing a hat backward in one shot and then wearing it forward in another shot, the student might want to reshoot to be consistent. Not everything can be worked out in preproduction planning; therefore, the student should go out and freeshoot (just like freewriting), either to get some back-up footage or to capture some spontaneous action and dialogue. During the production stage, helping the student determine whether they need to add or reshoot any footage should be the focus.

Postproduction

Finally, the postproduction stage of filmmaking is similar to the rewriting stage. At this step in the process, the student should be able to answer the most comprehensive questions about every aspect of the video, from the coherence of the narrative (global concerns) to specific choices about shot composition and editing techniques (local concerns). When looking at the global concerns, consultants can ask questions about narrative structure and scene development: How is the plot of the video progressing from scene to scene? Is there a specific argument the video is trying to convey? Referring the student back to their original outline or storyboard might be helpful at this time.

For local concerns, it can be helpful to rely on the concept of film grammar to discuss the visual and audio editing techniques used by the student. For example, just as a consultant might explain that a semicolon (and not a comma) should connect two independent clauses, a consultant might explain that continuity editing (and not montage) should be used to connect the shots of two characters in a conversation: it is easier for the audience to follow the ideas. The notion of film grammar can also be used to assess the relationship between the image and the sound. Consultants can also discuss the use of voice-overs, musical soundtracks, or sound effects and their relationship to the images with which they are paired. To make their videos accessible to all viewers, students should revise their original script to reflect the dialogue of the final cut of the video and use the final script to create captions and transcripts to accompany the video. During the postproduction stage, helping the student fine-tune and make final decisions about the global and local concerns of their video should be the focus.

Film Theory as Rhetorical Heuristic

While realist and formalist theories of film developed to explain film as an artistic form, we can translate these paradigms into rhetorical heuristics. These heuristics provide one basis for establishing a common language with students working on video projects. The type of feedback given by the consultants will vary depending on whether the student is going for a more realistic, natural look to the video or a stylized, technical use of the medium. These choices will be based on the student's purpose and audience for the video.

Consultants can provide feedback on the use of lighting, shot duration, camera movement, and continuity editing. On the one hand, a realistic or natural approach to film relies on some combination of natural light or three-point lighting, longer shot duration, little camera movement, and subtle editing techniques. On the other hand, a formalistic approach to film relies on some combination of high-contrast lighting configurations, shorter shot duration (thus, more frequent cutting), more camera movement, and contrastive editing. Switching between realist and formalist heuristics is advantageous, not only because every video project relies on some combination of these two basic approaches to filmmaking but also because each one contributes unique perspective, enhancing the student's visual and rhetorical aims.

ACTIVITY

The most informative practice of engaging in the process of filmmaking in preparation for tutoring multimodal projects relies heavily on being engrossed in process. Thus, activities and practices should first encourage some form of immersion in active creation of a video project.

Consultant-developed video projects need not be created solely for training purposes; writing centers are actively seeking new ways to create digital content for online audiences, as noted by David M. Sheridan (2010) in "Multiliteracy Centers as Content Producers." When designing your own video projects, you can continue to use the video-making process as a heuristic while creating content for your writing centers. These projects can be particularly useful for centers who cannot allocate dedicated staff to create content. More important, you can have an active hand in developing the multimodal praxis of your center, creating a legacy of material that can exist long after you leave your institution.

We provide two activities geared toward developing and engaging with a working knowledge of video production. The video-analysis assignment offers you the opportunity to evaluate a short video using film-analysis terminology. This short-form assignment provides a faster orientation to the world of film grammar and video making; it is suitable for writing centers with condensed training opportunities. The video-composition-project assignment asks consultants to create a short promotional video to inform students of your writing center's services. This assignment is better suited for writing centers with dedicated training courses, tutor-certification programs, and training opportunities that allow for long-term projects. Nonetheless, both video projects should allow you to make deeper connections with film principles in a manner that enriches your overall understanding.

Video-Analysis Assignment

Assisting students with video projects requires a foundational knowledge of the language of film, otherwise known as *film grammar*. This activity offers several terms and points of consideration for video analysis adapted from appendix C in *Multiliteracies and Emerging Genres* (Adsanatham et al. 2013).

Search the web for a long-form commercial of at least sixty seconds. Watch the commercial three times, paying attention to the images, sounds, transitions, texts, clarity, persuasiveness, and arrangement. After the third viewing, write a reflection on each of the following:

1. *Visuals.* Discuss how images, text, actors, and objects are used in the commercial.

   Reflection: How do the commercial's images infuse creativity and hold viewer interest? How are shots composed (e.g., framing, lighting, camera angle and movement)? Does the commercial have quality resolution? How does text aid in understanding the narrative? How does the video make accessibility accommodations? Do captions compete with embedded text?

2. *Sounds.* Describe how sound is incorporated in the commercial.

   Reflection: How does the commercial include musical accompaniment and draw emotion from the viewer? How does the music connect with its correlating images? If there are other audio elements juxtaposed with the images, how do they aid or detract from the commercial's narrative? Is the audio diegetic or nondiegetic?

3. *Persuasiveness.* Identify the commercial's use of the rhetorical situation (e.g., purpose, audience, context, message).

Reflection: What kind of rhetorical appeals does the commercial make? Are they effective in persuading the intended audience?

4. *Transitions.* Identify transitions used in the commercial.

   Reflection: How do the transitions connect the various shots of the commercial effectively? How does the commercial rely on montage or continuity editing?

5. *Clarity and arrangement.* Identify the balance among image, sound, transitions, and text in creating a clear message. Describe how the commercial's images and sounds create a progressive argument.

   Reflection: How does the flow of the commercial work as a whole? Is it focused and cohesive? How is the commercial sequenced? Does anything in the commercial feel out of place?

Suggestions and Considerations

Although the duration of at least sixty seconds might feel somewhat arbitrary, selecting a commercial with substantial length allows for more opportunities for deeper incorporation of filmmaking terms. Microfilms, music videos, and movie clips are other options for analysis.

Video-Composition-Project Assignment

Creating videos and working through the production process provide you with a foundation for understanding filming principles in action. This activity, therefore, requires you to (1) plan and outline, (2) film, and (3) edit a video project. Once finished, you will (4) write an accompanying interwoven reflection on the process. The goal is to create a two-minute commercial about your writing center. While this commercial should largely remain informative and address potential or existing misconceptions, your commercial should also relay this information creatively. Of importance, the video should address an audience of potential undergraduate students, fellow consultants, and writing center staff. In addition to the video, each stage of production should be accompanied by a reflective journal entry detailing the process of creating this commercial.

1. *Preproduction:* Determine what story your video will tell about your writing center. Decide what information is most relevant to the audience. Then, develop a storyboard for the video project. Envision what each scene will present to the audience. Include any relevant transitions. After scenes and settings are determined, draft a corresponding script for your storyboard. The script should include

elements such as dialogue, setting, and production notes. Once scripted, cast the video project and assign roles to available actors.

For your journal: Explain, if applicable, any significant research that went into the creation of the commercial's script. (For example, identify whether your video is a parody or draws inspiration from another source.) Discuss and detail any preplanning considerations that went into the making of the video (e.g., setting, location, casting, camera angles, lighting, and wardrobe). Explain how structural outlines or storyboards were used to envision the project prior to filming. When developing the video, reflect on how the rhetorical situation (purpose, audience, context, and message) inspired, changed, or guided the composition process. Explain the overall takeaway message for your audience.

2. *Production:* Using a developed script, film the commercial and bring the storyboard to life. Test out different shot angles, lighting, and settings. Allow for some spontaneity in the process and be sure to capture extra footage while shooting.

For your journal: After filming the video, write a description explaining the structure of the commercial and the filming process while shooting footage. Refer back to the storyboard and explain how the commercial adhered to or deviated from the plan or inspired any spontaneous freeshooting.

3. *Postproduction:* Edit the film to create a cohesive narrative. Based on the narrative and goals of the film, apply *continuity editing* and/or *montage editing.* Include any narration, additional sound mixing, and background music. Remember to add accessibility features to the video.

For your journal: Discuss the editing process for the commercial. Write a description of how scenes were structured and the reasoning behind the order in which they appear. Include information on reshoots, revising imperfections, and any audio-visual pairings used postfilming.

4. *Final reflection:* Reflect on the overall impression of the project as a writing consultant. In particular, describe how the video-composition project is similar (or dissimilar) to processes used in traditional writing compositions. Draw comparisons between the two, and also reflect on how this process could inform the way you would consult students with video projects.

Suggestions and Considerations

Given the availability of filmmaking technology, this activity can be completed using easily accessible resources. Consultants should consider filming their projects with camera phones and using free or low-cost composing software. With the rapid changes in audio and visual production technology, some research might be required to determine what equipment and software is appropriate for the project. University libraries and resource centers often have equipment and software available for loan or use.

CONCLUSION

Because film dominates communication in the twenty-first century, it becomes increasingly incumbent on writing centers to adapt the way they connect with and help students, both online and in person. Writing consultants are often hired because they have some relatively advanced writing skills and intuitions, which they have often developed by going through the writing process. Likewise, the best (but not the only) way for consultants to develop skills and intuitions about visual communication is to make their own video projects, simultaneously contributing to their center's resource materials for writers. Though it is not necessary for every consultant to develop an elaborate knowledge of film theory and production, we have tried to provide a foundational vocabulary upon which consultants can build their own approach to tutoring multimodal communication. And, by translating some familiar notions from writing tutoring into film-tutoring strategies, we hope consultants will become confident in their ability to help students compose multimodal projects with video components.

RESOURCES

The following is a list of resources for consultants on how to produce and/or evaluate multimodal projects with video components, including software, accessibility, and tutorials on the technical aspects of film.

Video-Editing Software

https://filmora.wondershare.com/

> Though video-editing software can be expensive, many programs are available for free, including Apple iMovie and Windows Movie Maker. And though video-editing technology changes rapidly, consultants can visit Filmora for annually updated lists of quality video-editing programs.

Videos about Filmmaking

https://www.youtube.com/watch?v=_rWcQdH7-wE

> In *How to Make a Short Film*, professors and students from Santa Fe University of Art and Design explain what it takes to make a short film and provide examples of students' short films.

The following YouTube channels offer video introductions to film history, theory, and production, including helpful tutorials explaining the technical aspects of how to use a variety of filmmaking equipment and software. Consultants can see these channels for examples and explanations of the technical terms discussed in the "Background Information" section of this chapter.

Filmmaker IQ: https://www.youtube.com/user/FilmmakerIQcom/
Videomaker: https://www.youtube.com/user/videomaker
Cinecom.Net: https://www.youtube.com/user/YapperDesign
DSLRguide: https://www.youtube.com/channel/UCzQ1L-wzA_1qmLf49ey9iTQ

Criteria to Evaluate Video Projects

Appendix C in Adsanatham et al. (see references) provides a student-generated list of criteria by which to evaluate video projects, including images, sounds, transitions, text, clarity, and persuasiveness.

Accessibility

http://www.washington.edu/accessibility/videos/
    The University of Washington's "Accessible Technology" page provides helpful
    guidelines and resources for creating accessible videos.
https://www.access-board.gov/
    In the event that students are required to meet accessibility standards dictated by
    law, consultants can refer them to the United States Access Board website.

KEY SEARCH TERMS

accessibility; blocking set; continuity editing; diegetic sound; formalism (film); montage editing; nondiegetic sound; realism (film); shot composition

REFERENCES

Adsanatham, Chanon, Phill Alexander, Kerrie Carsey, Abby Dubisar, Wioleta Fedeczko, Denise Landrum, Cynthia Lewiecki-Wilson, Heidi McKee, Kristen Moore, Gina Patterson, and Michelle Polak. 2013. "Going Multimodal: Programmatic, Curricular, and Classroom Change." In *Multiliteracies and Emerging Genres*, edited by Tracy Bowen and Carl Whithaus, 282–312. Pittsburgh, PA: University of Pittsburgh Press.

Alexander, Iain. 2012. "Short Films Will Become the Most Important Communication Tool." *Film Industry Network.* http://www.filmindustrynetwork.biz/short-films-become -most-important-communication-tool/14005.

Costanzo, William. 1986. "Film as Composition." *College Composition and Communication* 37 (1): 79–86.

Kolker, Robert. 2006. *Film, Form, and Culture. 3rd ed.* New York: McGraw-Hill.

Manchel, Frank. 1990. *Film Study: An Analytical Bibliography. Volume 1.* Cranbury, NJ: Associated University Presses.

Murray, Donald M. 2003. "Teach Writing as a Process Not Product." In *Cross-Talk in Comp Theory: A Reader*, edited by Victor Villanueva, 3–6. 2nd ed. Urbana, IL: NCTE.

Rose, Mike. 1980. "Rigid Rules, Inflexible Plans, and the Stifling of Language: A Cognitivist Analysis of Writer's Block." *College Composition and Communication* 13 (4): 389–401.

Sheridan, David M. 2010. "Multiliteracy Centers as Content Producers: Designing Online Learning Experiences for Writers." In *Multiliteracy Centers: Writing Center Work, New Media, and Multimodal Rhetoric*, edited by David M. Sheridan and James A. Inman, 189–204. Cresskill, NJ: Hampton.

12

PUBLIC SERVICE ANNOUNCEMENTS (PSAs)
Focused Messages for Specific Audiences

Alice Johnston Myatt

University of Mississippi

CHAPTER OVERVIEW

This chapter offers an overview of public service announcements (PSAs) and provides consultants with specific strategies for helping students assigned to either analyze or develop PSAs to understand the constraints and affordances of this particular genre. In general terms, PSAs are "messages in the public interest disseminated by the media without charge," and an important aspect of successful PSAs is the pairing of a focused message with a specific audience (Goodwill 2010, para. 2). Multimodal consultants can use rhetorical strategies and some basic design knowledge to guide students in their efforts to target segments of the public with this important multimodal genre.

ILLUSTRATIVE EXAMPLE: DEVELOPING A HEALTH-SERVICE PSA

Dinah is a third-year student in her university's nursing program, and she plans to build a career in the field of public-health policy. As part of a course she is taking on environmental health, she has been assigned to develop a sixty-second public service announcement on a topic related to environmental health and inner-city neighborhoods. Since Dinah's main interest is in improving healthcare options for teen mothers living in rural areas, she is less familiar with healthcare issues in urban areas. Her assignment requires that she craft a statement that will capture the interest of and spark change in viewers who for the most part have different cultural backgrounds and healthcare needs than the population Dinah is accustomed to studying, all within the space of one short minute!

Feeling something akin to writer's block, Dinah made an appointment with a consultant, and together they analyzed the assignment and

DOI: 10.7330/9781607328469.c012

brainstormed ideas. After doing some research, she decided to stress the health benefits of community garden spaces. She hoped her PSA could potentially put a spotlight on how community gardening efforts were being used to solve a problem (lack of fresh vegetables) faced by inner-city communities (her target audience). She decided on the tagline "Fresh food, healthy bodies" and planned to show the annual cycle of garden growth, harvesting, and consumption in four ten-second frames (using forty seconds of her allotted sixty seconds) that featured images from successful urban community gardens paired with healthy, smiling people to share her story. She determined that the balance of her time would be spent on captioning, transitions, and brief narrated voiceovers emphasizing key points, and credits. At that point, she confidently began her work and returned to the writing center with the finished PSA in order to get some objective feedback on the effectiveness of her message and use of visuals. Her work with the writing center consultants paid off when she received a gratifying request from her professor to use her work as an example for future classes.

BACKGROUND INFORMATION: WHAT YOU
NEED TO KNOW ABOUT PSAS

As a genre, the PSA has evolved to the point that the Federal Communications Commission (FCC) officially defines it as "any announcement for which no charge is made and which promotes programs, activities, or services of federal, state, or local governments (e.g., recruiting, sale of bonds, etc.) or the programs, activities or services of non-profit organizations (e.g., United Way, Red Cross blood donations, etc.) and other announcements regarded as serving community interests, excluding time signals, routine weather announcements and promotional announcements" (Goodwill 2010, para. 1). The cost of dissemination is borne primarily by the entertainment industry via movie studios (who might show PSAs as part of the brief clips prior to the start of films), radio stations (audio PSAs are a staple feature of radio stations), and television stations that fall under the jurisdiction of the FCC. Many newspapers also print public service announcements with no ad cost charged to the producers, and the internet has become an increasingly popular venue for the distribution of PSAs via websites and blogs.

Early in the twentieth century, PSAs became a popular method for the US government to take advantage of the move toward advertising to craft messages that could initiate dramatic and needed changes on a grand scale (Goodwill 2010, para. 4). With the involvement of the

United States in World Wars I and II, the genre took on some of the formal aspects of what media professionals today expect of PSAs—powerful images, calls to action, and short, succinct messages designed for specific purposes and audiences. Given the history of this genre, we can understand why it is vital to incorporate strategies for strengthening the visual, audio, and textual elements when designing strong PSAs.

PSAs are assigned to students from a variety of disciplines, and their use spans many and diverse fields. In business and marketing, public service advertisements might combine elements of formal marketing, such as branding, in order to get their message across to target audiences. In public policy and health sciences, they often serve to get important information—even lifesaving information—to target audiences. In rhetoric-based courses, PSAs are often assigned as an analysis project in order for students to discover how visual, audio, textual, and cultural elements combine to design a message that will persuade the target audience to take some form of action.

When working with PSAs, it helps to have a clear understanding of the student's discipline and the target audience, regardless of whether the assignment is to analyze or compose a PSA. In fact, without a clear sense of the target audience, a PSA will lack focus and very likely fail in getting its message across. This is especially important if the target audience is outside the cultural or educational experiences of the student, much as Dinah was unfamiliar with healthcare issues in urban communities. Thus, researching and understanding the target audience is essential, and it should be one of the first considerations to discuss with students who are working with the genre.

Once a target audience is determined, designers must consider which mediums best suit that audience. PSAs are truly multimodal in that they rely on linguistic, aural, gestural, and visual elements to convey their messages. They might be sound files (.mp3, .wav) intended to be played over airwaves on both high-definition channels like SiriusXM® and standard AM and FM radio stations. Many are developed in digital formats such as videos or digital posters, while printed posters and flyers are staples of clinics, doctors' offices, and educational sites. The PSA might be as basic as a bordered announcement in a community newspaper, or it might be as elaborate as a rich multimodal message played in a premium advertising spot during an internationally televised sports event ("Super Bowl" 2015). An example of the latter is the one-minute PSA video *Two Causes of Asthma* that aired during the 2010 Winter Olympics, reaching in excess of forty million viewers ("Prevent" 2010).

CONSULTATION STRATEGIES FOR PSAS

Consultants should think of the rhetorical features found in PSAs as occurring along a continuum from basic, one-mode/one-audience messages to more complex, multimodal messages that target multiple audiences via multiple mediums. Understanding the Gestalt principles of visual design as well as audio-design principles provides a solid foundation for the strategies discussed in this section. A rhetorical understanding of the interplay of audience, purpose, and context and of the classical rhetorical appeals (*ethos, logos, pathos,* and *kairos*), is useful in working with students, regardless of stage (initial or complete) or assignment (create or analyze). To see how these understandings contribute to the development of effective strategies, I interviewed University of Mississippi writing consultants to learn what works for them when it comes to PSAs and used their insight to build some helpful tips for consulting on a PSA project.

Determine the Type of PSA and Its Constraints

As with most types of tutorial interactions, consultants should begin by asking for a copy or description of the assignment. From the assignment, note the medium of the PSA and its length and distribution constraints. Most broadcast PSAs are either thirty or sixty seconds in length, although students might find examples of longer PSA videos on the internet, especially if such are housed on organizational websites. In composing or analyzing the message, consider the following questions and the design choices embedded in the answers—refer to Lindsay Sabatino's introduction in this collection for expanded discussion on the design elements mentioned here. Having answers to these questions will ease the transition into the production stage of the project; they will also assist in evaluating and analyzing completed PSAs.

- *Is the PSA static (poster, billboard, screen)?* In designing such, consider using a mock-up or sketch approach to create effective layouts using low-tech tools like colored paper, scissors, and markers to design the message. In review and analysis, notice the design elements of linguistic, visual, and spatial meanings: these are essential to composing a static message that nonetheless catches the eyes of audiences and delivers its message in just three to five seconds.
- *Is the PSA audio only, or does it combine audio with visual and textual elements?* Audio PSAs require careful attention to the design elements of linguistic and audio meanings; sounds and the words that accompany them are primary—for more information about creating audio, see Brenta Blevins's chapter on podcasts. If audio/visual, composers must

incorporate the design elements of visual, gestural, spatial, and multi-modal meanings, while analysis requires attention to how successfully the design elements are used to convey a focused message. In order to make PSAs accessible to all audiences, audio files should be accompanied with transcripts, and videos should include captioning, transcripts, and audio descriptions. To learn more about making audio and video projects accessible, see Brenta Blevins's chapter on podcasts and Patrick Anderson and Florence Davies's chapter on video projects, respectively.

- *What time parameters govern the final length of the PSA?* Be sure you know and observe time constraints; many professors give little to no leeway for compositions that are too long or too short. In fact, most require the final product to meet the time constraint within a one- or two-second margin.

Understand the Rhetorical Situation

Successful PSAs make effective use of the rhetorical appeals of *ethos, logos,* and *pathos* and of a sense of *kairos* to achieve their purpose. The rhetorical appeal of *ethos* relies on the credibility of the communicator, which in the instance of PSAs could be either an individual (Michael Jordan's 1987 *Don't Do Drugs* PSA ["Michael Jordan" 1987]) or an organization (Habitat for Humanity's 2016 PSA ["2016 Habitat" 2016]). Consultants might ask designers, "What is it about you or your work that makes this message credible?" Using sources and assets responsibly and ethically is another way of imparting *ethos* to the project. When a message appeals to the emotions of its audience, it is invoking the power of *pathos*, which is an appeal to sentiment or feelings. Many of us have seen heart-wrenching images of mistreated animals or starving children, and when such messages grab our attention, the rhetorical appeal of *pathos* is successful. Often, PSAs incorporate specific evidence and statistics, making use of the rhetorical appeal of *logos*. Appealing to the logic of audiences is *logos* at work, while the use of *kairos* situates a message within a relevant time frame or at an effective moment. Sending out a PSA on the need for flu vaccines in the height of summer would not be good use of *kairos*. Consultants who assist designers can use these appeals to focus on a goal for the PSA. As writing center consultant Adrienne Lay notes, "I usually tell these students (or myself) something similar to what I would tell them if they were turning something in via a writing format. And that is to define a clear goal. What do I need/wish to accomplish with this? And what specific choices can I make that will aid in getting this point across" (pers. comm.)? Each one of the rhetorical appeals discussed at the beginning of this section can be thought of as a strategy for making decisions and choices. For example, what images will drive the point of the message home to the audience, inspiring action (use of *pathos*)? What evidence selected will support the statements made in the message (use of *logos*)? What kind of information is needed to reinforce credibility (use of *ethos*)?

What if consultants are asked to respond to a completed PSA a student brings in for review prior to submitting it to their professor? Writing center consultant Alix Moody says, "Provide authentic help by being an interested audience for the project" (pers. comm.); her fellow consultant Dana Repel agrees, saying, "Be sure to always ask about the audience for the project—does the student have a clear sense of who the audience is/will be" (pers. comm.)? One strategy is to ask the designer to describe a specific person or group that will respond to the PSA.

Identify the Tagline

An effective PSA has a tagline—a one-phrase or one-sentence summary of the message that people will remember long after their initial engagement with the PSA itself. A classic example is the tagline from many US Forestry Service PSAs: "Only *you* can prevent forest fires!" (Video Archeology 2014) or the well-known "This is your brain on drugs" ("80s Anti-Drug Commercial" 1987). If we look back at the assignment Dinah was given, we get a sense of the value of viewing her early work on the PSA as a problem that needed a solution; recall that her tagline was "Fresh food, healthy bodies." If consultants are responding to a finished project, they should be able to quickly identify such taglines; otherwise, more work on this element is needed.

Decide on a Story

Every PSA should have within it a story that vividly stays with the hearer or viewer long after the message itself has been played. Dinah knew she wanted to show images of healthy children, smiling faces, and healthy teeth in those smiles. Her story would be about how cultivating, harvesting, and eating fresh vegetables would result in improved health for the community. When responding to or analyzing completed projects, ask, "What is the story? What is the narrative?" The message or meaning of the PSA comes from the interaction of linguistic, audio, visual, gestural, spatial, and multimodal design elements, and they should be woven together in such a way that an entire narrative—including backstory and afterword—can be imagined after viewing the PSA.

Develop an Outline and Script

The best way to design an engaging narrative is to make use of a mock-up or storyboard and a script. If the PSA project is static, the mock-up is best, as it can function as an outline for the project, and it includes the layout design, colors, images, fonts, and any recurring elements—see Brandy Ball Blake and Karen Head's chapter on storyboarding for more suggestions on using storyboarding in a session. The storyboard shows sequence; it portrays time and movement and is a step-by-step description (often visual and drawn by hand) of the progress of the message and the elements needed at each step of its production (Arola, Sheppard, and Ball 2014, 93). Unless static, most PSAs have some type of audio (especially narration), and if so, writing out a script in advance is a vital step and makes adding captioning much easier. Alix, whom we heard from earlier in this chapter, makes this connection, saying, "All of the elements of writing from a rhetorical standpoint are there: audience, purpose, context, and medium—all of these are things most of them are familiar with. . . . Often I will help the student to have structure or begin with structure like preparing a script to follow" (pers. comm.). An easy way to begin this process is to get the designer to answer aloud this question: What is the message you want people to remember? Write down the answer to that question; it often forms the basis of the script or outline.

Gather Sources and Assets

Kristin L. Arola, Jennifer Sheppard, and Cheryl E. Ball (2014) refer to the resources gathered and used in making a PSA as "sources" and "assets" (61). These assets need not be expensive or difficult to find; a good starting point is to go to the Creative Commons (CC) website and search for different resources (for more information on CC and attribution of multimodal sources, see Molly Schoen and Sarah Blazer's chapter on citations and copyright). In addition to including still images and photos, the CC search will return sound files and textual elements like unusual fonts students can use in developing their PSAs.

An important part of a PSA is the closing information provided to give the audience a way of finding more information or contacting the sponsoring organization. If needed, an ending credits screen also provides attribution for external sources and assets used in the PSA. Think back to the example we begin this chapter with: in addition to her story segments, Dinah prepared a six-second narrated introduction, a ten-second conclusion, and a four-second contact/credits closing, thus reaching her goal of a sixty-second PSA.

Consider the Technology

When working with designers, ask them to consider the affordances and purpose of the technology they might want to use. Why are they using a particular technical or digital tool? Using a technology tool just because it is available or is the latest trend is not a good reason to select it: the technology chosen should enhance and support the delivery of the message and the purpose of the PSA.

There is no need for consultants to be tech experts—if questions come up of a technical nature, the important thing is to know where to send students to get technical support on campus. Rather than try to become experts in technology, writing center consultants do better to route technical needs to staff trained in those areas. That said, it's worth noting that when students and consultants keep design principles and rhetorical strategies in mind, the end message is clear, focused, and effective regardless of the technology used.

Translate the Verbal to the Visual

Once the outline or storyboard has been developed, the script written, and the sources and assets gathered, it is time to assemble the elements into a cohesive whole. While many students are comfortable with assembling and editing media files, and many have had some grounding in taking a rhetorical approach to the development of messages, others are unfamiliar with the tools, rhetorical elements, and design principles essential during this process; at this stage, they might turn to the writing center for help. Experienced consultants recommend that designers pay attention to the medium and the content of the message. Is it successful in communicating the message? Logan Coney says, "Probably most of my time spent in a session, after going through how a multimodal looks, is spent helping a student reduce their content down to a manageable level" (pers. comm.).

At times, designers bring in a draft of a PSA and ask for feedback. Regardless of the mode of the PSA, understanding visual and aural design principles helps consultants provide feedback and suggestions in harmony with the principles of visual analysis and aural analysis. Visual analysis examines the way the concepts of figure-ground contrast, grouping, and color are used (see this collection's introduction), while audio analysis notes the ways the layers of sound and the pitch, rate, and intensity of voice and delivery are used in support of the message.

ACTIVITY: A PSA CONSULTANT-EDUCATION WORKSHOP

This workshop offers consultants an opportunity to gain familiarity with the genre of PSAs by analyzing PSAs and using the strategies detailed in the sections above. This workshop has three stages: analyzing PSAs, creating PSAs, and writing a reflection. Although it would be ideal to work through this activity with a group, you can adapt it to work through the exercises on your own.

Analyze PSAs

In this guided analysis, we begin with a static image and then move progressively via audio only to a more complex composition. Let's begin by reviewing this example of a static PSA:

http://www.adcouncil.org/Our-Campaigns/Family-Community/ Diversity-Inclusion ("Diversity and Inclusion").

Working in groups of three or four, discuss the following questions, and feel free to comment on aspects of the ad you find effective. Be prepared to share your conclusions with your fellow consultants.

- How does the PSA use figure-ground contrast? Grouping? Color?
- In what ways are the rhetorical appeals of *ethos, kairos, logos,* and *pathos* evident?
- Is the message effective? Why or why not? What would you change?

Next, let's listen to and analyze an audio example from the Radio Space website, a good source of audio PSAs: http://www.radiospace .com/sepsa.htm ("Public Service").

Again, we can use the questions and strategies introduced earlier in this chapter to discuss the effectiveness of the PSA.

- How does the PSA use layers of sound (foreground/middle ground/ background)?
- In what ways are the rhetorical appeals of *ethos, kairos, logos,* and *pathos* evident?
- Is the message effective? Why or why not? What would you change?

Now, let's view a multimodal PSA on domestic violence: https:// youtu.be/5Z_zWIVRIWk ("Super Bowl"). Discuss these questions:

- How does the PSA use figure-ground contrast? Grouping? Color?
- How does the PSA use layers of sound (foreground/middle ground/ background)?
- In what ways are the rhetorical appeals of *ethos, kairos, logos,* and *pathos* evident?

- How are the six design elements of the meaning-making process—linguistic, visual, audio, gestural, spatial, multimodal—at work in this PSA?
- Is the message effective? Why or why not? What would you change?

Create PSAs

Now that you have looked at these three examples, create a sixty-second PSA for your writing or multiliteracy center. Your PSA might provide tips for writers, explain common writing misunderstandings, share interesting facts about writing, or help writers understand writing situations and genres. Consider whether your PSA will be static, audio only, or video.

- What story do you want to tell about your center? What aspect of your center will you highlight?
- Who is your target audience?
- How will you use figure-ground contrast? Grouping? Color?
- How will you layer sound (foreground/middle ground/background)?
- How will you use the six design elements of the meaning-making process—linguistic, visual, audio, gestural, spatial, multimodal—in this PSA?

Once you have created your PSA, share it with another group or consultant for feedback. Discuss your rhetorical and design choices. Was your intended message received?

Reflection

Now that you have had opportunity to explore and create PSAs, reflect in writing on the following:

- How does this genre make use of the rhetorical strategies of *ethos, logos, kairos,* and *pathos*?
- In what ways do the rhetorical modes (textual, verbal, gestural, spatial, aural, visual) and appeals (*ethos, logos, pathos,* sense of *kairos*) combine to make meaning for audiences?
- What did you learn from these activities about the purpose of a PSA analysis? About a multimodal analysis in general?
- Based on analyzing and creating PSAs, what questions would you have for student designers? How do your experiences help you provide feedback on PSAs?

CONCLUSION

In discussing the rhetorical work of multimedia production practices, Jennifer Sheppard (2009) notes that instead of viewing multimedia as "just technical skill," we should pay "careful attention to practices of production [in order to] demonstrate the critical negotiations writers/ designers must undertake as they compose multimedia texts" (122). As seen in this chapter, effective PSAs certainly include attention to such rhetorical elements as audience, purpose, and context; however, in line with Sheppard's argument and keeping in mind that the outcome of a successful PSA will be "comprehension of the text," special attention must be given to the rhetorical choices PSA composers make, choices that are specific to the genre (123). These rhetorical choices require "diverse and significant literacies," and multimodal consultants will assist students beginning or analyzing such projects in understanding the complexities of designing the tightly focused and specific messages required of the PSA genre (123).

ACKNOWLEDGEMENTS

I am most grateful to the University of Mississippi writing center consultants who took the time to talk with me about helping students with multimodal compositions, including PSAs. Thank you, Sam Briete, Logan Coney, Adrienne Lay, Alix Moody, and Dana Repel!

RESOURCES

The resources in this section provide further background information on the genre of public service announcements; example PSAs; scholarship considering audience, visuals, and sound; and tools to create PSAs.

Background and History of the Genre
Dessart, George. 2016. "Public Service Announcements." *Museum of Broadcast Communications.* http://www.museum.tv/eotv/publicservic.htm.
Goodwill, Bill. 2010. "Public Service Advertising—Background and Future." PSA Research Center. www.psaresearch.com/bib9830.html.

PSA Examples and Models
EPA—https://www.epa.gov/newsroom/public-service-announcements
"Prevent Asthma Symptoms PSA"—https://youtu.be/njy1ZqMmw3s
Audio—RadioSpace Public Service Announcements: http://www.radiospace.com/psa home.htm
Centers for Disease Control (CDC) website—search for PSAs; there are many!

Audience
Lunsford, Andrea A., and Lisa Ede. 2014. "Among the Audience: On Audience in an Age of New Literacies." In *The Routledge Reader on Writing Centers and New Media*, edited by Sohui Lee and Russell Carpenter, 194–209. New York: Routledge.

Sound

Selfe, Cynthia L. 2009. "The Movement of Air, the Breath of Meaning: Aurality and Multi-modal Composing." *College Composition and Communication* 60 (4): 616–63.

Resources: Assets and Technology

Creative Commons—https://search.creativecommons.org/
Audacity™—http://www.audacityteam.org/
GarageBand™—https://itunes.apple.com/us/app/garageband/id408709785?mt=8

Visual Analysis

"Assignment Analysis" on the Excelsior OWL website: http://owl.excelsior.edu/research
-and-citations/assignment-analysis/
Hacker, Diana, and Danielle N. DeVoss. 2015. *Understanding and Composing Multimodal Projects*. Boston, MA: Bedford/St. Martin's.
Purdue OWL—https://owl.english.purdue.edu/owl/resource/725/01/

KEY SEARCH TERMS

design principles; public service announcements; PSAs; target audience; tagline

REFERENCES

Arola, Kristin L., Jennifer Sheppard, and Cheryl E. Ball. 2014. *Writer/Designer: A Guide to Making Multimodal Projects*. Boston, MA: Bedford/St. Martin's.
"PSA Samples: Causes of Asthma PSA." 2018. Salo Productions. *Saloproductions.com/public -service-announcements/psa-samples.*
"Diversity and Inclusion." N.d. Ad Council. http://www.adcouncil.org/Our-Campaigns /Family-Community/Diversity-Inclusion.
"80s Anti-Drug Commercial: This Is Your Brain on Drugs." 1987. YouTube video, 0:14. Posted September 16. https://www.youtube.com/watch?v=3FtNm9CgA6U.
Goodwill, Bill. 2010. "Public Service Advertising—Background and Future." PSA Research Center. www.psaresearch.com/bib9830.html.
"Michael Jordan Anti-Drug PSA 1987." 1987. YouTube video, 1:01. Posted February 4. https://youtu.be/rb8z2BMrd60.
"Prevent Asthma Symptoms PSA." 2010. YouTube video, 1:01. Posted February 25. https:// www.youtube.com/watch?time_continue=16&v=njy1ZqMmw3s.
"Public Service Announcements from Snowball Express." N.d. RadioSpace. http://www .radiospace.com/sepsa.htm.
Sheppard, Jennifer. 2009. "The Rhetorical Work of Multimedia Production Practices: It's More than Just Technical Skill." *Computers and Composition* 26 (2): 122–31.
"Super Bowl 2015: Domestic Violence PSA." 2015. YouTube video, 1:00. Posted January 27. https://youtu.be/5Z_zWIVRIWk.
"2016 Habitat for Humanity Public Service Announcement." 2016. YouTube video, 0:30. Posted September 15. https://youtu.be/SSVuN0tLJ84.
Video Archeology. 2014. "Only You can Prevent Forest Fires (Ad Council PSA)." https:// youtu.be/1LI81cWh3Fs?t=53s.

13

PROFESSIONAL IDENTITY AND SOCIAL MEDIA
Consulting Personal Branding Projects

James C. W. Truman

Auburn University

CHAPTER OVERVIEW

Writing centers see a great deal of job-related writing. Students bring in CVs, resumés, job letters, and especially personal statements to get feedback on how best to represent themselves to the world beyond the university as a future professional, a future graduate student, or whatever their goals might be. As part of this support for job-related writing, your writing center is likely to see writers using the idea of personal branding as way to position themselves on the job market. This might be an approach writers discover on their own, or their career center or advisor might direct them to it, or this might be a concept used in a class assignment. This chapter offers consultants information on personal branding elements and social media so they can help writers consider effective, holistic choices about their own personal branding.

ILLUSTRATIVE EXAMPLE: WRITING CENTERS, JOB-MARKET WRITING, AND PERSONAL BRANDING

Last semester, Karen, an undergraduate in a marketing class, brought an assignment to write a reflective essay to the writing center—she was scheduled to work with Sayler, a graduate student in the English Department. When Sayler asked why she was writing this reflective essay, she said it was part of her semester-long personal branding project and that it was to be posted to LinkedIn Pulse. While personal statements are very familiar to our consultants, the idea of a personal brand is generally not. Fortunately, Sayler had been introduced to the notion of personal branding in a web-design class in her master's in technical and professional communications program. Since she had been developing

DOI: 10.7330/9781607328469.c013

materials to build a message about her own personal brand that would be focused, clear, and consistent across multiple genres and multiple media, she was able to help Karen see that this reflective writing project was more than just a story to be posted on LinkedIn. Sayler was able to coach her in developing a coherent, cross-media approach, and she was able to support Karen as she made effective choices in relation to the larger project.

This broad perspective of integrating texts into a single, synchronized message is the core of personal branding; short, easily consumable texts, from logos, to biographies, to social media posts, to long-form reflective essays, work together to project a consistent message about the individual, their skills, the work they do, and the value they add to those with whom they work.

BACKGROUND INFORMATION: WHAT IS PERSONAL BRANDING?

The concept of personal branding emerged in the late 1990s as a holistic approach for individuals to control their public representation as professionals. We're all familiar with how the concept of corporate branding works; since the middle of the twentieth century, corporate brands like Coke, Pepsi, Nike, McDonald's, Starbucks, and so forth have been ubiquitous presences across the globe (Pendergrast 2013). However, these brands are more than simple images and catch phrases. A brand is a series of strategic rhetorical choices made in the construction of texts in multiple media that creates a consistent message about who the corporation is and what it does. Pepsi is a recognizable tricolored sphere logo, a catch phrase emphasizing youth (in the 60s "Come Alive, You're in the Pepsi Generation," in the 80s "The Choice of a New Generation," and in the late 90s "For Those Who Think Young"), and consistent messaging following the theme of youthful activity ("Pepsi" 2012). Personal branding as a concept takes this visual, textual, and thematically driven approach and applies it to individuals—most visible in celebrity brands like Oprah or Ellen, all recognizable by one name alone (Lair, Sullivan, and Cheney 2005; Shepherd 2005).

Personal branding is now almost ubiquitous in the corporate world (Gershbein 2015). But even academics have started to see personal branding as a useful mechanism for communicating their work. Kelly Marshall's (2017) column in *Vitae*, "Branding Yourself as an Academic," provides insight into the benefits of extending your reach through personal branding. At our writing center (and I speculate at many others), we don't necessarily see ourselves as being experts in how to communicate with specific potential employers—nor are we experts in the specific forms of professional writing. We do not see ourselves as replacing people who have deep knowledge of the genres of CVs, resumés, or job letters, as well as familiarity with job markets, employer expectations, and the variety of codes in play across the professions. We often collaborate with our university's Office of Career Services to do cross training with our staffs to ensure we are communicating with the professionals who do have this expertise.

Nevertheless, with the plethora of information out there framing the idea of personal branding, the thoughtful guidance of a consultant becomes even more useful. Personal branding has many elements, with experts coming from multiple angles, and there are plenty of books and online resources available to help students make choices (see the "Resources" section of this chapter). So much information can make it hard for a writer to figure out where to start. So, from a writing center point of view, we can boil down the core elements of personal branding to a few subgenres that can help the writers you're working with gain traction. These are not, of course, the only ways to be engaging with personal branding, but they can be useful to help a writer focus on the choices they need to make.

The Personal Branding Statement

One of the most fundamental elements of personal branding is communicating core information about oneself to an audience, and the short, one-sentence personal branding statement can help writers do this—as much as a person can say in "one out-breath," as recommended by the Undercover Recruiter ("7 Rules" 2016). The personal branding statement can be broken down into three elements:

- First, *you* are your brand—you want to communicate what makes you unique or stand out. This seems simple, but finding an authentic, substantive way to define yourself can take some deep reflective, introspective work.
- Second, you are asserting that you can *do* something for your audience, that you can add value; as Peter Montoya (2003) writes, "Your brand is a promise" (5).
- Third, you are addressing the *context* in which you will deliver that promise. This includes the limits of the audience you are addressing, as well as the other defining elements of the context—the field of work, a geographic region, or other setting or situation.

The Undercover Recruiter offers a particularly clear example of a personal branding statement from an HVAC salesman in Edinburgh,

Scotland: "John keeps families in Edinburgh warm through bespoke heating installations using only the most advanced German boilers" ("How to Craft" 2016). John clearly articulates his context (in terms of audience, "families," and geographic location, "Edinburgh"), the promise of value ("keeps families. . . . warm") and what's specifically unique about what he does ("bespoke heating installations using only the most advanced German boilers"). As the article notes, "This clearly tells you what John does, for whom and gives you an insight into how. I would say the statement is memorable, I for one think of a family keeping warm and snug over Christmas all thanks to the fantastic boiler man John."

Slogan versus Personal branding Statement

The personal branding statement is usefully distinguished from a slogan, though a statement can be usefully transformed into one. A slogan is designed to communicate your message in an even more concise form (like the US Army's classic slogan "Be All You Can Be"). Generally, your slogan should focus on what you *do*, not be too clever, and be under nine words long. (Montoya 2003, 117–18)

The Personal Logo/Graphical Icon

The most familiar element of any corporate branding is, of course, the visual graphic element (the term *branding* does come from the physical, visual marking of cattle and other livestock). When you think Pepsi, you immediately remember the globe graphic. So, for a personal branding project, you might be helping a writer develop their own personal logo, or graphical icon, to accompany their branding statement, slogan, or other materials. Montoya (2003) advises against images (especially photographs) that risk becoming clichéd (114). Generally, the best practice is for a logo to emerge from the writer's name or initials, framed creatively; a Google search for *personal branding logo* will confirm that. The fundamental design principle of less is more is usefully applied here, along with the design principles from the introduction to this collection.

Personal logo example. Sayler Hasty, our consultant from the illustrative example, developed her own personal logo as part of a web-design class. In figure 13.1, you can see how she used her initials as the primary visual, with an enclosing circle to give the logo a sense of boundary and structure, and that she added another element (the vertical arrows) to add balance and directional energy. She chose her colors, the aquamarine/blue-and-black contrast, to represent strength and focus, appropriate to her goal of moving into business/higher education

*Figure 13.1. Sayler Hasty's personal
logo (2016)*

administration. Hasty's personal logo can also be viewed in color at www
.multimodalwritingcenter.org. Her choice of a serif font, with its classical
tone, fit into her personal story of having completed an MA in literature,
for which she wrote a thesis on Victorian literature, before her technical
writing master's. Thus, her icon pulled together her personal experience and the administrative and technical work to which she saw herself
moving. In addition, Sayler most definitely followed the less-is-more
dictum to great effect.

Sayler did not, of course, create this image spontaneously but worked
with her colleagues at the writing center and in workshops to develop
this concise, yet not simple, personal logo. Asking consultants to develop
such a logo can be a useful training activity (see below).

Social Media

While personal branding existed before social media, a strong social
media presence is fundamental to personal branding (Tombrakos
2012). The world of social media changes very quickly—Vine was once
thriving, and then it was gone and is now just a memory, along with
MySpace and Second Life. But regardless of the platform being used,
what is relevant is that writers consider that what they're composing on
that platform will be read by multiple audiences, and the writer must
consider how each post participates in building a perception of them
as an individual, regardless of intent. Whatever writers post, wherever
they post it, they must be consistent with their brand choices since over
90 percent of employers use social media as part of their hiring process
(Jobvite 2013). Writers who have multiple social media platforms should

make sure a consistent brand is represented across all the platforms. As Joanne Tombrakos (2014) writes in "10 Reasons You Need a Digital You," "The line is increasingly blurred between professional you and personal you." Writing center consultants can help writers be aware not just of what *not* to post but also of how to craft thoughtful social media content that promotes a professional brand. While this process might be different across platforms, for clarity's purpose, I will focus only on strategies for managing LinkedIn.

LinkedIn: Of all the social media platforms, LinkedIn is the most important platform for personal branding. My colleague Emory Serviss, who teaches marketing at Auburn University's Harbert School Business School, calls a LinkedIn account the "table stakes" of personal branding; if you don't have a LinkedIn account, you're not in the personal branding game.[1] Helping a writer make thoughtful choices about how they represent themselves on LinkedIn is one of the most important things a consultant can do to support writers' personal branding projects. LinkedIn is not just about filling in basic information and picking a flattering headshot (though that is, of course, part of it).

LinkedIn summary statement: LinkedIn offers the opportunity to craft a biographical statement; in crafting this document, the writing center consultant is usually at their most comfortable. The LinkedIn summary statement is the biographical component of the profile that can let the writer extend their personal branding statement in rich and thoughtful ways and deepen their personal brand. LinkedIn even publishes examples of summary statements consultants can use to help writers think creatively about their statement. The "Resources" section at the end of this chapter provides information about these examples and links to a number of helpful articles.

LinkedIn Pulse: LinkedIn also offers a space for long-form blog posts, LinkedIn Pulse. This space provides a very useful opportunity for students to articulate an in-depth reflective essay that tells the story of who they are, what they can do, and why they should be able to do it. Writing center consultants are usually very comfortable working with long-form reflective thinking. We often support students to deepen their critical thinking about the message they are putting forth to employers and to graduate schools in job letters, resumés, and personal statements, all of which are much more than a simple articulation of their experiences.

These documents are an opportunity for the writer to reflect upon the work they've done and to synthesize their experiences into a coherent story that represents the best "intellectual autobiography" they can. This is high-level critical thinking, which is why employers and graduate schools ask for such materials as part of their evaluation process; they are not interested just in someone's ability to list their accomplishments but also in their ability to represent the depth of their critical thinking about those accomplishments. This genre has a lot to do within the limited forms of job letters, resumés, and personal statements. So, we help writers do this difficult intellectual work by asking fundamental questions:

- Who is the *you* you're representing here?
- What are the details that will *show* your audience this version of you?
- What does this version of *you* bring to the community you're looking to join?

This reflective process is usually more difficult than writers want to admit—but it can be transformative, and this is the work writing centers can be very effective at helping writers work through as they develop their own brand for professional and graduate-school applications.

CONSULTATION STRATEGIES FOR PERSONAL BRANDING ON SOCIAL MEDIA

Analyze Writers' Current Social Media Presence

Consultants can help writers think carefully about their social media presence, especially in terms of their professional identity online. In some cases, students might not have spent much time or effort developing a professional identity on social media. Consultants can discuss the importance of students' examining their social media presence with a professional eye. There are ways to separate private and personal life from public and professional life online, and thinking carefully about what information about them is widely available can help an individual begin to consider which aspects they choose to share in different online contexts, thereby creating their personal brand.

Help Writers Reflect on Their Brand

One important way to help students focus on their personal brands is to help them reflect on their experiences in productive ways. These questions can help consultants guide a writer:

- *Who are you? What makes you stand out?* Consultants can engage students in a conversation about their interests and concerns. Helping students determine what they represent as a person and/or a professional offers them an opportunity to articulate abilities, values, characteristics, and skills that make them stand out.

- *What's your promise?* We all have something to contribute, and consultants can talk to writers about what they can deliver for their coworkers and colleagues. Ask writers, What do you do? What value do you add?
- *What's the context?* As many chapters in this book address, context is everything. Helping writers think about the boundaries of what they do is just as important as helping them think about what they can promise. Consultants can urge writers to think about audience and the expectations of their fields or disciplines.

Get Beyond Clichés

Consultants might want to explore more specific, or achievable, ways of thinking about individualism. David Rendall (2015) urges people to get in tune with their "freak factor," which might seem like a risky term to use, but it's about making what might seem like a weakness into a strength. Taking this approach can help writers think creatively about developing their statements by getting a sense of what makes them unique.

Designing a Personal Logo

As Jackie Grutsch McKinney (2009) argues, consultants work to help students "read through" visuals to be able to make rhetorical choices about multimodal texts. We encourage consultants to talk through what they are seeing in a writer's design choices (or to have the writers talk through their own choices), which is analogous to reading a traditional alphabetic essay aloud, to help students think about their multimodal documents as full text. Through this process, consultants can help writers think about *why* they are choosing particular colors, forms, and fonts. Even for a small icon, these choices are complicated, and small, seemingly insignificant choices can mean the difference between a perception of competence and a perception of amateurism.

ACTIVITY

Since the genres involved in personal branding are so short and so personal, one of the most straightforward ways for consultants to develop strategies for working on these projects is to do them. Sayler was able to work more effectively with Karen because of her experience thinking through her own branding strategies—this process can work for us all! The following activities can be done in the order they're presented or on their own, and they focus on your identity as a consultant. If you haven't had much experience with your own personal branding, I recommend working your way through each activity.

Meta-analysis of Your Own Social Media Message

Thinking about your current social media message and how it gets received across the different online landscapes can be useful in determining the direction you take your personal brand. This activity can be fun but also possibly a bit sobering as you discover what sort of message it might have been unintentionally sending.

1. Go back through your social media posts, analyze them through the eye of a professional audience, and reflect on the sort of brand you are presenting right now.
2. What did you notice? What message are you communicating?
3. Now that you have an idea of the brand you've established so far, what kinds of professional posts or content might you develop to shore up or counter that identity.

This process can be used as a first step in setting up your own professional LinkedIn pages, building your own professional posts, and developing content for Twitter, Instagram, or SnapChat—and whatever other social media platforms you occupy.

Practice Reflective Writing

Many consultants already have the experience of developing personal writing center philosophies or other reflective projects. The tools of personal reflection (and the strategies developed while workshopping these projects) are easily transferable to helping students with the core reflective thinking used to generate both the shorter personal branding genres and the longer in-depth reflective texts. What is your tutoring philosophy, and how does it inform your consultations with writers? How did you come to this philosophy? How does this philosophy serve to situate you professionally as a consultant?

Build Your Own Personal-Brand Statement

Begin thinking creatively about how to consider the idea of your own uniqueness, of your promise of value, and of the context in which and the audience to whom you're offering that value. Consider how your own professional goals and personal brand will inform you as you move forward in your academic and professional careers.

Develop your own tutoring brand. What sort of role do you play as a consultant, what are your strengths when working with writers, and what are you able to deliver for writers?

1. Break down your tutoring brand before building the personal brand statement as a consultant:
   a. What's your context?
   b. What's your promise of value?
   c. What's specifically unique about what you do?
2. Transform your answers to these three questions into a concise yet meaningful statement.
3. Consider asking another consultant to workshop your ideas to practice developing useful questions about difficult issues like uniqueness.

These brand statements can be included on your consultant biography page on the website or WCOnline, or they can be published in other ways as part of your center's outreach, which can add real value to your center.

Design Your Own Logo

Along with (or instead of) the personal branding statement, you can design (with paper and pencil or digitally) your own visual logo. As you move your work to a visual format, meet with a consultant to discuss how your visual branding choices are conceptually connected to your personal branding statement. Consider the following:

- What are you trying to communicate visually?
- How will the colors, fonts, and images advance the message of your statement?

As you use the strategies discussed in this chapter to think about designing your own logo, it is also useful to consider the Gestalt principles discussed in many chapters in this collection and to consider Shawn Apostel's quick-and-dirty pathos strategies.

CONCLUSION

Personal branding is a challenge, primarily because it produces an illusion of simplicity. That simplicity leads people to believe there is a clear set of guidelines for building your brand; just look at the large number of publications with "listicles" with titles like "7 Steps to the Perfect

Personal Brand." However, as JD Gershbein (2014) says, "An extraordinary personal brand is not achieved in cookbook fashion. There is no system of absolutes, no cookie-cutter methodology." Your primary work as a consultant will likely be to help the writer get beyond their first impulse to see the *concision* of personal branding (the *compactness* of the genre and the *unity* of message) and confuse that concision with *simplicity*. Personal branding is a constellation of texts and practices, and it is *holistic* and *synergistic* in that it is greater than the sum of its parts. Your work will be, as with many consultations, to ask probing questions, to challenge assumptions made by the writer, and to play a skeptical audience member who will not take simplicity at face value. The strategies above should help you play that role more effectively.

Finally, remember there are multiple resources that are constantly changing available on the internet—a simple Google search will find many creative tools to help a writer make choices about representing their personal brand. For example, in December of 2016, *Forbes* published two columns by William Arruda (2016; 2017) titled "2017 Personal Branding Trends Part 1: The Death of Text" and "Part 2: The Proliferation of the Free Agent." This constantly changing landscape of best practices might help writers assess the lay of the land when it comes to personal branding at any given moment. Expectations might be changing, and you might need to help the writer read those different resources actively (only a few of which I have discussed here) and make informed, reasoned choices based on that field of knowledge. There is a lot to work with, which means a great opportunity for creative collaboration.

RESOURCES

Since there's so much constantly being produced about personal branding (this list is only a small percentage of what's available through a simple Google search), these resources will likely be out of date quite soon. But they are a useful starting point for helping writers navigate the expectations of their audience and the different choices for crafting these different genres, and I've included lists of search terms to help you find the most current resources available.

Personal Branding Statement

Hard-Copy Text Resources

Beckwith, Harry, and Christine Clifford Beckwith. 2007. *You, Inc.: The Art of Selling Yourself.* New York: Grand Central.

Chritton, Susan. 2014. *Personal Branding for Dummies.* Hoboken, NJ: John Wiley & Sons.

Kang, Karen. 2013. *Branding Pays: The Five-Step System to Reinvent Your Personal Brand*. Branding-Pays Media.

McNally, David, and Karl D. Speak. 2004. *Be Your Own Brand*. San Francisco, CA: Berrett-Koehler.

Montoya, Peter. 2003. *The Brand Called You: The Ultimate Brand-Building and Business Development Handbook to Transform Anyone into an Indispensable Personal Brand*. Peter Montoya Incorporated.

Online Text Resources

"How to Craft Your Personal Brand Statement." N.d. Undercover Recruiter. http://theundercoverrecruiter.com/how-craft-your-personal-brand-statement/.

Lake, Laura. 2017. "How to Write Your Personal Branding Statement." Last modified June 10. The Balance Small Business. https://www.thebalance.com/how-to-write-your-personalbranding-statement-2295809.

Locke, Abby. 2011. "Capture Your Personal Brand in One Sentence." Ladders. https://www.theladders.com/career-advice/capture-personal-brand-one-sentence/.

Marshall, Kelli. 2017. "Branding Yourself as an Academic." Chronicle *Vitae*. https://chroniclevitae.com/news/1681-branding-yourself-as-an-academic?cid=at&utm_source=at&utm_medium=en&elqTrackId=95c042d61d7e4eea84a31dc2775d3e08&elq=bb6a2bd767c143fe9cacbcf3fcd01638&elqaid=12364&elqat=1&elqCampaignId=5024.

"The 7 Rules of Effective Personal Brand Statements." N.d. Undercover Recruiter. http://theundercoverrecruiter.com/7-rules-effective-personal-brand-statements/.

Personal Branding Logo

Carson, Nick, and David Airy. 2017. "Logo Design: Everything You Need to Know." Creative Bloq. http://www.creativebloq.com/graphic-design/pro-guide-logo-design-21221.

Gendelman, Vladimir. 2015. "200+ Best Personal Logo Design Examples for Inspiration." Company Folders. http://www.companyfolders.com/blog/200-cool-personal-logo-designs-for-inspiration.

Johnson, Joshua. 2013. "10 Tips for Designing Logos That Don't Suck." Design Shack. https://designshack.net/articles/inspiration/10-tips-for-designing-logos-that-dont-suck/.

Stribley, Mary. N.d. "Personal Branding: How to Design Your Personal Brand Image In 10 Steps [Cheat Sheet]." Canva. Retrieved October 27, 2017. https://designschool.canva.com/blog/personalbranding/.

LinkedIn Summary Statement and LinkedIn Pulse

Conner, Cheryl. 2015. "Read This First, Before You Publish a Post on LinkedIn." *Forbes*. http://www.forbes.com/sites/cherylsnappconner/2015/11/25/read-this-first-before-you-post-on-linkedin/#439036965340.

Guiseppi, Meg. N.d. "Personal Branding Makes Your LinkedIn Summary Dazzle." *Job-Hunt*. Accessed January 31, 2017. https://www.job-hunt.org/personalbranding/branded-linkedin-summary.shtml.

Reilly, Kate. 2016. "7 LinkedIn Profile Summaries That We Love (And How to Boost Your Own)." *LinkedIn Talent Blog*. April 21. https://business.linkedin.com/talent-solutions/blog/linkedin-best-practices/2016/7-linkedin-profile-summaries-that-we-love-and-how-to-boost-your-own.

Smith, Jacquelyn. 2014. "Here's What to Say in Your LinkedIn 'Summary' Statement." *Business Insider*. http://www.businessinsider.com/what-to-say-in-your-linkedin-summary-statement-2014-12.

Stec, Caryl. 2016. "How to Publish on LinkedIn Pulse: A Beginner's Guide." *HubSpot (blog)*, January 7. https://blog.hubspot.com/marketing/linkedin-publishing-beginner-guide #sm.0000rg1qvzokecy810o15jls6gbdy.

Social Media

Tolliday, Daniel. 2015. "How to Use Social Media to Build Your Personal Brand." Social Media Examiner. http://www.socialmediaexaminer.com/use-social-media-to-build -your-personal-brand/.

Tombrakos, Joanne. 2012. "7 Reasons You Need a Vibrant Digital Profile." *Forbes*. http:// www.forbes.com/sites/85broads/2012/11/30/7-reasons-you-need-a-vibrant-digital -profile/#53008aab4e90.

Tombrakos, Joanne. 2014. "10 Reasons You Need a Digital You." Huffington Post. http:// www.huffingtonpost.com/joanne-tombrakos/10-plus-reasons-you-need_b_5272970 .html.

Van Dijck, José. 2013. "'You Have One Identity': Performing the Self on Facebook and LinkedIn." *Media, Culture & Society* 35 (2): 199–215.

KEY SEARCH TERMS

*(You can use **brand** or **branding** to get different results.)*

personal branding statement; personal branding statement versus slogan; personal brand taglines; creating personal brand; personal logo design tips; personal branding LinkedIn strategies; LinkedIn personal branding playbook; LinkedIn personal branding examples; personal brand social media; personal social media strategy; personal branding through social media

NOTE

1.   I am indebted to Professor Serviss's expertise and suggestions for this project. Professor Serviss teaches MKTG 3010, which involves an extended LinkedIn-based personal branding project. He has forgotten more than I will ever know about personal branding, and I am thankful for his advice, wisdom, and resources as I developed this chapter.

REFERENCES

Arruda, William. 2016. "2017 Personal Branding Trends Part 1: The Death of Text." *Forbes*, December 21. http://www.forbes.com/sites/williamarruda/2016/12/18/2017-person albranding-trends-part-1-the-death-of-text/#a5a50b324e4f.

Arruda, William. 2017. "2017 Personal Branding Trends Part 2: The Proliferation of the Free Agent." *Forbes*, January 03. http://www.forbes.com/sites/williamarruda/2016/12 /20/2017-personalbranding-trends-2017-part-2-the-proliferation-of-the-free-agent /#12b7dfd5b084.

Gershbein, JD. 2014. "Please, No More Advice on Building My Personal Brand." *Forbes*, June 15. http://www.forbes.com/sites/groupthink/2014/06/15/please-no-more -advice-on-building-my-personal-brand/#225d36e13176.

"How to Craft Your Personal Brand Statement." 2016. Undercover Recruiter. http://theundercoverrecruiter.com/how-craft-your-personal-brand-statement/.

Lair, Daniel J., Katie Sullivan, and George Cheney. 2005. "Marketization and the Recasting of the Professional Self: The Rhetoric and Ethics of Personal Branding." *Management Communication Quarterly* 18 (3): 307–43.

Marshall, Kelli. 2017. "Branding Yourself as an Academic." ChronicleVitae. https://chronicle vitae.com/news/1681-branding-yourself-as-an-academic?cid=at&utm_source= at&utm_medium=en&elqTrackId=95c042d61d7e4eea84a31dc2775d3e08&elq= bb6a2bd767c143fe9cacbcf3fcd01638&elqaid=12364&elqat=1&elqCampaignId=5024.

McKinney, Jackie Grutsch. 2009. "New Media Matters: Tutoring in the Late Age of Print." *Writing Center Journal* 29 (2): 28–51.

Montoya, Peter. 2003. *The Brand Called You: The Ultimate Brand-Building and Business Development Handbook to Transform Anyone into an Indispensable Personal Brand.* Peter Montoya Incorporated.

Pendergrast, Mark. 2013. *For God, Country, and Coca-Cola.* New York: Basic Books.

"Pepsi Slogans and Logos Throughout the Years." 2012. G&M Distributors. https://gmdist .com/blog/pepsi-slogans-and-logos-throughout-the-years/.

Rendall, David J. 2015. *The Freak Factor: Discovering Uniqueness by Flaunting Weakness.* Charleston, SC: Advantage.

"The 7 Rules of Effective Personal Brand Statements." 2016. Undercover Recruiter. http://theundercoverrecruiter.com/7-rules-effective-personal-brand-statements/.

Shepherd, Ifan. 2005. "From Cattle and Coke to Charlie: Meeting the Challenge of Self Marketing and Personal Branding." *Journal of Marketing Management* 21 (5–6): 589–606.

"Social Recruiting Survey Results." 2013. Jobvite. http://web.jobvite.com/rs/jobvite/ima ges/Jobvite_2013_SocialRecruitingSurveyResults.pdf.

Tombrakos, Joanne. 2012. "7 Reasons You Need A Vibrant Digital Profile." *Forbes.* http://www.forbes.com/sites/85broads/2012/11/30/7-reasons-you-need-a-vibrant-digital -profile/#53008aab4e90.

Tombrakos, Joanne. 2014. "10 Reasons You Need a Digital You." Huffington Post. http://www.huffingtonpost.com/joanne-tombrakos/10-plus-reasons-you-need_b_5272970 .html.

14

COPYRIGHT AND CITATIONS FOR MULTIMEDIA SOURCES

Molly Schoen and Sarah Blazer
Fashion Institute of Technology, SUNY

CHAPTER OVERVIEW

This chapter discusses how students can ethically incorporate images, videos, and other multimedia materials into their work. Topics discussed include attribution, copyright, fair use, and finding multimedia resources. Consultants can use examples and strategies provided to help students practice small changes toward more responsible multimodal composing.

ILLUSTRATIVE EXAMPLE: THE MENSWEAR MYSTERY, CREATIVE INFLUENCES, AND ETHICAL ATTRIBUTION

For six months, Sarah walked past an exhibit outside FIT's Writing Studio, struck by an image embedded in a menswear student's rendering of his collection. This image looked just like the work of an artist named Yellena James, whom Sarah had discovered on Etsy a few years before. In fact, Sarah had two of her pieces hanging in her living room. But there was no credit to James on the work hanging in the glass case, and Sarah felt sure the student had copied or appropriated James's work. When the opportunity came up to work with Molly on this chapter, Sarah learned how she could solve the mystery. Using reverse image searching, a process we explain later in the chapter, she took a photo of the image through the glass case and uploaded it to Google Images. Our search of the photo alone did not yield results from James's work, but it did lead Sarah to a blog entry the menswear student wrote in which he posted the same images, this time with the note "Based on a series of paintings by Yellana [*sic*] James."

Mystery solved—for the most part. We were heartened to see the student credited James's work when he posted his designs publicly. But we then had other questions. Why did the professor who chose to put

DOI: 10.7330/9781607328469.c014

it on display not ask this student—or any other student whose work was exhibited—to attribute influences? Looking at the student's illustrations more closely on his blog, we realized these works hadn't just inspired the student; parts of James's works had been copied and depicted as prints on several garments. Did the professor know the image wasn't the student's own? Did James know?

The menswear mystery raises questions about how writing center consultants can and do encourage and motivate students to cite images and other multimedia material *even* when their professors do not request or prioritize it. What might have happened if a consultant working with this student to prepare his final presentation on the collection had discussed with him the need to attribute his image sources? Would it have led to a realization that the student actually copied another artist's work? Might there have been an opportunity for the student to imagine himself in James's position—his work unduly appropriated by another artist?

Finally, if greater awareness and knowledge about fair use and copyright prompts consultants to raise issues professors are not raising, writing center directors can initiate campus-wide conversation about fair use and copyright so faculty do their part to inform and encourage students about the ethical use of multimedia materials.

BACKGROUND INFORMATION

More than ever, students are incorporating multimedia elements into their assignments. From videos in blog posts to high-resolution images in PowerPoint presentations and audio clips in online portfolios, multimodal elements can yield more dynamic, engaging work. Students, in general, and those in art and design fields in particular, are becoming more adept at finding, using, and creating audiovisual content. Just as attribution and copyright are important when borrowing text, they are also important factors to consider when using images, video, and audio. Yet many students do not know when copyright issues come into play, nor do they know how to properly cite copyrighted materials (Muriel-Torrado and Fernández-Molina 2015). Even citation manuals can be vague in these areas, as new media formats and platforms emerge rapidly.

Fortunately, because of fair-use laws in the United States, students (and educators) may incorporate others' intellectual property into their academic work without permission, so long as credit is given. Just as with quoting text in a paper, a citation is needed, but explicit permission from the publisher is not. So, why should students bother learning about copyright at all? Here are a few important reasons:

- Knowing the basics of copyright improves the quality of student work because students can provide thorough credit lines to outside sources used.
- Not *all* uses of copyrighted work are acceptable in the academic sphere, so a student should be able to distinguish what's allowable and what isn't.
- A basic awareness of copyright enables students to better safeguard their own original work against unauthorized uses.

Many students go on to have professional careers in fields impacted by copyright laws, such as art and design, journalism, science, and advertising. In order to best be prepared for their futures, a rudimentary understanding of intellectual property is essential.

INCORPORATING MULTIMEDIA MATERIALS

Because intellectual-property issues are often very complex, a consultant is better off knowing where to *find* helpful resources rather than trying to *know* everything there is to know about copyright.

Students might not even realize images or videos must be credited. Social media sites from Twitter to Pinterest make image and video sharing so simple many do not consider the implications of what they're doing: republishing someone else's original work. For example, posting a photo of a magazine spread on Instagram might be considered acceptable for casual uses (Wang 2015), but it can also be unethical. Neglecting to include information about a work is a disservice to others who might be interested in it and leaves its creator without recognition.

Social media blunders are one thing, but in academic and professional spheres, the stakes are higher. Neglecting to properly attribute an image or video might result in a lower grade or an accusation of plagiarism. If a student's use of copyrighted material is publicly shared, there is the risk of legal action from the work's copyright holder. Consider what might have happened in the case of the menswear student mentioned earlier.

Therefore, because not all students recognize all materials need to be credited, consultants should help catch unattributed photos, videos, or diagrams and explain to the student how and why they should be cited.

Fair Use

In the United States, fair use is a legal doctrine that allows limited use of copyrighted material without permission from the copyright holders.

(Other countries have similar laws called *fair dealing*). We experience fair use frequently in everyday life: from excerpts of novels in book reviews, to song parodies, to video clips in news broadcasts ("Fair Use"). Without fair use, permission would have to be obtained and royalties paid in these circumstances—an onerous burden that would diminish the quality of both culture and information in our society.

In the academic world, fair use comes into play to promote research and scholarship. It would be difficult for a film professor to teach a class without showing copyrighted works or for a biology teacher to teach without using scientific research and images. Fair use for students means they could share a complete copyrighted work, like a song or painting, in class but not in a public environment. For example, a student could use a Beatles song as the audio in a class video project but could face trouble if the video project were publicly posted to YouTube. However, smaller portions of a work—such as a short song clip or a small, low-resolution image of a sculpture—may be shared publicly, provided the use of that work favors at least two of the four factors of fair use, discussed below.

It should be noted that any original creative work or research is automatically copyrighted by its creator(s) (Harvard). One need not register a copyright for, say, a sculpture in order to maintain its status as intellectual property. If someone were to use photos of that sculpture without the artist's permission, though, the artist could most definitely take legal action. To determine whether use of someone else's intellectual property falls under fair use, there are four factors to consider.

1. *Purpose and character of the use.* Using copyrighted material for nonprofit, educational reasons demonstrates fair use. For example, say a student uses and cites images of contemporary art for an internship presentation at a museum. This could be considered fair use since the use of copyrighted images is for noncommercial reasons. A fashion brand's use of those same images in its advertisements would likely not be considered fair use because the images are used for profit.

   Modifying copyrighted material instead of copying it entirely also demonstrates fair use. Suppose students in an audio-engineering class are interested in overdubbing a clip of a nature video with a newly recorded narration. They intend to show off their completed work publicly on YouTube. Copying the original narration verbatim is not transformative, but writing a new script—perhaps a satire of the original—is. In order to be considered transformative, the modified work should make a new commentary in relation to the original work.

2. *Nature of the copyrighted work.* One has more leeway in using materials from factual works, such as a biography, than from a creative, expressive work, such as a novel. This is because sharing facts benefits public knowledge and because factual information is often found from multiple sources, unlike a unique creative expression. A filmmaking student could make a video on the life of author Harper Lee but could not make their own adaptation of *To Kill a Mockingbird* for public viewing without consent from Lee's estate.

3. *Amount and substantiality of the portion of copyrighted work used.* The less of a work one uses, the more likely that use is to fall under the fair-use category. It is perfectly reasonable to quote a small excerpt of a work; without it, reviews and analyses would be dull and unhelpful. But one should not use any more than necessary. Just as a student shouldn't quote entire pages of a book for an essay, they should not use images of a fashion designer's entire fall collection when only one photograph is needed to illustrate their inspiration.

4. *Effect of the use upon the potential value of the copyrighted work.* If the unlicensed use of a copyrighted work harms or could potentially harm that work's income-earning potential, this is a case that violates fair use. An example of this is a developing case between mega clothing retailer Zara and over twenty independent designers. The designers allege Zara stole their designs for pins, patches, and other accessories. Because Zara is the world's largest fashion retailer, it is able to manufacture these accessories at lower prices than the corresponding items on the designers' websites (Porter 2016). This use hurts the independent designers' business.

There is also an unofficial fifth factor of fair use, and that's good faith. Where it applies to fair use, good faith means the user made their best attempt at using copyrighted material ethically. Giving credit to the original author of the work demonstrates good faith. But if someone deliberately tries to hide the fact that they are using someone else's work, or if they transform it in a vulgar, offensive way for no justifiable reason, that does *not* demonstrate good faith.

Putting it all together, fair-use claims are more likely to be supported if two or more of the four factors can be applied favorably to the situation. However, there is no hard-and-fast rule about what constitutes fair use and what doesn't. The laws are deliberately vague because the nature of creative work itself varies so much that each case merits individual consideration.

The good news for students is that anything they use *within academic confines* is generally acceptable. There are limits. Students should not, for example, photocopy an entire book and distribute copies to their classmates.

Workarounds

If all this talk of fair use and intellectual property is enough to make your head swirl, you are not alone. Fortunately, there are several workaround strategies composers can take without sacrificing the quality of the assignment's content.

The simplest workaround might be to link or refer to a work without including it. For example, with digital projects, instead of *uploading* copyrighted images or videos, students may simply *link* to a URL of the material instead. This avoids copyright infringement while still including the copyrighted work in context. The only caveat to this is making sure the website they are linking to is a legitimate source. If the linked site contains false or incomplete information, it reflects poorly on the student's work. For example, if a student wants to illustrate a blog post with an image of a lithograph print, they should try to find that image on the artist's official website or the website of the museum or gallery that owns it. Other websites, such as Tumblr, Flickr, or Pinterest, are often rife with misinformation. They might have the wrong artist or title listed, and the image itself might be poor quality or have been retouched to the point that it is markedly different from the original artwork.

Creative Commons

Instead of using a commercial stock image to illustrate a point, a student could search for royalty-free images on Creative Commons. Creative Commons (CC) is a nonprofit organization that enables individuals to share their own work or find somebody else's work to use. CC's worldwide affiliates have developed easy-to-understand licenses anyone may apply to their work, from photos to audio recordings, literary works to scientific research, and more. These licenses are customizable so the work's creator can both share *and* protect their work. For example, a landscape photographer might choose a CC license to allow others to reuse their images for free, but only for noncommercial purposes, and only with attribution. A musician might give a Creative Commons license to a recording that enables others to use it for any purpose, including commercial ventures, but with the stipulation that it may only be copied and not transformed or "sampled" into a new derivative work.

All results should be scrutinized. There is no registration process for a Creative Commons license, so it is the student's responsibility to verify that the actual author or owner of the work posted the CC-licensed content. This can be done by examining the Profile or About page of the individual or publisher who posted the materials. Anybody could download a photograph from the internet and fraudulently repost it, so use caution when determining what's available.

Public Domain

Instead of using copyright-protected media in their assignments, students might opt to search for works in the public domain. Items in the public domain are out of copyright and are therefore free to use without restriction. Copyright terms are temporary and eventually expire. In the United States, with very few exceptions, anything published prior to 1923 is in the public domain (Harvard). So a student might choose to use a historical photograph as an illustration rather than a contemporary one. Other works, such as many of the documents and photographs published by the US government, are meant for public consumption, so they are in the public domain from the time of their creation.

Shakespeare's plays, Vivaldi's symphonies, and the US flag are all in the public domain. The only catch to using work in the public domain is differentiating between the original work and later-published, copyright-protected versions. Vivaldi's *music* is free to work with, but most *recordings* of his works are under copyright. A violinist could compose their own work based on the melody of a Vivaldi concerto, for example, but to use a 2006 recording of that concerto as background music in a publicly shared video would be a copyright violation.

Attributions

Whether the audience of a project is one professor or the entire internet, students should *always* attribute any materials that are not their own work. Just as citing text is necessary to avoid plagiarism, images and other media also must be credited. In most cases, attributing multimedia materials can be done with a combination of captions and a works cited or list of illustrations page.

Captions

Captions provide basic information beneath an image or video. Typically, they answer the who, what, when, where, why, and how of the subject. Caption styles vary widely depending on the type of media depicted and the publisher's style guidelines. A caption for an art image typically includes the artist's name, title of the work, year of creation, materials used, dimensions, and the museum or other institution that owns the work. Captions for journalistic images usually include the

Sample art-image caption: *Figure 14.1. Henriëtte Ronner,* The Musicians. *C. 1876–1877. Pencil and watercolor on paper, 13.5 × 17.87 in. (34.3 × 45.4 cm). Amsterdam, Rijksmuseum.*

Sample news-photograph cutline or caption: *Matilda II, the Algonquin Hotel's resident cat. (Ozier Muhammad. New York Times.)*

photographer's name, the names of people in the photograph, and a general description of the image.

MLA, APA, and Chicago style manuals all include information on captions and image citations. Students can find the correct formatting by consulting a manual or by asking their professor for an example. In many instances, there are no exact rules for captions. Students working on a presentation might opt to keep their image captions brief to avoid cluttered-looking slides. Alternatively, they could include a list of all image captions at the end of the presentation.

Citations

Citations for audiovisual media are similar to citations for articles and text-based documents. However, complications arise owing to the evolving nature of digital media. Owing to the different publishers and format, a citation from an image taken from a printed book looks different than a citation for an identical image found online.

When citing online materials, list the website that *originally posted* the content. Do not, for example, include a Pinterest link; rather, do some research to track down the original file. (Research methods are discussed later in this chapter).

Citations for multimedia resources can be frustrating to create. Sometimes there might not even be a preferred citation for a new media format, such as virtual reality. But style manuals are designed with some flexibility in mind, so students should make their best efforts. When in doubt, providing more information is a safer bet than leaving something out!

FINDING IMAGES

Much of the information discussed in this chapter involves finding media and information. For any course project that mandates using outside sources, students must think about how to locate them. How do they do this? And how do they find accurate information about these materials?

Sometimes, a student has a specific work in mind to use in a project but is unable to gather all the necessary citation information about it. It's safe to say we have all at some point found an image we liked online and saved it without noting anything else about it, like the photographer's name or the website from which it was downloaded. How do you retrace your steps to find this information? Try the following techniques with your student.

Metadata Viewing

Digital images come with metadata, or information about the image, embedded within them. Depending on the type of camera or scanner used, different kinds of information are stored inside the image. For example, an iPhone camera automatically records the date and time of capture, as well as the GPS coordinates of where the photo was shot. Digital images published by museums or professional photographers might include embedded information with the title of the work and its copyright holder. This metadata can often provide good hints at what an image is about and where it's from.

What can be gleaned from this information? Consider the following example: a student took a photo of a sculpture at a gallery last year. She would like to use this image for inclusion in a presentation for her art history course, but she can't remember the name of the gallery or the artist who created the sculpture. Viewing the metadata of this image, she could retrieve the GPS coordinates from where the photo was taken and use that to identify the gallery. Noting the date the photo was taken, she could then examine the gallery's website for past exhibitions to get a better idea of who the artist of the sculpture is.

Reverse Image Searching

One of the reasons images can be hard to find online is because search engines are queried by text, not visual information. Fortunately, image-recognition technology, such as Google's Reverse Image Search, is changing that. Reverse image searching is like Shazam but for pictures. The popular smartphone app Shazam can "listen" to a few seconds of a recorded song and then identify the artist and title of that song. On a parallel plane, reverse image searching "sees" an image and retrieves similar or identical results. By viewing other websites where these similar and identical images appear, one can gather more information about an image and often find a higher-quality version of the picture.

Beyond identifying mystery pictures, reverse image searches can be utilized in other clever ways. They can be employed to find larger-size or higher-resolution versions of an image. They can be used to browse visually similar images, helpful for finding inspiration.

Creative types can also use reverse image searching to safeguard their own work. Suppose an art student has images of their drawings on their blog. They want to make sure no one is posting those images elsewhere, at least not without giving proper credit. By doing reverse image searches on their own drawings, they can see where else it has been published online, allowing them to contact those website owners and ask them to either take down or attribute the images in question.

CONSULTATION STRATEGIES FOR COPYRIGHT AND CITATIONS

Determine Whether Copyright Issues Are at Play

Listen carefully when your student describes their project. Will it include using or sampling others' materials? Will it be shared openly or only within the classroom or a password-protected website such as Blackboard? These considerations help determine what precautions might need to be taken in regards to copyright. As a general rule, use of these materials is fine in a classroom setting, whether in person or on a password-protected website. And, as with anything else, anything that is not the student's original work *must* be attributed.

Help the Student Understand Fair Use

If the student's use of someone's intellectual property will be made publicly accessible, the student should either first seek permission from the
copyright holder or be confident it qualifies as fair use. Omitting the
copyrighted work and finding a copyright-free alternative are two other
options. Keep the four factors discussed earlier in mind when helping a
student determine whether or not their use of a source falls under fair use.

Know the Workarounds

Students can avoid copyright infringement by simply linking to legitimate sources. Consultants should explain to students that while providing a link is a good copyright workaround, students still must ensure
they are linking to a credible source. Furthermore, Creative Commons
provides royalty-free images students can use, and works in the public
domain are fair game since they are out of copyright.

Discuss Attribution

Captions should provide information on the who, what, where, why, and
how of the visual media. What's most important is that consultants help
students understand the importance of citing materials. Citation can
be tricky with emerging technology, so if new technology has yet to be
accounted for in a particular style manual, play it safe by encouraging the
student to include as much information about that source as a possible.

Use Metadata to Find an Image

As mentioned earlier, metadata provide good hints about an image and
where it's from. To view this metadata from a Windows computer, right
click on the image's filename and select Details. On a Mac, the best way
to view an image's metadata is to open it in the Preview program. From
there, select Tools > Show Inspector from the menu bar. A student can
also quickly view image metadata using Adobe Bridge if it is installed
on the computer or by searching for an online image metadata viewer.

Ensure Accuracy with a Reverse Image Search

Reverse image searching has *many* uses. It works for identifying digital
images on the web that have no information or misleading data, such as
those posted and reposted across social media. It also works with unique,

unpublished images. You could take a photo of anything from a plant to an animal, a building to a dress, and Google can often identify the content of the image.

To do a reverse image search, go to http://images.google.com, click on the camera icon, and either upload your image or provide a link to it. Google will then display results based on the visual attributes of the image provided. If there are no satisfactory matches, you could refine your search by adding keywords, such as *20th century collage.*

ACTIVITY

Millions of images and videos uploaded to the web have little or no identifying text. What information there is might be inaccurate. To practice finding optimal images, try the following quick search:

1. Pick a specific subject—for example, artist Piet Mondrian or a topic like vintage wallpaper designs—and do an image search on two of the following popular, commercial websites: Google Images, Flickr, or Pinterest.

2. Compare the results, including both the image quality and the availability of descriptive data about the artwork. Are there inconsistencies? How can you tell which images and captions are accurate?

3. Now try the same search on a more reputable source. For art images, Artstor is a great option, but if your institution doesn't subscribe to it, try the Google Cultural Institute, which contains images from reputable sources only. How do these results compare with the results from the commercial websites?

Using Creative Commons-licensed audiovisual materials is one of the best ways someone can use others' work ethically and without infringing copyright. Try these steps to find CC media.

1. First, determine the type of media needed (image, video, audio) and the subject. Let's say a student is looking for images of snow leopards to use in their blog.

2. Go to https://search.creativecommons.org/ and select the website you wish to search. In this case, we'll try Flickr, since millions of photographers host their images there.

3. Type your search term(s) and hit enter.

4. The search redirects us to a page of image thumbnails on Flickr. Click on one you like.

5. Find the CC info on the page by looking for small, round icons or text that says "Some Rights Reserved." Click on the link to view the details of the license.

6. From there, you can ascertain whether or not the image can be used. The CC license will clearly explain how you are free to use the image and under what terms (such as providing attribution or by not modifying the original).

Remember, you should try to determine that whoever posted the CC-licensed image is the actual owner of the photograph. If something looks amiss, it's better to use another image. For more practice, go to the Search or Advanced Search pages on different websites and try filtering by "Creative Commons licenses." SoundCloud, Wikimedia Commons, and Google Images include CC status where applicable.

CONCLUSION

While new and emerging technologies can be challenging to effectively and ethically use in a student's own work, there are also new tools to address these hurdles. Improved search-engine functionality, image-recognition technologies, web and smartphone apps, and Creative Commons licenses offer innovative ways to both find and use multimedia resources. Alongside academic resources, such as style manuals, LibGuides, and university copyright offices, there are many places to gain understanding of how citations and fair use come into play.

Knowing the basics of copyright law is beneficial to students because it empowers them to better control the output of their own work. By knowing how to license their work with Creative Commons licenses, and conducting periodic reverse image searches to see where else online images of their work might be popping up, students can address any possible cases of copyright infringement head-on. Recognizing the importance of giving credit where credit is due, even in an informal classroom presentation, improves students' research skills and better prepares them for their future careers.

RESOURCES

Citations

https://sites.google.com/a/colgate.edu/colgatevr/citing-images
    The Colgate University Visual Resources Library has information on citing images.
https://owl.english.purdue.edu/owl/resource/560/01/
    The Purdue Online Writing Lab (OWL) explains how to cite all kinds of audiovisual formats.

Copyright, Fair Use, and the Public Domain

http://www.collegeart.org/fair-use/

> The Code of Best Practices in Fair Use in the Visual Arts, published by the College Art Association (CAA), focuses on fair use as it relates to those working in the visual arts. The CAA website on fair use also includes infographics, hypothetical scenarios, FAQs, and webinars that make it easier to understand the topic.

http://fairuse.stanford.edu/

> Stanford University's Copyright and Fair Use website includes information on and examples of fair use.

http://law.duke.edu/cspd/

> Duke University's Center for the Study of the Public Domain

https://copyright.columbia.edu/basics/fair-use.html

> The website of Columbia University's Copyright Advisory Office includes a Fair Use Checklist, which can help you determine if your use of copyrighted material is within the limits of fair use or not.

https://www.copyright.gov/fair-use/more-info.html

> For more information on Fair Use, visit this website.

Better Web Searching

Google Advanced Image search: https://www.google.com/advanced_image_search

Google Reverse Image search—click on the camera icon to begin: https://images.google.com/

Creative Commons search: https://search.creativecommons.org/

KEY SEARCH TERMS

captions; copyright; citations; multimedia; audiovisual; resources; plagiarism; intellectual property; art; images; fair use; attribution

REFERENCES

"Fair Use in a Day in the Life of a College Student (infographic)." 2016. Association of Research Libraries. http://www.arl.org/focus-areas/copyright-ip/fair-use/3831-fair-use-in-a-day-in-the-life-of-a-college-student-infographic#.WIuTqLYrI8Z.

Harvard University Office of the General Counsel. 2016. "Copyright and Fair Use." http://ogc.harvard.edu/pages/copyright-and-fair-use.

Muriel-Torrado, Enrique, and Juan-Carlos Fernández-Molina. 2015. "Creation and Use of Intellectual Works in the Academic Environment." *Journal of Academic Librarianship* 41 (4): 441–48. http://dx.doi.org/10.1016/j.acalib.2015.05.001.

"More Information on Fair Use." N.d. Copyright.gov. Last modified July 2018. https://www.copyright.gov/fair-use/more-info.html.

Porter, Nia. 2016. "Zara Under Fire—Again—for Allegedly Plagiarizing Indie Arist." Racked. http://www.racked.com/2016/7/20/12235004/zara-tuesday-bassen-plagiarize.

Ronner, Henriëtte. C.1876—C. 1877. *The Musicians.* Watercolor and pencil on paper, 13.5 × 17.87 in. (34.3 × 45.4 cm). Rijksmuseum, Amsterdam. Bequest of Jonkheer P. A. van den Velden, The Hague.

Wang, Emily. 2015. "Instagram Is Full of Copyright Loopholes—It Made My Career, but It Could Break Yours." Quartz. https://qz.com/424885/i-got-a-job-posting-photos-of-my-dog-on-instagram-but-others-arent-so-lucky/.

GLOSSARY

affordances. Potentials and limitations for a particular mode (linguistic, visual, audio, gestural, spatial).

alternate text or <alt> tag. Word or phrase used to describe visuals or images. Websites use <alt> tags in HTML in order to adequately describe page contents, such as images or operable elements like "buttons," making them accessible through screen readers.

artifacts. Examples of work in an ePortfolio to demonstrate progress or display accomplishments, such as videos, audio, images, text, infographics, posters, data, and so forth.

artist statement. Statement offering creative individuals an opportunity to communicate the purpose, philosophy, and inspiration of their visual work through the written or spoken word.

assessment ePortfolio. Academic or professional ePortfolio that displays artifacts representing experiences and completed projects.

attributions. Crediting the original author of any materials, such as text, images, and any other media.

audience. The addressed and imagined recipient of a text. In this collection, audience regularly goes beyond reader to include viewer, user, and listener.

audio description. Verbal description of important visual content occurring in a video that is not already conveyed in the dialogue. These descriptions include set details and character costumes, actions, locations, body language, facial expressions, and all on-screen text.

audio meaning. Noise, music, and sound effects.

brochure. Portable, printed information in a format meant to advertise, inform, persuade, or demand action.

captioning. On-screen textual representation of the audio for visual content, such as videos. Captions also provide basic information beneath an image or video.

close-up shot. Close-range shot in which the subject or a feature takes up most of the frame.

cohesion. Creating unity across modes.

content-management system (CMS). Computer application used to organize, facilitate, and support the creation and modification of digital content. Typically used in web-design software such as WordPress.

context. The situation in which a genre is composed and received. Context takes into account the cultural, social, and physical factors that influence and inform how writers/designers/artists and readers/viewers/listeners engage and experience a text.

continuity editing. Editing film in a way that reduces conflict between two shots, producing a "natural" transition and attracting as little attention as possible to the cut.

curator's notes. Explanation providing the context and purpose of the inclusion of an artifact in an ePortfolio.

CRAP. An acronym for contrast, repetition, alignment, and proximity coined by visual designer Robin Williams in her book *The Non-Designer's Design Book.*

delivery. How something is said or presented. Delivery includes employing vocal varieties in pitch, rate, and intensity (such as tension, roughness, breathiness, loudness range, and vibrato).

developmental ePortfolio. EPortfolio that includes artifacts to illustrate the progress, growth, and reflection of learning.

DOI: 10.7330/9781607328469.c015

diegetic sound. In video production, sound that happens on or off screen but has not been edited in.

elements of art. The seven visual components of art: color, form, line, shape, space, texture, and value.

ePortfolio. Collection of digital artifacts that demonstrate, document, and reflect on a writer's experience.

ethos. Character or credibility developed by the writer.

F-shaped layout. Web-page format that directs users' eyes to track information following the F-shape, starting at the top left-hand corner, moving horizontally across the top, then moving down and moving across the next row of content.

fair use. A legal doctrine that allows limited use of copyrighted material without needing permission from the copyright holders.

field or background sounds. Sounds added to the foreground in order to simulate real-world conditions and natural reality. These sounds can also come in the form of music and are meant to create a particular mood or emotion.

figure-ground contrast. The Gestalt principle of creating a distinction between the figure and ground to separate one image from another.

figure or foreground sounds. The most important sound; the sound the listener must be immediately aware of and identify with.

font. Design of all alphabetic and numerical characters and punctuation of documents and projects. Fonts are either serif—small strokes or tails on the letters—or sans serif.

formalism. In film, creating and conveying ideas, concepts, and meanings that are not contained in any single shot.

framing. The position of the camera in relation to the staging.

Gestalt principles. Principles from a German movement in psychology that refer to the ways we organize information and perceive objects in relation to the whole visual field.

gestural meaning. Body language, behavior, and sensuality.

ground or middle-ground sounds. Contextual sounds the listener is aware of but pays little attention to.

grouping. The ways our eyes organize information and group them together.

high camera angle. The camera pointed down on the subject, typically to make the subject less powerful or important and to establish the viewer's dominance over the subject.

hue. Color, such as yellow, red, blue.

infographic. Multimodal texts that combine words, visuals, and data to convey complex information. Infographics are typically organized in seven ways: statistics, information timelines, process, geography, comparison, and hierarchy.

kairos. Situating a message at the opportune time or effective moment, considering place, time, and context.

linguistic meaning. Language, including delivery, vocabulary, positioning, word choice, information structures, and the overall organizational properties of the text.

logos. The writer's appeal to reason or logic.

long camera shot. A shot providing a wide range of the setting and less intimacy with a subject.

low camera angle. The camera pointed up at the subject, making the subject appear powerful and the viewer insignificant.

medium camera shot. A shot allowing the audience to see the whole subject in detail.

middle or level camera angle. A neutral, eye-level camera shot.

montage editing. Editing of film to increase or highlight the conflict between two shots and call attention to the cut.

multimodality. Meaning shaped by the interaction among multiple modes (linguistic, visual, audio, gestural, spatial) and how they are combined to create a message.

multimodal meaning. Relationship among multiple modes (linguistic, visual, audio, gestural, spatial).

pathos. The writer's appeal to the audience's emotion.

personal branding. A holistic approach that allows individuals to control their public representations as professionals. Individuals can take visual, textual, and thematically driven approaches to communicating core information about themselves to an audience.

podcast. A digital audio recording made of such auditory elements as speech, music, and sounds and that can be listened to via computer, media player, or smartphone.

prezilepsy. A disoriented feeling caused by the zooming and panning movement Prezi offers, which can be disruptive and unsettling to viewers when it is overused.

principles of art. Principles used by artists to organize elements of art: balance, emphasis, movement, proportion, rhythm, unity, and variety

proximity. The Gestalt principle of grouping objects based on their distance from one another.

public domain. Items out of copyright and therefore free to use without restriction.

public service announcement. A static, audio, or video message in the public interest disseminated without charge.

purpose. The reason behind creating a text. Whether the goal is to inform, educate, persuade, entertain, analyze, or problematize (or some combination of these), writers create texts with meaning and purpose.

realism. In film, capturing natural movement and space to replicate raw reality.

remediation. When new and older media are blended. Often new media are informed by older media (e.g., a book is adapted into a movie).

rule of thirds. In video or photography, dividing the shot into a grid of nine sections and positioning the most important objects where the lines intersect to produce a compelling visual dynamic. The subject or point of interest should appear along the lines in one-third or two-thirds of the grid, but not in the center.

saturation. Purity of a color or strength of the color.

shot. In video production, the outcome of the interplay between the set (staging and lighting) and the camera (framing and camera/lens movement).

showcase ePortfolios. Professional ePortfolios that display the creator's best work.

similarity. The Gestalt principle of grouping objects together based on their similarity in shape, orientation, color, or texture.

spatial meaning. The arrangement of elements on a physical plane, in environmental spaces, and in architectural spaces.

staging. In video production, the arrangement of people and objects against a background or environment.

storyboard. A communication tool with roots in the film industry that helps artists, authors, filmmakers, and other creators plan stories while addressing multiple modes within the work.

style. How a message is delivered, including word choice and devices such as metaphors and similes.

tagline. Short text—one phrase or one sentence—summarizing the writer's message that people will remember.

texture. One of the elements of art: how something feels or how it looks as if it might feel.

three-point lighting. Setting up the lighting on a subject that includes a key light placed near the camera, a fill light to remove undesired shadows, and a backlight to distinguish the subject from the set, creating a three-dimensional look.

tone. The mood or attitude of a piece.

transcript. Static textual representation of the audio for a podcast or video.

value. Amount of black or white in a color.

visual meaning. Colors, images, font, page layout, perspective, and screen formats.

voice. Individual's personality expressed through unique wording.

white space. The part of a page left unmarked, often referred to as *negative space* in visual arts. Negative space is the space between objects and can help create balanced and proportionate compositions.

Z-shaped layout. Web-page format that directs users' eyes to track information following the Z-Shape, starting at the top left-hand corner, moving horizontally across the top, across the center, and then horizontally across the bottom.

ABOUT THE AUTHORS

Lindsay A. Sabatino is assistant professor of English and director of the writing center at Wagner College. Her research and pedagogical interests focus on multimodal composition, digital literacies, the relocation of writing centers into libraries, online tutoring, writing studio spaces, and faculty development. She has published in *Computers and Composition, Writing Lab Newsletter, The Peer Review,* and *Praxis.*

Brian Fallon is associate professor and founding director of the Writing & Speaking Studio at the Fashion Institute of Technology, SUNY. His career has focused on promoting the collaborative learning practices of peer tutors, especially through his work with the National Conference on Peer Tutoring in Writing. He is a recipient of the Ron Maxwell Award, has published in *The Writing Center Journal,* and has contributed to *The Oxford Guide for Writing Tutors.*

Patrick Anderson is a visiting professor of philosophy at Grand Valley State University. He earned his MA in English and his PhD in philosophy from Texas A&M University, where he was a graduate writing consultant at the Texas A&M University Writing Center. In addition to his primary research in social-political philosophy, he also holds a graduate certificate in film and media studies and has published in the *Quarterly Review of Film and Video.*

Shawn Apostel is assistant professor of communication at Bellarmine University. His research interests include teaching with technology, digital ethos, e-waste reduction, learning space design, and technical and visual communication. His work has been published by *IGI Global,* the *CCDigital Press, Lexington Books,* the *New Forums Press, Kairos,* and *Computers and Composition Online.*

Jarrod Barben received his bachelor's degree in writing and rhetoric at the University of Utah and is a lab coordinator for the Salt Lake Community College Student Writing & Reading Center and the English department's Online Plus Writing Fellows Program.

Brandy Ball Blake is the director of the Naugle Communication Center at Georgia Tech and has also served as the professional and technical communication coordinator at the Stewart School of Industrial and Systems Engineering. In these roles, she has worked extensively to develop initiatives that help students improve communication.

Sarah Blazer is assistant professor and associate director of the Writing & Speaking Studio at the Fashion Institute of Technology, SUNY. Her pedagogical and research interests center on developing and advancing humane, inclusive, and effective tutoring and teaching pedagogies through writing center staff education and college-wide outreach and collaboration. Her work has been published in *The Writing Center Journal, College English,* and the *TESOL Encyclopedia of English Language Teaching.*

Brenta Blevins is assistant professor of writing studies and digital studies at the University of Mary Washington. She teaches and researches multimodality/multiliteracy, digital and online pedagogy, and the literacy and rhetoric of virtual reality (VR), augmented reality (AR), and mixed reality (MR). Her publications have addressed multiliteracy centers, multimodality, and digital media and pedagogy.

RUSSELL CARPENTER is executive director of the Noel Studio for Academic Creativity and associate professor of English at Eastern Kentucky University. Recent books include *Writing Studio Pedagogy* and *Sustainable Learning Spaces*. He is editor of the *Journal of Faculty Development*.

FLORENCE DAVIES is an administrator at the Texas A&M University Writing Center. She received her MFA in writing and literature from Stony Brook University. She is currently working on her second novel for young adults, centered on the coming-of-age experiences of black girls and their mental health. She can be found on Twitter as @thewriterflo.

KATE FLOM DERRICK is the senior program coordinator for the Searle Center for Advancing Learning and Teaching graduate and postdoctoral program at Northwestern University. She was a peer tutor and staff member at DePaul's University Center for Writing-based Learning for nine years. She lives in Chicago with her husband, daughter, and cats.

LAURI DIETZ is the associate director for Faculty Support & Pedagogy at Stanford University and former director of the University Center for Writing-based Learning at DePaul University. She has published and presented on peer writing tutor professional development, ePortfolios, undergraduate research in the humanities, and the scholarship of teaching and learning.

CLINT GARDNER is the program manager of College Writing and Reading Centers at Salt Lake Community College (SLCC). His writing center research includes the development of online writing tutoring practices and systems, as well as the impact of working as a peer writing consultant in community college writing centers.

KAREN J. HEAD is executive director of the Naugle Communication Center and associate chair and associate professor in the School of Literature, Media, and Culture at Georgia Tech. Her book *Disrupt This!: MOOCs and the Promises of Technology* describes the pressure on professors to embrace new technologies in the STEM era.

ALYSE KNORR is assistant professor of English at Regis University and editor of Switchback Books. She is the author of three poetry collections, one nonfiction book, and three poetry chapbooks. She received her MFA from George Mason University, where she co-founded Gazing Grain Press.

JARRET KRONE is an instructor of rhetoric and writing at the University of Colorado at Colorado Springs. His publications and research interests focus on digital rhetoric, digital pedagogy, writing and multiliteracy center studies, and peer-to-peer mentorship.

SOHUI LEE is assistant professor and faculty director of the Writing and Multiliteracy Center at California State University Channel Islands. Coeditor of the *Routledge Reader on Writing Centers and New Media*, she has published extensively on multiliteracy centers, multimodal composition, and creativity (*The Writing Center Journal, WLN, Praxis, Computers and Composition*).

JOE MCCORMICK, former developer of the Salt Lake Community College Student Writing Center online tutoring system, holds an MA in teaching English as a second language for the University of Durham (UK) and now works in Florida as a software developer.

COURTNIE MORIN is an instructor at Eastern Kentucky University and the University of Kentucky, where she teaches first-year composition, rhetoric, and applied creative-teaching courses. Courtnie's publications focus on pedagogical best practices for both the classroom and writing center.

ALICE JOHNSTON MYATT is assistant professor in the Department of Writing and Rhetoric at the University of Mississippi, where she teaches writing and works with the university's writing centers. Her research includes online tutoring and teaching environments, tutor education, and intersections of writing program and writing center administration.

MOLLY SCHOEN is the visual resources curator at the Fashion Institute of Technology, SUNY. In this position, she assists history of art faculty with their image, research, and technology needs; she also promotes visual-literacy concepts throughout campus.

JAMES C. W. TRUMAN is assistant director of university writing and is responsible for the Miller Writing Center at Auburn University. As part of a university-wide initiative, he works with students and faculty to enhance the culture of writing and writing instruction across campus. He received his PhD in English from UNC Chapel Hill.

INDEX